THE PLEADER

The
Pleader

An Autobiography

Len Murray

MAINSTREAM
PUBLISHING

EDINBURGH AND LONDON

First published in Great Britain in 2002 by
MAINSTREAM PUBLISHING (EDINBURGH) LTD
7 Albany Street
Edinburgh EH1 3UG

ISBN 1 84018 642 9

A catalogue record for this book is available from the British Library

Typeset in Garamond

Printed in Great Britain by
Creative Print and Design Wales

CONTENTS

FOREWORD

A striking and, some would say, fundamental feature of the structure of the Scottish legal profession is the division between solicitors and members of the Faculty of Advocates. At one time it was total: a solicitor who wished to speak to an advocate in the Parliament House had to seek out the advocate's clerk and seek permission to approach the great man – it was invariably a man. The Second World War put paid to all of that, as many returning warriors used their gratuities to pay the Faculty's entry fees, and women claimed their right to plead alongside, and against, the men. By Act of Parliament passed in 1990, solicitors were given the opportunity to qualify for the right to plead in the highest courts; and, even before that, many who wanted to exercise their forensic skills in the most challenging forum joined the Faculty of Advocates after perhaps ten years of professional practice: the old barriers tumbled down.

Len Murray points to the anomaly that solicitors have to pass certain extra examinations to earn the right to plead in the higher courts, whereas members of the Faculty of Advocates gain instant access to all courts; and he suggests that all would-be pleaders, whether solicitors or advocates, should have to work their way up from the District Courts to the House of Lords. But what justifies the tradition is that no advocate can appear in any court whatsoever unless he is instructed to appear, by a solicitor who, if he is doing his job properly, has first ascertained that the advocate is fit to plead in that court. Solicitors deal directly with the public, with regular clients who have no effective means of discovering if their solicitor – who may be excellent at giving advice – is any good on his feet.

But Len's clients were lucky. He was good on his feet. It was partly a natural gift and partly the result of an education that was clearly designed to develop the analytical skills that any lawyer must have, and the verbal skills without which the court cannot be persuaded to accept the results of the analysis.

This book is eloquent of the gift, the education and the skills. One of

Len Murray's achievements has been to become an after-dinner speaker of some renown throughout Scotland. In that role, he uses language with great clarity and economy. He also displays a fine sense of dramatic timing, so that any tale he embarks upon grips the listener and holds him until Len lets the punch line loose. I remember seeing him in full flow and realising that he was recording his after-dinner speech. I was astonished at the apparent vanity of recording his own words, and upset that he had not seen fit to record mine. But the explanation was simple: Len played his own speeches back the following day in the solitude of his own study, not to laugh at his own jokes but to calculate which had been successful and which had belly-flopped. Only the fittest would ever be repeated. It was typical of the careful preparation that characterised all Len's work: nothing was left to chance. Nothing, neither the brevity, the gravity, nor the humour was too unimportant to be neglected. Len rightly recognises that, for the pleader, as for the after-dinner speaker, the real work is done before he gets up on his feet, and after he has sat down at night to analyse his performance.

For most members of the Faculty of Advocates, part of the attraction of the work is that most of the clients are once-only clients; there is no lasting relationship to distort the objectivity of the advice. For the solicitor it is no less attractive that, from case to case, from crisis to crisis, he builds up a relationship with his clients that may endure for decades and create a relationship of trust that is personally rewarding. But, to succeed in that type of relationship, you have to have some personal warmth, warmth of a kind that advocates do not need and sometimes lack.

The warmth of Len's relationships with his clients is evident, but it has never seemed to impair his objectivity. When he wins a laugh it is more often at his own expense than at the expense of some unfortunate whose brush with the law Len has sought to mediate. I feel sure that in writing this book Len has been engaging in the literary equivalent of listening in his study to the recording of his after-dinner jokes. Only this time he is inviting the reader to pass judgement on the performance.

Anyone who has practised successfully in the courts knows how rewarding intellectually and personally it is to attempt to use all one's gifts, training and experience to advance on behalf of the client the arguments that he would have wanted to put for himself. It is not dishonest to present the client in the best possible light, any more than it is dishonest for a hairdresser to use his or her skills to put a few highlights into an otherwise boring head of hair, or for a mortician to put a smile on the face of the dear departed: people expect it and are not deceived. What one can learn from Len Murray's career, and from the cornucopia of anecdotes that decorate his book, is that practising the law as a court pleader is fun and infinitely varied. No two days are the same. Nothing is ever repeated without a new twist. All that is certain is that the next moment will bring a surprise. What is important is that the pleader brings a well-calibrated mind to the task so that he can ride the sudden storm, seize the unexpected moment and outwardly pretend that everything was planned and expected. Len demonstrates that the trick is to keep a still head while all around shake theirs. The only pity is that he never chose to practise advocacy in the highest courts; he had much to teach.

Baron McCluskey of Churchhill

CARISSIMAE UXORI FILIISQUE

APOLOGIA

For many years I resisted the idea of writing a book about my experiences as a lawyer in Glasgow. My objection was always twofold. In the first place, when clients come to instruct a solicitor they do so in what has been traditionally called 'the confidential circumstances of solicitor and client'. This means that whatever they tell their lawyer will be regarded as confidential between the lawyer and the client and those confidences will be respected for all time, even after the client's death. The very last thing that a client expects is that his lawyer will one day breach those confidences by telling the world about them. In the second place it might be regarded as an appalling arrogance to think that anyone might be interested in what I have to say about anything!

I was finally persuaded that it would be possible to put some chapters together without breaching the confidence of any client, and I have tried to do so in the following pages.

Over the years I obtained an enormous amount of satisfaction and enjoyment in practising law in my native city of Glasgow. I hope that some of that enjoyment will be conveyed to and shared by those who take the time and the trouble to read what I have written.

I could not have written this book without the help of so many people: my wife for her forbearance while I spent endless hours at my desk; my erstwhile clients who unknowingly gave me so much pleasure; my fellow Glaswegians for their enormous sense of humour, without which I could never have survived the pressures of legal practice; my publishers for all their patience over many months; but perhaps above all I must express a huge debt of gratitude to my good friend George Wilkie, not just for his encouragement but for all his help in getting this material together in an acceptable form.

TONY MILLER – THE CRIME

The old Bakelite phone burst into action. Its raucous sound split through the almost cathedral hush of my room, clamouring for attention. A gravel voice charged with emotion and panic shouted from the earpiece: 'Len Murray? I really need your help. My son has been charged with capital murder.'

The adrenaline was immediately flowing. Accepting this would mean my second capital murder case within a year and as a young lawyer I was instantly elated. Little did I know that in the coming months as the case unfolded it would become a nightmare that would stay with me for many years to come.

Outside, the sun had waved its golden paintbrush over the grime-laden Victorian buildings of that erstwhile 'second city of the Empire', my native Glasgow. It was a city that could be as mean and dangerous as it could be generous. It was afternoon and its inhabitants meandered around the streets on that warm August day in 1960, with no knowledge of the drama unfolding in my office.

Alf Miller and his wife sat opposite me. Archetypal Glaswegians: hard-working, honest, probably not well off by any standard. Pass them in the street and you would not give them a second glance.

Mrs Miller, small and tidily dressed, sat saying nothing. Occasionally she would squeeze her hands together, looking at the floor, then the ceiling, then the floor again; anything to distract her from the panic inside. Alf, holding my attention with pleading eyes, his voice quivering slightly, his head shaking with disbelief, launched into the family's problem. Their 19-year-old son Tony had been charged that afternoon, along with a 16-year-old boy called James Denovan, with murder.

The incident had taken place in the recreation ground of Queen's Park in Glasgow some months previously. It had come to light while Denovan was being held on remand in connection with another case. In the course of an interview he had broken down and blurted out how he and Tony Miller had carried out a series of attacks on homosexuals in Queen's Park and one of them had died. Denovan had acted as the lure, distracting the victim. Miller then came from behind to assault and rob him. All of their victims were homosexuals who had never reported the crime to the police.

Denovan had shocked the authorities in the remand home with this dreadful story and the police had been called in. An investigation was immediately launched and now Miller and Denovan had been charged with murder or, more correctly, capital murder.

In those days certain types of murder were still capital crimes and involved the death penalty in the event of conviction. One such type was a murder 'in the course or furtherance of theft'. In this case the assault from which their victim died was carried out during their robbery of him and so it fitted one of the criteria for a capital crime.

If, then, Tony Miller were convicted he would hang. James Denovan would not hang because he was too young.

'Surely they can't hang Tony, can they?' asked Mrs Miller, who had hardly taken any part in the discussions so far.

'Why do you ask that, Mrs Miller?' I enquired.

'He was only 18 at the time. He's too young to hang.'

His mother thought that no one under 21 could be sentenced to death and I had the dreadful task of telling her that 18 and not 21 was the minimum age for hanging. It was a task for which I would never have volunteered but it was the first of many unpleasant duties that I would have to perform during this case in the months to come.

I arranged to go to see young Tony at Craigie Street Police Station in the south side of the city where he was being held. He was a slim, rather sallow youth with hair drilled into place with oil. His thin face was pale. I don't know if it was from the shock of arrest or just from his lifestyle. He sat in a tiny cell, originally painted white but now covered in graffiti that had been there for years. The air had a pervasive smell of urine and strong disinfectant. He did not say very much at that stage but I did not expect that he would. The shock of it all was obvious in him. My meeting with him was less than an hour in length. It was hard work but I got from him what was required in the way of instructions to represent him.

The following day he appeared in Glasgow Sheriff Court along with James Douglas Denovan. They were marched into the small courtroom at

2 p.m. precisely by two policemen. Each was firmly gripped by the shirtcuffs. They stood before the sheriff and they were both charged with murder.

The allegation was that on 6 April 1960 in the recreation ground of Queen's Park they had assaulted John Cremin, struck him on the head with a piece of wood or other similar instrument, knocked him down, robbed him of a bank book, a watch, a knife and £67 of money and 'did murder him'. It was also alleged in the charge that the murder was committed in the course or furtherance of theft and thus it was a capital murder.

There were various other lesser charges of assaults and robberies which were alleged to have taken place in the months of March, May and August of that year and they all related to incidents involving men in the Queen's Park. The court appearance was a brief, formal one and the two were remanded to Barlinnie Prison to await their trial.

While interviewing the various witnesses whom the Crown intended to call and obtaining statements from them I started to build up a picture of the case against Miller. To represent him I instructed two Junior Counsel, Irvine Smith and Alistair MacDonald. I had instructed them the year before in what was my first capital murder trial so we were used to working with each other. Both would achieve distinction with judicial careers on the shrieval bench – James Irvine Smith in Glasgow and latterly North Strathclyde, and Alistair MacDonald as sheriff in Orkney and Shetland.

The victim, John Cremin, was a man in his 50s, a homosexual, a thief and an individual mourned by few. However, his life had been taken, apparently, in the course or furtherance of theft. Accordingly, under the terms of the Homicide Act, anyone convicted of taking that life (even a 19-year-old) was liable to be hanged.

In preparing for the trial I consciously built up a kind of emotional barrier between Miller and myself. The previous year when I had my first capital murder case I was frightened for my own sake, frightened of how I would react if my client were to hang, frightened of the emotional effect that it would have on me. This time I wanted to ensure as far as I could that I would be unaffected. I did not realise that I would fail so miserably.

The case against Tony Miller was formidable. There was a tremendous amount of evidence against him and it seemed to me that clearly there was a very substantial risk of his being convicted.

I saw Tony quite often at Barlinnie Prison (a soulless place that still gives me shivers when I pass by) and I met with his parents regularly to keep them posted. As our enquiries went on I had little good news to give them. The more we investigated the case against their son the stronger it seemed to become.

An oddity about the case was that when Cremin's body was found it was first thought that death had been from natural causes. He had been wearing a cap that night and this hid any injury. Only when a post mortem was carried out and a massive subdural haemorrhage was found was it realised that this was no natural death. Only a severe blow on the head could have caused such a haemorrhage. The two doctors who carried out the post mortem were two of the country's most experienced and respected pathologists, James Rentoul and Walter Pollock Weir. They had no doubt that a hefty blow from a flat-surfaced object, such as a piece of wood, somewhere about the left temporalis muscle (on the left side of the head) had caused the fatal injury. Accidental death, they said, could be ruled out. It was murder.

The evidence implicating Miller and Denovan in the murder charge came from several sources. The pair had been in the habit of frequenting the Cathkin Café in Victoria Road in Glasgow's south side. It was a rendezvous for many of the local teenagers. A number of their friends had told the police how Miller and Denovan had often boasted in the café of what they had done to Cremin. Some of them even spoke of one ghoulish moment when the two accused pointed out the very spot in the recreation ground of Queen's Park where Cremin had been assaulted and had 'flaked' in their words. Denovan had callously suggested that they observe two minutes' silence for him. In addition Miller and Denovan had been seen in possession of Cremin's bank book and they had also been seen with brand-new bank notes such as a bank would issue on a withdrawal. The evidence against them was overwhelming.

TONY MILLER – THE TRIAL

The trial began in Glasgow High Court on Monday, 14 November 1960. The presiding judge was Lord Wheatley, who would subsequently be appointed to the post of Lord Justice Clerk, the second highest judicial office in the country. The prosecutor was James Law, who would become an eminent QC.

Only a capital murder trial could have packed the public benches in the way they were that damp Monday morning when the trial began in the North Court of Justiciary Buildings in Glasgow's Saltmarket. The penalty in the event of conviction was death. That guaranteed a great deal of public interest and press coverage. Looking along at the press benches, the reporters were packed like sardines and their photographers (without their cameras) squeezed in so that they could identify the relevant witnesses who gave evidence.

By the second day of the trial the issue had become confined to the capital charge only because both Miller and Denovan had tendered pleas of guilty to all of the other charges. All that was left then for the jury to decide was the capital charge. Indeed, the issue had become even narrower – which of the two of them had struck John Cremin on that fateful night? This was crucial because in terms of the Homicide Act of 1957 only the one whose hands had dealt the fatal blow could be hanged (an effort to ensure that there could be no repeat of the scandal of the Craig and Bentley case in England in the 1950s). Denovan was only 16 and so no matter what role the jury thought he might have played in the affair he would not hang. Miller, however, could.

When the Crown case closed on the Tuesday, Tony Miller did not give evidence on his own behalf. That was a decision that had been taken by his advisers. We felt that nothing was to be gained by his giving evidence and a great deal might be lost. Apart from any other consideration, we were sure that he would not make a good witness on his own behalf.

James Denovan, however, did give evidence and in the course of that he claimed that the three-foot length of wood used as the murder weapon had been wielded by Tony Miller and not by him.

By the Wednesday morning the evidence was over. The advocate depute, James Law, made his final submissions to the jury. He invited them to hold that Miller had struck the blow and he asked that they should find him guilty of capital murder. Since Denovan had been acting along with Miller he should be convicted of non-capital murder.

Irvine Smith addressed the jury with his customary passion and ability. It was an outstanding address coming from surely one of the greatest advocates. He invited the jury to hold that they could not say which of the two had struck the fatal blow since there was only the evidence of Denovan to that effect. They should treat Denovan's evidence with caution. The proper verdict in his submission was a verdict of guilty but of non-capital murder. Charles Macarthur, who represented Denovan, asked the jury to hold on the evidence that Miller had struck the fatal blow. If they did that then they could not find his client guilty of capital murder.

That afternoon I sat at the bar of the court throughout the 70 minutes or so of Lord Wheatley's charge to the jury. It was superb. Lord Justice General Clyde would later describe it as 'a model of clarity' and it would become the model on which many Scottish judges and sheriffs were to base future charges to juries for years to come.

It was the first time that I was to hear that great definition of 'reasonable doubt' which I would hear so many times in the course of my professional life. Lord Wheatley described it as 'such a doubt which, were you to meet it in the conduct of your own important affairs, would give you pause'. At the mention of that last word Lord Wheatley took off his glasses and, focusing his eyes on the window above the jury, he paused. It was very dramatic.

The judge told the jury also that the consequence of their verdict was not their concern and warned them that they must be unaffected by the consideration that a verdict of guilty of capital murder would involve the death penalty. That was none of their affair, he said. If they were to find that Miller had committed the murder and it was committed in the course or furtherance of theft then he said they 'must steel themselves to it'.

As the jury retired at two minutes past three that afternoon I reckoned that not even the forensic brilliance of Irvine Smith was going to be enough to save the life of Tony Miller.

Counsel and I went along to the gown room to await the jury's return. Nowhere does time pass more slowly than the room where you wait for a jury's verdict. That was especially so in the days of capital charges. We all sat nervously round the oval table in the gown room. With us were Charles Macarthur and Laurence Dowdall, who was Denovan's solicitor. Laurence, who was my great idol in my younger days, had been through that wait so often over the years. It was only the second time that I had experienced it and I hated it just as much that day as I had done when I had experienced it for the first time.

An eternity seemed to have passed since the jury went out. Then it came, the jingle of the bell high on the wall of the gown room which summoned us back into court. I checked my watch. It was three thirty-five. The jury had only been out for just over half an hour.

We trooped back all of us and took our places around the D-shaped table in the well of the North Court. The jury were already in place and not one of them would meet our occasional inquisitive glance. We all knew then what the verdict was going to be.

Miller and Denovan had already been brought up from the cells to their places in the dock and they sat there, both ashen. Escorting police officers sat bolt upright at each end of the dock wearing their white gloves and with batons resting on their knees. The tension was showing on them as much as on the rest of us. The judge's door onto the bench opened. The macer called out 'Court' as he preceded Lord Wheatley. The chaplain brought up the rear. We all rose at the shout of 'Court' and as we stood I was unable to control a nervous twitch in my knee. His Lordship bowed to the jury and then to us. We bowed in return. He sat down. This was the signal that everyone could sit. Donald Stevenson the Senior Deputy Clerk of Justiciary was clerk of the court. He remained standing and turned to the judge. He bowed and then paper in hand he faced the jury.

'Ladies and gentlemen,' he asked in a flat, emotionless voice, 'who speaks for you?'

The foreman rose, grim-faced. Donald Stevenson first took from him the formal verdicts on the charges to which the accused had pled guilty the day before. Coming to the third charge on the indictment, which was the charge of capital murder, he asked in a quiet voice: 'What is your verdict on charge three as regards the accused Miller?'

There was a long silence. I said to myself: 'Wait . . . wait.' This was the moment I had dreaded since 30 August when I was first instructed in the case.

'Guilty of capital murder.' The foreman's voice was surprisingly strong. I sensed that it had taken a special effort for him.

'And is your verdict unanimous or by a majority?'

'Unanimous.'

Another juror, a man in the back row, was weeping quietly.

'What is your verdict on charge three as regards the accused Denovan?'

'Guilty of non-capital murder.'

None of us at the bar of the court spoke. I for one could not. I was choking back my emotion.

Donald Stevenson sat down to write out the verdicts in longhand in the Minute Book of the court. It took him four minutes to do that. Nothing could be heard but the quiet weeping of the juror and the movement of the clerk's plain nibbed pen over the parchment page. He finished. He rose and asked the jury if he had correctly recorded their verdict and he read it back to them. They nodded in agreement.

The formalities were over and the verdicts had been recorded.

The advocate depute moved for sentence. Neither Irvine Smith nor Charles Macarthur had anything to say since the sentences were prescribed by law. They both sat back in their chairs, not looking at each other as though trying to be somewhere else.

Lord Wheatley then spoke for the first time since the jury had returned with their verdict:

'Anthony Joseph Miller, in respect of the verdict of capital murder just received for which the law imposes but one sentence, the sentence of the Court is that you be taken from this place to the Prison of Barlinnie, Glasgow, therein to be detained until the seventh day of December next and upon that day within the said Prison of Barlinnie, Glasgow, between the hours of eight o'clock and ten o'clock forenoon you will suffer death by hanging, which is pronounced for doom.'

At the mention of that last phrase he touched his wig with the black tricorn which was always available to the judge in capital cases and which had replaced the black cap but a few years before. The sentence on Denovan was that he be detained during Her Majesty's Pleasure.

The two accused were turned around by the escorts and led out of the dock, almost being hustled down the stairs to the cells. A door slammed and they were gone. The jury were discharged by Lord Wheatley and excused from further High Court jury service for ten years and further Sheriff Court jury service for life. His Lordship rose, bowed to the jury and then to the Bar and walked off the bench. The trial was over.

There was something unreal about this. At the age of 27 and with only three years' experience as a qualified lawyer I had heard a sentence of death upon my client – a boy of 19. I did not know how I should be reacting. So many thoughts were rushing around my mind – was this real or would someone come along and say it was only in my imagination? Would a juror suddenly rush back into court to say it was all a mistake? How was Tony Miller going to cope with this? What of his parents? His mother had not been in court that day and his father had left the court before the verdict. Would they know yet? How would they react? Should I try to find them?

My Counsel and I went downstairs to see Tony. The enormity of it all had not reached him. We spoke nervously. We would appeal. There then began the fight to save Tony Miller's life.

As we left the North Court a cold wind was blowing up the River Clyde. Already the news vendors were selling the *Evening Citizen* and calling out the headline: 'Miller to hang.'

TONY MILLER – THE APPEAL

The hours were ticking away. We had to act fast or Tony Miller, sitting in Barlinnie Prison, would hang. Grounds had to be found to convince the Appeal Court that Lord Wheatley had erred in law with his direction to the jury.

The appropriate Act was one which had been passed in 1926 in the wake of the scandal of Oscar Slater's case. Oscar Slater had been convicted of the murder of an 82-year-old woman, although he had an alibi and the evidence against him was insubstantial to say the least. Following numerous calls for a pardon or a retrial, evidence emerged which exonerated Slater and he was released from prison after serving 18 years. The newly constituted Court of Appeal quashed his conviction on the grounds that the original judge had misdirected the jury. In Scotland the Appeal Court effectively cannot look at any matter of fact. A jury's view of the facts of a case is final. What the Appeal Court *can* look at is any question of law or any alleged misdirection by the presiding judge. What we were interested in, therefore, was whether there had been any mistake in law or any misdirection of the jury. This meant a very minute study of what Lord Wheatley had said in his charge to the jury. It had been a very careful and painstaking charge but we had to scrutinise it to see if we could find in it any possible ground of appeal.

We found three. The first ground was that Lord Wheatley had erred in law when he directed the jury that they could not consider culpable homicide as a possible verdict in the case. Lord Wheatley had made it clear to them that there was no room for such a verdict. 'If it was homicide at all, it was murder,' he had said. Most judges would have given a jury the option of bringing in a verdict of culpable homicide had they wanted. That would have been one way for the jury to avoid returning the capital verdict, which was one that juries did not like bringing in.

Lord Wheatley was never a judge for soft options. As a matter of law he thought there was no room for culpable homicide so he took that option away from the jury. The question that we were taking to the Appeal Court was whether he was right in doing so. We were arguing that the jury should have been left to decide whether this was murder or culpable homicide.

The second ground of our appeal involved the evidence given by James Denovan, the co-accused. In his evidence Denovan said that he had no idea that Miller was going to strike such a severe blow. He did not mind being party to an assault but he did not want any unnecessary violence. Miller, according to him, had struck the fatal blow. Lord Wheatley had told the jury that if they were to disbelieve Denovan in this then there was not enough evidence to convict Miller of capital murder. The jury had convicted Denovan, so they must have disbelieved him at least in part. Thus, ran our argument, because they had disbelieved Denovan on this point there had not been enough evidence to convict Miller of capital murder.

Our final ground was, if you like, the blanket cover that the verdict was contrary to the evidence. We had ten days in which to lodge our appeal. We lodged it on 25 November, some nine days after Tony Miller had been sentenced to death. In the meantime Tony's father had enthusiastically begun the task of collecting signatures on a petition to the Secretary of State asking him to recommend the exercise of the Royal Prerogative, which could commute the sentence to life imprisonment. The first signatures on that petition were the signatures of the parents of an 18-year-old boy from Hounslow in Middlesex who had been hanged just a fortnight before the beginning of our trial.

In April of 1960, Alexander Stirling, who had been convicted of a double murder, had been reprieved at the last moment after a petition to the Secretary of State for Scotland. That gave us great hope. Now Stirling's father also publicly gave us his support.

On 30 November the High Court fixed 7 December as the date for hearing the appeal and at the same time postponed the date of execution. My Counsel worked extremely hard in preparing the appeal. Lord Wheatley's charge was positively dissected, hours of preparation were put in and every legal precedent of any relevance was canvassed. Independently of the appeal, the petition to the Secretary of State was going ahead and gaining momentum every day.

We were not optimistic about our chances in the Appeal Court. It was not a court that commanded much respect from the profession as a whole as it was hard-line and only a tiny proportion of criminal appeals ever had any success. It was the last resort in Scotland, and, unlike England, there was, and is, no appeal to the House of Lords in criminal matters. Indeed, it is no secret that the legal profession was becoming so disillusioned by the Appeal Court and its approach that there was open unrest in many quarters. It was felt that the court was often much less than fair and there was talk of conferring jurisdiction on the House of Lords simply to have another appellate court.

The petition for reprieve, however, was another matter. It had to succeed and there was every reason to think that it would. Tony Miller was only 19. He had never previously offended at all. He came from a good home. No member of his family had ever been in any bother and the killing was obviously not premeditated. There was also another factor. Many saw a parallel between Miller and Denovan on the one hand and the English case of Craig and Bentley on the other. Craig had been sent to detention while Bentley had hanged. Many still remembered the injustice of that hanging and the parts played in that injustice by Lord Goddard and Sir David Maxwell Fyfe, the then Home Secretary. In the light of all those factors I could not see Tony Miller being allowed to hang.

I went up to Barlinnie each week to keep him posted as to our progress.

There was always a cold welcome awaiting me from the dark grey stones. Stepping through the main gates was ever disturbing. My head automatically turned to the small area within the prison where executed prisoners were buried: no gravestones or proper burial for them. (Today that area now lies under 300 centimetres of tarmacadam.)

It was a small cold room that was kept for solicitors' visits to their clients. I will never forget the harsh sounds of keys rattling on chains, the continuous clanging of metal doors and faint echoing shouts in the distance from prisoners and officers. Tony was brought to the room under escort, neatly dressed in prison clothes, a blue and white striped shirt and dark-blue serge trousers. As he sat in front of me I could see there was a look of total resignation in his eyes. With each visit it would become more pronounced.

I found those to be strange meetings. He seemed to be becoming more distant or perhaps more resigned to his fate. As we talked his eyes would look around the room as if trying to shut out the inevitable. I felt as though he was not very interested in whether the appeal succeeded or not, or even whether the petition was successful or not. At first I put it down to his nature. In all my dealings with him he never had been a good communicator. However, as each visit passed, I realised that in fact it did not matter to him whether his appeal was successful. His attitude was that if it were the will of God then he would be reprieved. If it were not God's will then it would not happen. I found this an extraordinary attitude in one so young. In those weeks following his conviction Tony Miller was acquiring maturity far beyond his years and far beyond anything he had shown so far.

Our appeal was heard as scheduled on 7 December. The judges were the Lord Justice General Lord Clyde, along with Lords Carmont and Guthrie. Within minutes of the appeal beginning it became apparent that my worst fears were going to be realised.

Had we been able to nominate the trio of judges that we would *not* want to hear a criminal appeal then we would have picked the three that presided. Lord Clyde was not a popular judge and was very right wing in his ideas. Lord Carmont had written his name indelibly on the copper plate of the history of Glasgow by handing out exemplary punishment to razor slashers when that particular evil had been reaching epidemic proportions in this city. He had done more than anyone else to stamp it out and had gained enormous public support in doing so. However, he had certainly not made many other contributions to our law and in all conscience and charity he was neither the best lawyer nor the best judge on the bench. It was rather disheartening to realise that at least two out of the three judges were not likely to display much sympathy.

Some of the comments that came from the Bench during the hearing of the appeal astonished me. I remember the Lord Justice General saying of Miller to Irvine Smith: 'But the man did not even have the courage to go into the witness box.' Until the end of the nineteenth century it had not been possible for an accused person to give evidence on his own behalf. It only became competent in 1896. Since then it has always been a recognised and respected right of an accused person not to give evidence. Indeed successive generations of judges and jurists have always insisted that there is no obligation upon an accused to give evidence and have upheld his right not to do so. Accordingly, to hear Scotland's most senior judge make that comment was something which was regarded by those of us who heard it as at least disappointing! At that moment it became perfectly obvious to all present that this was a purely academic exercise that was doomed to fail.

The appeal was in fact dismissed in a surprisingly short time in the course of the morning as being 'completely devoid of substance', a description which I and many others felt to be thoroughly unwarranted. The grounds were not the strongest but they were argued with consummate skill. They were rejected by the Appeal Court almost with contempt and in that most unsatisfactory of ways – without any reasons being given. This was a capital case. A boy's life was at stake but we were made to feel that it was an impertinence to bring that case into the Appeal Court. We were left with a thoroughly unpleasant taste in our mouths.

A new date for the hanging was fixed – 22 December – some 15 days ahead. There was no other appeal court to which we might go and all that was left was our petition to the Secretary of State for Scotland asking him to recommend the Royal Prerogative.

TONY MILLER – THE EXECUTION

It was almost like a military operation. Alf Miller had set up tables in the city centre collecting signatures. Forms were sent to factories and workplaces throughout Glasgow and the west of Scotland. Railway stations were manned with canvassers and Members of Parliament were lobbied. Support was received from Lord Packenham, Baroness Wootton, Bessie Braddock MP, Barbara Castle MP and Alice Cullen, who was then MP for Gorbals. Thousands were now signing the petition and messages of sympathy and offers of help were coming from all over the country.

When I eventually sent that petition through to the Secretary of State, John S. Maclay, it had some 30,000 signatures from people in all walks of life and from all corners of the country. I am sure that no Scottish petition for the Royal Prerogative had ever had as much support. Just a week before the date for the hanging I received information that one of Tony Miller's grandparents had at one time suffered from mental illness. No mention of that had ever been made before, whether at the trial or in the petition, and accordingly I passed the information on to the Secretary of State in the hope that it might be of some assistance.

On Monday, 19 December there was still no word from the Secretary of State. The press announced that he had postponed a short holiday and they speculated that the probable reason for the postponement was so that he could consider our petition for reprieve. That afternoon, some time after four o'clock, my receptionist advised me that there was a gentleman there from the Scottish Office who wanted to see me. A slender, pleasant-looking man wearing a grey pinstripe suit and carrying a bowler hat entered the office. In his hand he held an official-looking envelope.

He proffered it, telling me that it was from the Secretary of State. I realised that I was now holding in my hand the official response to our petition. I was sure that within moments I would be reading that the Secretary of State had recommended to Her Majesty that she exercise her Prerogative of Mercy. I was convinced that the petition had been successful.

I remember slitting open that envelope very carefully and taking out the letter. Both the messenger from the Scottish Office and I were still standing just inside the door of my room. I went round to my desk and sat down. I unfolded the letter nervously. It read:

> Sir,
> I am directed by the Secretary of State to inform you that after careful consideration of the case of Anthony Joseph Miller he regrets that he is unable to find sufficient grounds to justify him in advising Her Majesty to interfere with the due course of the law.
> I am, Sir,
> Your obedient servant

It had been signed by an official at the Scottish Office.

'Christ, I don't believe it.' I stared at the letter. This had to be a mistake. Something had gone wrong. I looked up at the messenger in utter horror. He had known what that letter contained. He looked at me for a moment or two and then his eyes drifted to the floor, embarrassed by it all. His had not been a pleasant task and there was no doubt that he had not enjoyed it. My eyes went back to the letter, reading and rereading, still wondering what had gone wrong.

'If you will forgive me, Sir.' It was the messenger from the Scottish Office and I realised that he was anxious to go. He must have felt intrusive.

I went downstairs to my senior partner's room, knocked and went in. I sat down still dazed by it all. I tossed the letter over to him and he read it several times over.

'Willie,' I asked, 'What the hell do I do now?'

'Pray,' he said.

I could not believe what was happening. They were actually going to hang the boy. Here we were in the latter part of the twentieth century, supposedly in a civilised community, and a 19-year-old boy was going to hang. What kind of society were we, or more accurately, what kind of government did we have? What good would hanging him do?

In a daze I drove across the River Clyde, past the very court building where he had been sentenced, towards Govanhill. I had to speak to Alf and his wife. I wended my way through the Gorbals, dodging youngsters who were playing football in those depressing streets surrounded by the eerie shapes of the old Victorian tenements. The weather was closing in. I sat in my car outside the Millers' house for an age, mentally tracing the shape of my windscreen and watching the wipers clear the water from the glass for the hundredth time. I kept putting off the dreaded meeting.

Eventually I forced myself to the door of their house. My knocking echoed through the close. They were out. God, I was so relieved. If that meeting had gone ahead it would have been the most difficult of my life. I later learned that they had been to see Alice Cullen MP.

Alf came to see me the following morning. He had learnt of the decision the previous afternoon while at the prison visiting his son. It would be difficult to say which of us was the more stunned. I remember thinking how vast a change there had been in that man during the three or four months that had passed since our first meeting. He had become old beyond his years and he looked bent and haggard. Mrs Miller kept to herself and stayed mainly at home.

I think that I felt more sympathy for that man that morning than I had ever felt for anyone. I had to take a positive approach even at this late stage. All that I could think of was a direct approach to Her Majesty and accordingly Tony's father and I sent separate telegrams to Buckingham Palace that morning. We now had less than 48 hours. There was nothing more we could do but wait.

No reply was received from Buckingham Palace on the Tuesday. That night I telephoned Alice Cullen. She promised that she would do what she could the following day. However, we were running out of time. Tony was due to hang on Thursday morning.

Wednesday came. It was a very long day but it came and went with no word. I had stayed in my office hoping for news, hoping that each time the telephone rang there would be word of intervention by Her Majesty. The telephone did ring – many times – but not one of the phone calls was the one I had hoped for.

That night the enormity and horror of it all came home to me in a way it had not done before. The following morning they were going to hang that boy. Of course he was no angel and of course he had taken a life. But at the same time by what right did our society think they could take his? 'Thou shalt not kill,' said the Lord. He did not add any proviso. Killing was wrong whether by an individual or by the state. An enormous feeling of anger and revulsion grew up inside me that evening and I well remember the feelings of bitterness and resentment, which I was probably feeling for the first time. Until the Miller case I had probably been in favour of capital punishment. It was something that we had always had. My profession is traditionally conservative and I suppose I was as conservative as any. But I realised that this case had made me a bitter abolitionist. The barbarity and futility of it all were inconsistent with our claims to be a civilised society.

Not only were they going to destroy a life that did not belong to them, but, in addition, a punishment far greater than any other that man could ever possibly devise was being handed out to two totally innocent individuals – the parents of the condemned boy.

What had they done to be so cruelly punished in this way by society? What was their crime? Tony Miller probably did not matter because within a matter of hours life would be no more to him; but our society, yours and mine, was going to place on the backs of his parents a cross heavier than any parent should be expected to bear.

I sat in my office alone. It was early and I had been there since 6 a.m. The same telephone that had begun the nightmare was sullenly silent. Outside, tramcars moaned their way over wet slicked cobbles. As they passed each street junction their wands sparked a blue rain from the overhead connections. It had been foggy the night before. People criss-crossed the streets through the slow rising light. It was like viewing a Lowry painting through a net curtain. Still no phone calls.

My heart jumped as the clock struck 8 a.m. At that moment a young man took the final 14 steps of his life – from his cell to the scaffold in Barlinnie Prison. A hood was placed over his head and a rope was draped round his neck. At 8.02 on the morning of Thursday, 22 December 1960, Tony Miller, 19 years of age, was hanged. It would be the last execution in Glasgow.

Note: The last man to be hanged in Scotland was Henry John Burnet at Craiginches Prison, Aberdeen, on 15 August 1963.

CHILDHOOD

As I reflected on the events of the murder trial, I could not help but think back on how fortunate I had been to have a happy childhood free from peer pressures and anxiety. My only memory of an enemy seemed to be Adolf Hitler, who, I was convinced, had taken an instant dislike to me.

My parents, my sisters, my brothers and I lived in Knightswood, a council housing estate in the west of Glasgow. Most of my memories are happy ones because I was more fortunate than many other children at the time. Throughout my childhood I always enjoyed comparatively good health and I had loving parents. Their principal object in life was to serve their God and do their honest and level best for their family. Consequently my brothers and sisters and I always had much to be thankful for. I was the youngest of five children and was probably spoiled by my two elder sisters. My father was headmaster of a primary school in Glasgow and while that meant we were never wealthy it also meant that we always had food in our stomachs and clothes on our backs. I was much more fortunate, for example, than many of my school friends who had to suffer what must have been the enormous indignity of wearing the immediately identifiable garb which was provided to the needy by the local authority.

We lived in an environment that was generally secure and free from fear until the war started and brought the terror that became known as the Clydebank Blitz. History is not likely ever to forget those two nights in March 1941 when the German *Luftwaffe* brought so much misery to that town.

Knightswood is only a few miles from Clydebank and we were directly affected by the air raids. Early in the war the government of the day had provided air-raid shelters and in Glasgow the Anderson shelter was the most common. They were called after the minister who had authorised their general use. They were strange things made of widths of corrugated steel, each of which was curved at one end. Three widths were bolted side by side to form each of the side walls of the shelter, the curved ends forming the roof, and two straight pieces formed either end. The whole thing was sunk into the ground to a depth of about four feet. The roof, sides and ends were covered with clods of earth, which provided not just an effective camouflage from the air but also a very effective shock proofing. The Anderson shelter became a common sight not just in the back gardens of Knightswood but indeed throughout the country.

To us they were more than air-raid shelters. They were second homes; they were garden sheds; they were our play-dens; they were an integral part of our lives. Mothers vied with each other in making their Anderson the most comfortable in the area. A floor of railway sleepers covered in linoleum was basic equipment. Fitted carpets were not yet de rigueur in the homes let alone the air-raid shelters of Knightswood but a rug was usually thrown on top of the linoleum. Bunk beds lined the walls. A Primus stove in a biscuit tin served as the cooker, and candles mounted in cut-out cocoa tins hanging from the sides of the shelter gave us all the light we needed. There was always a supply of food for emergency use.

My mother, in common with most, was convinced that the Nazi hordes were coming and that some day before long we would need to hide in our outsize foxhole until some unidentified ally came to liberate us. With that in mind, water, dried egg, powdered milk and those tasteless wartime water biscuits were stored in our shelter as our emergency rations. Any night the sirens warbled their unforgettable warning my brothers and sisters and I made our way happily to the garden and to our beloved Anderson. There was a sense of adventure about it for us that was always in marked contrast to the apprehension of our parents. My father was very religious and I have memories of our spending most of our waking time in the shelter praying. My brothers and I were oblivious to the dangers of high explosive bombs and landmines. Worries were things for adults, not for children like us.

The first night of the Clydebank Blitz in March 1941 was horrible. Four hundred bombers of the *Luftwaffe* had brought death to five hundred and twenty eight people and injury to thousands more. The damage caused to homes and to property was worse than anything that Scotland had ever experienced in its history. These were things that passed our understanding as children. We had had an unforgettable time in our Anderson 'coorying doon' in our bunk beds after family prayers, loving the fun of it and counting the bomb blasts we heard before drifting off to sleep.

Dawn brought the All Clear. It was time to emerge into that cold March morning and see what damage had been done. Mercifully, Knightswood showed little sign of damage compared with the devastation that had been done to neighbouring Clydebank. But worse was to come. That night, the second night of the blitz, we were all packed off to the Anderson at our bedtime even although the sirens had not yet sounded. My parents had a premonition that the *Luftwaffe* would come back. They were right.

In total, over the two-night period, the Clydeside death toll was near 1,200. The area was obliterated beyond recognition. Scotland's Civil Defence Commissioner said of Clydebank: 'I have never seen men and women behave with such courage.'

One theory which has endured through the years is that bad weather and heavy cloud only hours before the raid began confused the German aircrews, fooling them into thinking that the Great Western Road, which runs 20-odd miles from Glasgow to Dumbarton and which was glistening in the rain that night, was the River Clyde. The leading navigators and bomb-aimers, peering through a gap in the heavy cloud got a glimpse of the shimmering boulevard, concluded that it was the river and thus that they were on target. They then decided to get rid of their deadly cargo immediately. The result was that stick after stick of bombs and incendiaries fell on residential Clydebank and the surrounding areas, and not the shipyards on the Clyde.

My father and mother always followed us to the shelter but not until Mother had gathered together the family valuables like birth certificates and insurance policies and brought them with her for safekeeping. I never did understand why. What use were the copy birth certificates? Why trouble to bring the insurance policies? Perhaps she wanted to deny some *Feldwebel* the chance of cashing in her eighteen pounds' worth! It was difficult to imagine some *Wehrmacht* officer stealing her policies and then presenting them to the City of Glasgow Friendly Society impersonating my father and demanding payment. But Mother, God be good to her, would have no more gone to the air-raid shelter without her marriage certificate, our birth certificates and the insurance policies than she would have gone without her children.

We got to the shelter just on time. Hardly were we there when the air-raid sirens sounded. Within minutes the bombs began to fall. The crack of the high-explosive bombs was almost non-stop and the deep roar of the landmines provided an accompaniment which terrified even the most brave-faced of us.

I had changed into my pyjamas in the upper bunk, which I shared with one of my brothers, and as I lay there hiding under the bedclothes I was saying my prayers with a new level of devotion. At about half past six the following morning we were nearly deafened by the roar of a landmine. We were certain that it had struck our house. It was as close as that. Instantly awake, we all had the same thought: the house had been flattened. Perhaps we found some consolation in the knowledge that Mother had the birth certificates and the insurance policies with her, but I don't remember.

My father could resist the uncertainty no longer. He had to see the extent of the damage. He took the spanner which was standard equipment in the Anderson shelters and in spite of my mother's cries to wait for the All Clear he unscrewed the sliding panel which formed the door of the shelter and slid it upwards to open it.

I sat up in my bunk to see what my father was doing. I was still sitting up when a landmine fell on Munn's farm about 400 yards away from our house on the other side of the Forth and Clyde canal. The blast hurled my father to the far end of the shelter and the same shockwave threw me backwards in my bunk bed. My sisters and my mother were screaming. Suddenly being in an Anderson shelter during an air raid was not quite the fun it used to be.

Blood poured from Father's head where he had struck the end wall of the shelter. Not much, but enough to alarm us. In the event the cut was superficial and all was well. With the help of my mother he got up and closed down the door. This time it would remain closed until the All Clear had sounded.

We did not have long to wait until we heard the distinctive monotone of the siren. The doors of shelters were being opened all over Knightswood as their occupants emerged into the morning, terrified of what they might see. My father emerged from our shelter convinced that the shockwaves of the landmine had wrecked our home. In fact they had not. Miraculously, not even a pane of glass in the house had been broken. It was divine intervention, said my parents.

My mother, sisters and brothers followed my father from the shelter and I was to bring up the rear. I dropped down from the bunk bed and to my surprise I collapsed on the floor of the shelter. I struggled to get to my feet but I could not. I realised in a flash that I could not walk. I was crippled! I screamed out. My mother reached me first and the terror that she was showing matched the panic I was feeling. The blast from the landmine must have done it. Through my tears I told her that I could not walk. My father ran back to the shelter when he heard me cry out and swept me up into his arms.

Terror and panic must have been the emotions that engulfed my parents as they realised that their youngest child was probably crippled for life. If only my father had not opened the door of the shelter before the All Clear had been signalled. Running with me in his arms to the house he shouted to my mother to telephone the doctor. Mother ran on ahead to open the door. My sisters were running alongside my father trying to hold me, trying to comfort each other or me, I did not know. I could not grasp what was happening. How could a seven-year-old appreciate what it would be like to be paralysed?

My father ran up the stairs, clutching me tightly in his arms. Mother had already reached the living room and was shouting to my sisters to see if either of them could remember Doctor Gallagher's telephone number. They could not. She began a frantic search through the telephone book for his number.

Meanwhile my father had brought me into the living room. He laid me gently down on the settee while he looked anxiously at this youngest child of his who might never walk again. The cause of my immobility was there to be seen. Both my legs were tightly stuck through one pyjama trouser leg.

TO BE OR NOT TO BE

The scene was one of those terrible careers conventions. You know the kind of thing I mean. Hundreds of disinterested children are herded back to their school for an evening to ask questions of experts they do not know about, careers and professions which they have no intention of following: the kind of exercise which seems so totally futile to the outsider. There was the usual gaggle of careers and professions represented, and a huge crowd of kids who thought it was probably better than staying at home and doing their homework.

The first part of the evening, during which each representative of a profession had the opportunity to speak to the assembly, had come to an end. The representatives of the various careers and professions had split up and gone their respective ways to sit in classrooms, soon, they hoped, to be inundated by questions from curious and interested children.

It was a then partner of mine, now on the shrieval bench, who was representing the Law Society of Scotland that night, and off he went to his classroom to sit in glorious solitude. There was not a child waiting for him. No one, apparently, was remotely interested in hearing what the law might offer as a career. But above the glass and wood partition separating the classrooms he could see that the career next door, accountancy, was obviously much more attractive to the youngsters than his as there was a vast queue of them waiting there. The queue spilled out of that classroom and down the corridor towards the entrance to his own. He almost envied accountants. Why should law be so uninteresting to young people?

At the end of the queue was a young girl of perhaps 11 or 12 who glanced in at his empty classroom several times, obviously struggling with either conscience or curiosity. Soon enough her curiosity, or perhaps even innate sympathy, overcame her and she left the queue, took the few steps necessary and entered my partner's classroom. This was it. He was about to face his first young aspirant to the profession. What would she ask? Would he know the answer? He put his hand on the bundle of material prepared by his professional body and felt reassured. The answer to any question this curious child might ask would surely be there in that bundle of material. Nonetheless he felt the inadequacy of his position sitting at a teacher's desk alone in a primary school in Grangemouth, with the awesome responsibility of being the one representative of the Law Society of Scotland. It is difficult to look like a lawyer when sitting on your own in an empty classroom in Grangemouth.

The young girl approached almost timidly. Her question was not obtuse. 'Are you a lawyer?'

He reckoned he knew the answer to that one: 'Aye.'

'Is it good bein' a lawyer?'

He decided that he could not improve on his first answer. 'Aye.'

Came the crunch question: 'Is it better than workin' in Asda?'

My friend's answer was classic and probably true:

'Marginally.'

That one word sums up the practice of the law in Glasgow quite admirably and far, far better than many volumes. Personally I cannot vouch for the comparative truth – I have never worked in Asda – but I imagine that my partner's reply was pretty accurate.

The other story, which appeals to me about joining the legal profession, is a story which is probably apocryphal. The farmer in Dreghorn, in Ayrshire, had only one son. The community anticipated that he would follow in his father's furrow. Amazement was expressed when it was learnt that come the following October the son was off to Glasgow to study law. A neighbour was unable to restrain his curiosity and asked why. The reply was immediate: 'He's aye been gye fond o' stickin' his nose intae ither folks' business so he micht as weel get peyed fur it.'

I was not persuaded by either of these considerations when I decided to take up the law as a career. I have never tried working in Asda and I have never been unduly interested in other folks' business. What attracted me was one thing only – the means of earning money. Not a lot but enough to keep body and soul together.

'A loaf of bread the Walrus said is what we chiefly need.'
So wrote Lewis Carroll and I knew what he meant!

To explain properly I really have to go back a bit in time. It was in 1951 that I first went to Glasgow University not to study law but to do a degree in Arts – modern languages to be precise. I had discovered while I was at school that the only subjects for which I had any aptitude (apart that is from swinging the lead and dodging classes!) were modern languages. I had done well in Latin. I had various school prizes for French and Spanish, both of which I could and still can speak reasonably. I could get by in Italian and Portuguese. I was already an Associate of the Institute of Linguists. I had won the Hispanic Council of Great Britain Essay Competition at the age of 14 and thus studying modern languages at university was the obvious and natural progression. I don't imagine I had ever thought of doing anything else.

I was well into the second year of my degree course when my father died. Although he had been a headmaster, in those days teaching did not provide the pension that it now does and all my mother had was her state pension. One of my brothers had already left home and was married. The other had just qualified as a teacher and his income was scarcely enough to pay the rent for the council house in Knightswood which we occupied. I had no income while a student: bursaries were not then what they would later become.

The future was still bleak and uncertain when I contracted TB Meningitis. Today it is a disease which is rarely known and when detected readily curable. In those days, however, things were rather different. Only a year or so before it had been inevitably fatal and even in 1953 it was still terrifying. There had been no complete cure as yet and those very few who survived were either deaf or blind or crippled. Streptomycin was in its infancy as a cure for tuberculosis and while medicine knew it had found a cure it had still not yet mastered the drug.

When I was taken to Belvidere Hospital in Glasgow I was quite ill. Indeed I was unconscious for two or three days. I remember coming to with my mother and two sisters standing around my bed. At the foot was a schoolteacher, John McDermott, later to become a priest, who had been a member of my father's staff. He was an immensely kind man and even his visit to me (whom he scarcely knew) was an act of great kindness. I remember that he asked me how I felt in those first few minutes of consciousness and then he went on to tell me that I was very lucky: if I had taken ill the year before I would have been dead! Some luck!

I spent six months in Belvidere Hospital. Six months of intramuscular streptomycin injected each morning at an ungodly hour into alternate thighs. And every morning for 13 weeks the dreaded lumbar puncture. A member of the nursing staff would kneel on the bed, turn me over onto my left side and then pull my knees up with her left arm under them. Her right arm would go round my neck and her hands would link somewhere about my middle. My spine was thus arched so that what felt like a double zero knitting needle could be pushed into the tiny space between I think the fourth and fifth lumbar vertebrae and what seemed to me to be gallons of cerebrospinal fluid were drained off and streptomycin was pushed in. After 13 weeks the punctures were reduced to only six a week. The day off was wonderful!

I never thought that six months could seem so long. When I came out I had to consider what I was going to do. I had part of a degree in modern languages but I had no money and I certainly could not afford to go back to university to finish that degree. Then a friend of mine had a brilliant idea, or so he thought. An apprenticeship in law. If I were lucky I might even get a pound a week. That would be wealth beyond the dreams of avarice. When I was flush I occasionally bought a half-pint of cider which cost sevenpence ha'penny in the union. Here was the prospect of my earning a pound a week!

THE APPRENTICE

Following my illness, the convalescent period was so long that it necessitated I drop out of university. In those days there was no readily available gap year. It was a disaster. But there always seems to be a good fairy somewhere and when all seemed black, up popped an opportunity to become an apprentice in a city law firm.

> The Law is the true embodiment
> Of everything that's excellent
> It has no kind of fault or flaw.

It was W.S. Gilbert who wrote those words with his tongue stuck very firmly in his cheek. When I started my apprenticeship all those years ago I had in my innocence no idea whether Gilbert was right. I would soon find out. The apprenticeship for law in my day was quite different from the period of training of today. Now most entrants to the legal profession in Scotland come via the universities. There is an alternative whereby an entrant may be admitted by taking examinations set by the Law Society of Scotland, but only a tiny proportion of entrants do it that way. By far the majority are graduates in law from one of the Scottish universities which offer a law degree. After graduation the aspiring young entrant then does a diploma in Legal Practice at the university and that takes another year. The diploma subjects, which tend to concentrate upon the practicalities of the job, are taught by the profession rather than by the academics, so it is, if you like, a kind of halfway house between the purely academic degree and the entirely practical real-life profession. Once you have completed the diploma then you must find a traineeship with a solicitor. Not an easy thing incidentally. You are a trainee for the first year, a trainee solicitor for the next year, and after that you receive that prized piece of paper which enables you to practise the skills that you have spent some five or six years acquiring.

In the 1950s, however, things were rather different. There was no diploma. It was introduced into the profession as recently as 1980 and was perhaps the biggest single advance in professional training since 1825 when the professional apprenticeship was introduced. In 1980 there was another change – the title 'apprentice' disappeared and the less artisan 'trainee' was introduced.

For us in 1954 the apprenticeship and the degree were done simultaneously, with the day divided between the university and the office. Our classes began at 8.30 a.m. (we were always on nodding terms with every milkman in Hillhead) and they went on till 10.30 a.m. Then it was on to the office via the university union (the students' club), or the refectory (only if you were really stuck), or Greengates coffee shop for what we regarded as a well-earned cup. Half past four saw another class or two. It was a long day, but I think all of us reckoned that the three years involved in that pretty hard grind were worth it. At least so we constantly told each other.

Out of term we were full time at the office but during the 30 weeks or so of the academic year our attendance at our masters' place of business was part time. It was really amazing how many solicitors then in practice did not realise that there were no classes at eleven o'clock in the morning and no class outings in the good weather that required their apprentices to be away from the office for two or three days on the trot!

Like the training period of today, apprenticeships obviously varied but they were always accompanied by the signing of a formal indenture. I still have mine and I am sure that the style was first devised by some ancient Roman. It still amuses me to read it. In terms of that indenture my employers were my 'masters'. I was 'bound apprentice' to them for a period of three years, during which time I had to serve them 'honestly, faithfully and diligently'. My mother (my father being dead) was my 'cautioner' and by and large she was to guarantee that I was to be of good behaviour. God help her, she had no idea what she might have been letting herself in for! In terms of the indenture I undertook to behave 'civilly and respectfully' towards my masters and to abstain from 'bad company and vicious practices', whatever they might have been. (It is one of the great regrets of my professional life that I never did find out what they were.) I also undertook that I would not absent myself from my masters' business under penalty of two days added on for every day that I was off. What do you think the reaction would be if such a requirement were to be introduced generally into our industrial relations scene today?

My masters for their part undertook to teach me their profession 'in so far as they themselves know it and in so far as the apprentice is capable of learning'. We never did reach a definitive view on either of those aspects! Still it was good fun.

Traditionally the apprentice's first job was drafting his indenture. All he had to do was lay hands on a standard style and change the names so it was no big deal. The standard indenture had been framed many, many years ago, so the language was pretty archaic.

Throughout the city the tasks of the apprentices varied. A coal fire in solicitors' offices was still commonplace in the 1950s and one fellow apprentice had the job of cleaning out the fire in his master's room first thing every morning. I was slightly better off. My office had no coal fires. Through the good offices of my former headmaster I had obtained an apprenticeship with a small two-man firm in Glasgow, Levy & McRae. One of the partners – Abraham Levy, the senior – was advanced in years and was never in the office for more than perhaps four or five hours a day. The other partner, Willie McRae, was my master, a very energetic individual who worked like a horse – seldom fewer than 11 or 12 hours a day – and was an intellectual genius. Unfortunately he expected me to become the same.

One of the benefits of doing an apprenticeship in a smaller office, as I would discover, was the fact that you learned how to do literally everything that went on. For example, I would soon be able to nip down to the post office and buy stamps as well as anyone else on the staff. But all of that was ahead of me. The other office staff (all female) consisted of two full-time typists, two part-time typists and a part-time filing clerk who also answered the telephone on a switchboard that even Alexander Graham Bell might have considered obsolescent.

I well remember my first day as an apprentice. I had never worked in an office before. Indeed my only previous jobs were as a casual post office worker at Christmas time, a barman in a Glasgow pub, and a tourist guide. Those latter two were held during summer vacations from the university. My job experience then was not terribly extensive and my curriculum vitae was not bulging with positions of responsibility.

I reached the office about 8.30 a.m. on my first day but nobody else came near for the better part of half an hour. My apprentice master arrived shortly thereafter and summoned me to his room. He asked if I knew Latin, which I did. He handed me an ancient dusty leather-bound tome, foolscap in size and about 400 handwritten pages long. He wanted a translation by 5 p.m. that day! I dutifully touched my forelock, retired to the little corner in the general office that had been cleared for me and opened up the tome. It was, as I had feared, entirely in Latin, closely written and about 300 years old. It was a chartulary or register of, I think, the Montrose Estates. I was in no condition to appreciate either the beauty of the calligraphy or the antiquarian value of the volume. My thoughts were much more practical. How in the name of the Almighty was I going to be able to get this done on time?

Three years before I had passed my Higher Latin examination (I never did understand how) but translating Caesar or Livy or even Ovid was child's play compared with this. There was no prospect of my finishing that translation by the end of my apprenticeship let alone by the end of my first day. What was I to do? Here was I given my first task in my very first real job and I was not going to be able to do it. I was a failure. I had visions of the shortest apprenticeship in law ever on record. How could Mother ever possibly meet her guarantee to my employers?

I would later as an apprentice take to myself a motto '*Ne illegitimi carborundum*'. Courtesy and decorum forbid a literal translation. It does however suggest that those born out of wedlock should not be allowed to grind you down. I did not have the words in those days but I had the thought and so off I went. Out came the newly acquired Parker ballpoint and I put pen to paper for the first time in my new position.

I must have written about twenty pages when I realised it was lunchtime. I was halfway through my first working day, halfway to my time limit and only about six pages through that latter-day tartan Doomsday Book when my master appeared at the door of the general office. He shouted over to me: 'Bring in what you've done.'

Oh heavens, here it comes. I'm about to be found wanting. Still he's bound to understand. I went into his room with my pages and the chartulary. He took the pages from me.

'Christ, is that all you've done?' I gathered he was not pleased. 'You've been sitting out there all morning and you've only got through the first six pages of that chartulary!'

I had the feeling that he was not going to understand. Maybe being a law apprentice wasn't such a good idea. Suddenly being a teacher seemed a better option.

'Well, I'm sorry but I did classical Latin and that book is medieval Latin,' said I – making my first ever plea in mitigation. It sounded rather unconvincing even to me. I wasn't prepared for what came next. All of a sudden the hostile tone and the glowering look disappeared and he threw back his head and laughed!

'Don't worry, son. I was too busy this morning to show you anything so I thought I'd just give you that to keep you out of mischief.' With that he took the pages of my morning's endeavour, ripped them up and threw them into his waste bin. He threw the chartulary onto a bundle of titles in the corner of his office.

'Let's go for lunch and this afternoon I'll give you some real work to do.'

That moment I think was my first professional crisis because I did not know whether to shout out with delight or with anger. There was a mixture of unmitigated relief and blind fury swirling around inside me but I'm not sure which, if either, I displayed. I remembered what my indenture said about my behaviour so I contented myself with my thoughts. I already knew that my master was a bachelor and at that moment I was convinced that his father had been one as well.

That kind of thing was not untypical in the life of the apprentice of those days. Many a poor sucker had been sent to one of the law stationery suppliers and told to ask for a notarial instrument. The staff of the suppliers were accustomed to such a request from apprentices. They usually responded with a degree of tact and sympathy when they told the hapless apprentice that a notarial instrument was a deed drawn up by a notary public and not some kind of implement that could be purchased over the counter. The sheepish-faced rooky would retire and go back to his office wiser than when he had left. Fortunately I never had to go to the stationer's.

THE SENIOR PARTNER

My encounters with Abraham Levy were not all that frequent. He was in his late 60s when I first met him and a very respected member of the profession. The social gulf between him and me was considerable. He was perhaps no longer very knowledgeable in the law but he was full of common sense and a bit of a philosopher, always ready with sound advice. Words of advice from him were words which I could never ignore, for I knew even then that in my chosen profession there is no substitute for experience. The truth of that, incidentally, has been proved to me almost every day that I have been involved with the legal profession.

The earliest words of advice I recall him giving me were that a solicitor's first duty is to protect himself from his client – advice that is even more apposite today than when it was first given to me. It is advice that a lawyer ignores only at his peril. Over the years of my apprenticeship I developed a respect and indeed an affection for him. He had a quietly dry sense of humour and always enjoyed a joke at his own expense. He drew enormous pleasure from telling a story of his early career. He was Jewish. Indeed he was the first Jewish solicitor to set up in business in Glasgow. Consequently he attracted enormous support from his co-religionists, not just from Glasgow but from all over the country. A solicitor in Leeds referred a young Jewish tailor from that city to him. Mr Levy (for he was never anything but Mr Levy to me) soon discovered that the young tailor wanted to buy first-class properties in Glasgow at second-class prices. The young man had ideas of expansion, ideas which in the view of the senior partner of our firm were way beyond the young man's true station in life. Mr Levy wasted, as he put it, a few lunches in the Royal Scottish Automobile Club on the young man before packing him off back down to Leeds totally convinced that spending any more time or money on him would be futile. He lived to regret the day he threw Montague Burton out of his office!

He used to view me with considerable reserve. In spite of his lifetime in the profession he had had only two previous apprentices. One of them,

Manuel Kissen, went on to the Bar and became one of the country's most respected judges in the 1960s, while the other was Willie McRae, who had become his partner some five years before I joined the firm. Clearly he did not have much experience in handling apprentices. There were the other problems of course: I lived in a council house and I never wore a hat.

I always had the impression that he thought it somewhat odd that anyone of my background and appearance should consider himself worthy of joining the legal profession. To him the badge of office of the solicitor was a hat. I did not have one, so how I hoped to qualify as a solicitor he just did not know. Things, however, improved for me when he somehow discovered that I had an interest in chess. He sent for me one day and asked me if there was any truth in this rumour. I told him there was. He asked where I played and when I told him that I was a member of one of the First Division clubs in Glasgow and I regularly played competitive chess in the Glasgow League he looked at me with a growing element of disbelief. Obviously he had never come across such a phenomenon before. Not only did this boy from a council house who didn't wear a hat think he could qualify as a solicitor but he played League chess as well. His curiosity was aroused. 'We'll have a game,' said he. It was not just a forecast – it was a command. An evening was fixed and I was duly summoned to his flat in Hyndland.

I put on my best suit for the occasion – or should I say my other suit – and rang his doorbell bang on the stroke of half past seven. He must have taken all of 20 seconds to answer the door – 20 very long seconds! In that time I stood hoping that he had forgotten our contest. He hadn't.

'Good evening, Murray.'

'Good evening, Sir,' said I dutifully.

He stood back to let me into the hallway of his gracious flat. He showed me into his lounge – sumptuously furnished – and there in the centre of the room was the ivory battlefield with the pieces laid out. Would this be my Bannockburn – or perhaps my Waterloo?

'You'll have a sherry.' I had no idea if this was a question or an instruction. It sounded like the latter. I did not know whether any answer was expected nor did I even know if I would like sherry for I had never even tasted it. University union cider was still the farthest frontier of my experience with drink. The sherry was in a ship's decanter and the glasses were crystal. I do not think I had actually seen either in real life before that night. Into two of the crystal glasses he poured a generous measure of alcohol.

The more we spoke the more I relaxed. The sherry was not as bad as I feared it might be. By the time we sat down at the chess table, I was ready to take on any Grand Master that the USSR would have allowed over its frontiers. But it was only then that I realised how difficult this game was going to be. I had no fear of his ability because I had been accustomed to playing chess in the top leagues over the last few years, whereas he had not played competitive chess for quite some time. Nonetheless, the outcome terrified me. This was a game that I could neither win nor lose. Diplomacy dictated that I should not beat him, yet at the same time my ego would not allow me to lose.

Accordingly I duly played out an honourable draw, but it had to be handled in such a way that he was not conscious of my, as it were, pulling any punches: such an insult, if detected, would be unforgivable. I managed it and he was delighted. And from then on I was accepted. The outward sign of that acceptance was that, whereas up until then he had always addressed me by my surname, from then on he always addressed me by my Christian name. More than that, he started to introduce me to his clients – a thing that Willie McRae had assured me he would never do. It became quite common for him to call me through to his room and say, 'Walter, [or whoever was the client for the day] I would like you to meet my apprentice.' (I was only his apprentice on those occasions.) 'He plays a good game of chess you know.' It was never: 'He's dead keen on the law and he works very hard.' However, I always dreaded another summons for another game: the strain would have been far too much!

At that time the firm was mainly concerned with conveyancing, that is the buying and selling of property; with executrices (the winding up of estates); and with a little fairly low-key debt recovery court work – all aspects of practice from which I would turn away in latter years. But I did receive a good basic grounding in these aspects of general practice and that would stand me in good stead for the future. And on my famous visit to Hyndland I learned the art of diplomacy. There was virtually no criminal work at all. In my three years there the firm had only one common law criminal trial, a simple charge of theft; and there was only one sheriff and jury trial which concerned an allegation of causing death by reckless driving.

That was not at all unusual; there were very few solicitors who were interested in the criminal courts for purely financial reasons. There was no criminal Legal Aid in those days. There was none in Scotland until it arrived here in 1964, many years after it had been introduced into England. People who found themselves in the dock by and large could not afford a lawyer. The result was that the profession tended to look down its Dickensian nose at those who practised in the criminal courts.

I remember the senior partner once discussing my future intentions with me. At the time we spoke I had no idea what I wanted to do and I told him so. In the course of our discussion he told me that people thought lawyers spent their working lives addressing juries. Well, he said, he had never addressed a jury in his life and he doubted if I ever would either. Time would show him to be very wrong in that respect.

UNIVERSITY

Glasgow University spreads itself over the west end of Glasgow like an old damsel's skirt. Until recently its spires and buildings commanded attention on the city's horizon. Now new monstrosities of architecture hide it away from the public gaze. For many centuries it has produced famous and not-so-famous scholars, politicians, scientists and, of course, lawyers.

The students in the Faculty of Law at Glasgow when I was there were quite different from the students of any other faculty. As we were part time we had little contact with the other students. Our visits to the union were only for a quick coffee after lectures in the morning and we were never as deeply involved in student affairs as the other students were. Although most of our lectures were given at university, our classes were at different hours (or rather half-hours) from those of other faculties. We arrived at 8.30 a.m., when I think only the janitors were about; we left about 10.30 a.m., when the other faculties would be halfway through a lecture hour. The result was that in the mornings we never really had the occasion to meet students from other disciplines. Thus we made our own corporate life and I suppose we were very much more insular in our ways than other students.

The most vital qualification for completing our course was a sense of humour. Whether we had it when we joined or whether we acquired it in the course of passing through the Faculty I don't suppose I shall ever know but undoubtedly it was critical.

I remember for example our final-year celebration dinner that was held (prematurely for many as it turned out) after our written conveyancing examination but before the oral. Those of us who attended the dinner had high expectations of success but in many cases the expectations were confounded. Our Professor of Conveyancing was the principal guest and he was joined by other professors and lecturers. All the students turned up in dinner suits and there could have been no greater evidence of our poverty. Grandfathers, uncles, next-door neighbours, pawnshops, secondhand clothes shops and I hate to think where else had been visited. The air was pungent with a cocktail of camphor and mildew.

We were all anxious to create an impression and were on our best professional behaviour because, who knew, some of us might very soon be qualified as solicitors. Yes, Sir, No, Sir, four or even five bags full, Sir, was the order of the evening, but an order which sadly became misted over with the fumes of alcohol as the evening wore on.

Our Professor of Conveyancing, John M. Halliday, who was in his first year in the Chair, was the main speaker. He had yet to conduct his oral examination of us and those who kept that thought in mind behaved accordingly. In the middle of his speech one of our number could contain himself no longer, however, and shouted some comment which indicated that he did not believe that the written paper had been as fair as it might have been; a sentiment, incidentally, which all of us felt but few had enough courage to express. It was also a thought my friend would never have expressed to the good professor without the fortification of the evening's alcohol.

But when he added that in his considered and professional opinion the professor was nothing but a rotten so-and-so whose family tree was as short as man could imagine, then we all knew that he had gone beyond the bounds which sober discretion would have dictated. To compound it and to stamp his own indelible fingerprint upon the knife, as it were, he added: 'Remember me. My name's ******.'

The good professor did as he had been enjoined to do and the poor man failed his oral.

They were in some ways a strange bunch our professors, but every one was a character. There was one, Professor John Boyd, who told his class of

Mercantile Law before the December class examination that they could omit the lectures on bankruptcy because there would be no question in the examination based upon it. When he drew up the examination paper he had obviously forgotten this and included a question on the subject. Since none of my contemporaries ever did a single stroke more than was considered necessary, there were vast numbers of failures in the examination. An impromptu and invisible protest meeting was held and a resolution was passed. For weeks thereafter every single member of the class cut out from the newspapers every single coupon advertising everything and anything and filled it in, giving the name and address of the hapless professor. He was besieged not just by sackloads of mail but by salesmen driving up to his home to give him a test drive in the Lotus or Maserati which they claimed he had sought. Estimators from Pickfords arrived to quote him for a removal he had never planned. Royal Marine Commandos acquainted him with the joys of life in the seaborne infantry and there was a steady drop through his letterbox of articles which, the suppliers guaranteed, would come in plain brown wrappers.

It was a successful tactic. It was not necessary for the class to march up and down University Avenue waving irrelevant and irreverent banners. Within a couple of weeks the good Professor Boyd came into the class one morning, held up his hands in abject surrender, apologised most amiably, and the campaign came to an end. If truth were told we spent months searching for an excuse to do the same thing to somebody else on the academic staff but we never found one.

The great story of the lie detector emanated from that same era. One of the members of the Senate had proposed that the Faculty should invest in the purchase of a lie detector. Bear in mind if you would that this was in the days before lie detectors became fashionable; one might almost say before lies had become fashionable. At any rate, a proposal was put forward at the Faculty meeting and argued moderately and sensibly. But one of the other professors took violent exception to the whole idea and he heaped so much scorn and ridicule on it that the worthy dons were taken aback by the savagery of the attack. The proposer came back just as heatedly accusing his opponent of knowing nothing about the subject and finishing up with the challenge that his opponent had never even seen a lie detector.

'Seen one?' said his opponent very quietly, 'I married one.' The Faculty voted against the acquisition.

Another of the great characters of that time was Andrew Dewar Gibb, QC, then Regius Professor of Scots Law. Dewar Gibb was a truly unforgettable character in the nicest possible way. Politically he was a virulent nationalist and his politics frequently emerged in the course of his lectures. But he was an intellectual genius, a member of both the English and Scottish Bars and, according to legend, had more degrees than a thermometer. He was a dapper little man and such hair as was left to him was already white. He had a fairly high-pitched voice but a very quiet one. In spite of his lack of size and lack of voice he commanded immense respect from his students. Whenever the class became too noisy he restored total silence by the simple expedient of speaking even more softly. We all, of course, had to strain to hear him and he could thus drop a hush on any group of noisy students. He was, I suppose, the very epitome of the university professor, constantly detached from it all but at the same time a man for whom we all had enormous affection.

In his later years he became a temporary sheriff and often sat in Glasgow Sheriff Court. There he really came into his own. In the nature of things most of those of us who pled before him were his former students and this was immensely satisfying to him. His dry humour was irrepressible. There was an occasion when one of his former students, by now qualified, was pleading before him in court and Dewar Gibb had to correct him on some point of law. 'I suppose we should put your misunderstanding down to some defect in your early learning,' said he, with a twinkle in his eyes.

On another occasion the charge being tried before him was one of assault within a bookmaker's shop. While the bookmaker was being questioned by the procurator fiscal, Dewar Gibb interrupted to ask, quite without warning: 'How many pay-in windows are there in this shop?'

'Thirteen, Sir,' said the witness.

'And how many pay-out windows?'

'One, Sir.'

'Hmm. Thought so.'

Those really were halcyon days. I suppose that in the Faculty of Law we acquired an arrogance and a conceit. But these were not for us as individuals but rather for our Faculty. We insisted that the students in the Faculty of Arts were nobodies. After all, we argued, the only people who went into Arts were those who could not get into any other Faculty. We regarded the fellows (though not necessarily the girls) of the Faculty of Science as detached from reality as they would all end up as boffins. We thought the engineers were scruffy, and the medics we laughed at. Every medical student, from the day of their first matriculation, always had a stethoscope visibly hanging from their pocket. They might not have attended their first class or bought their first book on medicine but nonetheless there they were with their stethoscope, which had to protrude from the pocket no matter the occasion, and no matter their dress.

To be fair, the students in our own Faculty were not beyond the reach of our uncharitable tongues either, although in many cases our lack of charity was almost justified. We had more than our fair share of first year students-cum-apprentices who would turn up complete with bowler hat. Nothing appeared more incongruous than a 19-year-old face with a bowler hat stuck on the hairy top. Those, of course, were the fellows who belonged to the legal factories; those vast oceans of law offices where everybody was anonymous and where partners would not even know who their apprentices were, let alone speak to them.

Our afternoon classes in the Royal Faculty Hall in the city centre were an event. They began at four-thirty and not at four o'clock as untold generations of masters had been led to believe by their not so very keen apprentices. One particular class was difficult to forget. The lecturer, who was a practising solicitor in Glasgow, would stand at the lectern and for the next 55 minutes drone on in one of the most soporific and monotonous voices imaginable, finishing each lecture at exactly the same point as the equivalent lecture the year before. He was considerate enough, however, not to have changed even his little jokes in all the years he had been 'lecturing'. The result was that many of us simply acquired a set of his notes from someone who had already done his class, took up a position outwith his line of vision (that was easy enough as nearly every position was outside his line of vision) and promptly fell asleep.

One of my fellow students (now the holder of high judicial office) decided to put the lecturer's powers of observation to the test. Our lecturer always had a glass of water on a table to his right and quite near the lectern. At 5 p.m. precisely the right hand would stretch out unseeingly, pick up the glass of water, bring it to his lips and he would drink. The glass would be put down and on two more occasions before 5.25 p.m. when we wakened and exited the same process would be repeated until the glass was drained. On this particular evening, shortly before the lecture was due to begin at

4.30 p.m., the lever of a fountain pen was activated and two large drops of royal blue Parker Quink dropped into the glass of water. It turned a startling and revolting blue. In came our lecturer. We sat back waiting for a reaction but none came: he had not noticed.

At 5 p.m. predictably the right hand went out and settled round the glass. This was the moment. The hand swung inboard like some deck-top derrick. He had to see something was wrong. The glass was lifted. The eyes did not budge. How would he react? Would we discover that he had some other tone to his voice? When I tell you that not one of us was asleep you will realise how electric was the tension. The glass reached his lips and still not a sign of detection. A swallow. The jib-like arm went down, swung outboard and the glass was replaced on the table. That man finished his glass of water as usual and I am sure that to this day he did not realise what had happened.

There is an alternative school of thought, of course, that says that our predecessors at that self-same lecture in each previous academic year throughout the period that he had been lecturing had done exactly the same thing and he had determined in his own monotonous and unchanging way always to ignore the joke. Until comparatively recently I used to see him fairly regularly in town. Every time that I did I was tempted to ask him what the truth was but I never did.

In those days it was compulsory to attend the class of Civil Law. The adjective 'civil' in that context should not be contrasted with 'uncivil' or 'military'. In fact it referred to Roman Law, a subject which had a far less important effect on the development of Scots Law than the academicians of my day liked to pretend. It was in my book far and away the least interesting subject in the entire degree. The only consolation in my year was our professor, Tony Thomas. He was an Oxford man with the most outrageous Oxbridge accent I had ever heard. Had it been used in a Brian Rix farce it would not have been out of place.

It was our professor's first appointment in Scotland. Indeed it was probably the first time he had ever been over Hadrian's Wall and you can imagine how a fellow like that would go down with the shower of Glasgow hooligans that we undoubtedly were. We refused to take the man seriously, which was not difficult because we could hardly even understand him.

One day, however, early in the first term, he was redeemed. He had been spotted, cloth cap, muffler and all, standing on the terracing at Celtic Park.

The news spread like fire through brushwood. The guy was human after all – if only the story were true. We could not possibly wait until Celtic's next home game so an enquiry had to be set up immediately. There was but one way to do it. The very next morning, before his accent could cut us through, one of my intrepid colleagues was on his feet: 'Sir, are you interested in football?'

It was a revelation. Our Oxford Don displayed a knowledge of football in general, and Scottish football in particular, that put us all to shame. It transpired that he had gained his blue at Oxford in football. From that day on, Oxbridge accent and all, he became what in Glasgow is called 'a bear' – he was adopted as one of us. All of a sudden we displayed an interest in the Institutes of Gaius and of Justinian that none of our predecessors had ever witnessed and an interest which a few days before would have been unthinkable.

Professor Thomas stayed on in Glasgow for some time. Rumour has it that he never got over Celtic's defeat in the European Cup final of 1970 at the hands of Feyenoord of Rotterdam and that the disappointment drove him back over Hadrian's Wall.

QUALIFYING

At last the great day had come. I was standing looking at a very ordinary piece of foolscap paper (for these were those far-off days long before A4 paper had ever been imagined) pinned by four drawing pins on to a green baize noticeboard which still stands near one of the gates of Glasgow University. We had been there for about 20 minutes, a group of us, all waiting for the last of the degree examination results to appear and each of us was trying to appear nonchalant. The results were to come out at 2 p.m. and we had gathered before then at the traditional noticeboard, waiting for the smartly dressed janitor to come marching round the corner of what was then the Queen Margaret Union and is now the John Macintyre Buiding.

Suddenly he appeared, as smart as he had been in the uniform of the Scots Guards, which he had worn a few short years before. He marched right up to the noticeboard, paying no attention to any of us. Unrolling that all-important sheet of paper he pinned it with military precision, stepped back and inspected it (for a moment I expected him to salute), then marched off in the direction from which he had come.

We surged forward. This was the *momento de verdad*. Our eyes were all on that list, desperately looking – had we passed? The names were arranged alphabetically. I expected the letter 'M' to appear before the Macs and I looked there. No Murray.

My heart had hit somewhere about my knees before I realised that the Macs had been listed before the Ms. A reprieve. Keep looking. On down, seven or eight names, and there it was, 'Murray, L.G.'. That was it. I had done it. I do not know whether I had expected to pass or not. I do not know whether the overwhelming sentiment was one of relief or disbelief. No more studying or so I thought in my innocence. Certainly no more exams to sit. I would have but a few weeks to wait and my apprenticeship would be over. I could then apply to the Court of Session to be admitted and soon I could call myself a solicitor.

I remember that when we saw our names on that noticeboard, typewritten on that very ordinary and very plain but oh-so-valuable sheet of paper, the nonchalance earlier affected disappeared instantly and joy without measure took its place. With those who had not made it we commiserated briefly, but our commiserations, however sincere, afforded precious little consolation to those who could now look forward to a summer studying for resits. They soon drifted away while those of us whose names were on the board remained, savouring it all. Perhaps we feared that one of the janitors would come along and tell us that the list was wrong and substitute another. None did and so we stepped down University Avenue and into the union.

There was no champagne. There wasn't even any drink. There was coffee and a celebratory sandwich. In no time at all each of us had been mentally translated from a final year apprentice and graduand of Glasgow University with not tuppence to his name to a highly successful solicitor or a QC. We were part of an enormous practice or a High Court judge or a procurator fiscal who was the scourge of the criminal classes, or even a highly paid adviser to some enormous corporation.

We enjoyed our pipe dreams or more accurately our Craven A reveries that afternoon. Then it was back to the office to report to an unbelieving master who obviously dwelt silently upon how much academic standards had fallen since his day, back to an office staff whom one viewed now with a newly acquired superiority. However improbable it might have seemed to them, I was about to become a solicitor.

The few weeks until the end of my apprenticeship were almost interminable. When that end came my salary would multiply five times! Heavens, undreamt of wealth was almost within my grasp. A discharge of my indenture was prepared, ready to be signed the first working moment of the day after expiry. Mother would never be called upon to honour her guarantee, whatever that might have been worth. My work attendance had been without blemish and so I did not incur the threatened penalty of two days extra for every day's absence. I would now be free to indulge all those vicious practices that I had foresworn for the past three years, even although I had still not discovered what they were. And, of course, I knew it all. I suppose that like everyone else joining our profession I thought that I was God's gift to the human race in general and to the legal profession in particular.

A few weeks later my discharge had been signed. My masters had certified that I had really, truly and bona fide served them as an apprentice. My application for admission as a solicitor had been granted and I now held in my hand that most treasured material possession of mine, as highly treasured today as it was all those years ago: my certificate of admission as a solicitor in Scotland.

Now I could set out like a twentieth-century Cortez to colonise the world, but my imperialist ambitions were confined to the walls of my native city. I wished then that lawyers could walk about town with some badge of office hanging from their pocket as the stethoscope hung from the pockets of the medicals. I never did find one, but it was amazing how many excuses I found to carry a Sheriff Court process in my hand. With its court backing showing, I carried it in such a way that the world and his wife, or even his mistress, would read it and conclude that I must be a solicitor.

I did not ever stop to wonder what the future might hold. Perhaps it was just as well. The profession which I had just joined was about to undergo a revolution, a revolution that had already started and which has continued throughout the years I have been in the law. What mattered to me at that time was that I was there. I was a member of 'the Club' and I was inordinately proud of my membership. I can say in all honesty that that pride has never abated.

FIRST PARTNERSHIP

My first partnership began in the summer of 1958, a year after I qualified. A friend of mine, Joe Friel, had acquired the business of a solicitor who had died. He was about to leave his then position as an assistant to a firm of solicitors in Glasgow and set up in practice. He asked me if I would join him. At first I was hesitant. I had married only 12 months before and we were expecting our first child. My wife and I were getting by on my salary as a qualified assistant, although the £14 I was being paid for my week's work was not taking us very far. We agreed, Joe and I, that he would go into the practice on his own. I would help out as and when I could. If in a few months it appeared that the practice could sustain us both then I would join him. That in the event was what was to happen.

The office that we took over was tiny with an overall area of probably something in the order of 300 square feet. It was situated two flights up in dingy railway property in the city centre. In those days all railway property was dingy and smelled of damp. You approached it through a close, which led to a D-shaped stairway. There was a main office, probably about 15 feet by 12 with two windows to the front. Off that was a small interviewing room. That was it. There was one telephone and an extension in the interviewing room. The furniture, were it still in existence, would have been snapped up by any American interested in wobbly Scottish antiques.

Before our partnership was formed, my real contribution came in the evening. Three nights a week we had an evening surgery in a tenement flat in Tradeston, one of the poorer districts of Glasgow. That office was bigger. It was only one flight up and we had the use of two rooms, the rest of it being occupied by a succession of families who vied with each other for being the dirtiest. One room was a waiting room while the other was an interviewing room and each Monday, Wednesday and Friday from 7.30 p.m. until 9.30 p.m., one of us (I two evenings, he one) would take the bus to Paisley Road to hold our own court.

There was no such thing as the Legal Advice and Assistance Scheme in those days so we went there hoping for whatever business we could get. The drill was always the same. Before seeing anyone I pulled out two or three half crowns, assuming I had that amount of money, stuck them on the front corner of my desk as a badly veiled hint to the prospective clients, then shouted them in, one at a time. We charged on average five shillings for our interviews in those glorious pre-decimal days, the days of real money. In today's currency that was twenty-five pence per interview and we felt delighted if we came away with two or three pounds for our hour and a half surgery.

Both Joe and I had a council-house-type background. Both of us knew what it was to be short of money and, above all, both of us were conscious that there but for the Grace of God (if I may borrow from Miguel de Cervantes) went we. The motto of the Law Society of Scotland is '*Nihil humani alienum*' ('Nothing alien to humanity', meaning that a solicitor concerns himself with all human affairs). We practised that motto in Tradeston.

We didn't do it just for the money. We did it for the experience, for the contact, and in the hope that something more than a five-bob interview would come. Frequently it did. Oddly enough, one of our more prosperous clients, who was to send us a fair amount of business in days to come when he himself had advanced in life, first came to us at our five-bob evening surgery.

I suppose that it was while servicing those evening surgeries that I realised just what a laugh there could be in the practice of the law in Glasgow. People would come and talk to us about matters that they would never dream of taking to the city-centre solicitor who was tainted with that remote haughty image which the profession had at that time, at least in the minds of the people of Tradeston.

Remember that in those days the profession was only beginning to open its doors (and that only an inch or two) to the vast majority of the population. With the passing of the Legal Aid (Scotland) Act 1949, which came into effect the following year, Legal Aid had been introduced, but only on a very limited scale, and only to bring or defend civil actions in the courts. There was no Legal Aid in criminal cases of any kind, and, more importantly, there was no Legal Advice and Assistance Scheme whereby, as now, ordinary men and women could walk into a solicitor's office and get advice at the expense of the state. The profession by and large was one which priced itself out of the reach of the ordinary man in the street and it was a profession riddled with elitism, class-consciousness and nepotism.

Our evening surgery in Tradeston was different. Joe and I were both young; we could relate to these people, and above all we were dead keen. So they came to see us. And they came about all sorts of things. There was a man who wanted to instruct me in an appeal against the refusal of an award of Infidelity Benefit. I had not known that the state rewarded adultery. A woman wanted a divorce from her husband from whom she had been separated for six years. She had with her three children who were all under five and my colleague's quick glance at the children drew from her the response: 'Aye, but he keeps comin' back tae apologise.'

After about six months of our association I gave up my job as a qualified assistant and took the plunge. The two of us were now in full-time partnership with our tiny city-centre office and our evening surgery in Tradeston. There followed for me the happiest months of my professional career. We had joined the profession we had chosen, but it was not a profession which did anything to welcome us. We were different. We had no fathers or uncles already practising law, ready to hold out a helping hand. We came from council houses and neither of us wore a hat! We had no connections, but we did have a few things on our side, although perhaps we did not identify them as advantages at the time. We were both young and poor as church-mice. Above all we were determined to succeed. Our energy knew no bounds, we were prepared to go anywhere, work until any hour, and to turn down nothing; and the fun we got from our enthusiasm was endless.

I suppose the fact that my partner was a bit of a joker in the most unlikely situations helped immensely. We had to make an alteration to accommodate me in the city centre office, so a tiny cubbyhole was partitioned off with a little waiting area formed in the general office. The trouble with the waiting room was that it was never empty. That would not have been so bad but the people who came to see us by and large were ignorant of things like body deodorants and probably didn't have bathrooms, or showers either for that matter. So there was always an incentive on us to see them as soon as possible, attend to their affairs and get them out and down the stair. Those days taught me the art of interviewing in the shortest possible time.

On one particular day there were about half a dozen people squeezed almost shoulder to shoulder in our waiting room, which would have made a splendid lift for a maximum of four people. Most of them were there to see my partner, who was under considerable pressure. It was a warm day and the atmosphere was pretty foul. He came through from the interview room and asked if I could help out.

'Of course,' I said, enthusiastically, 'I'll go and see one.'

'There's a new client outside called Cannon,' he said. 'Maybe you could see him. I don't know what it is about but it's a new case.'

Every time you saw a new client there was always the possibility that the fellow wanted to buy up the busier half of Argyle Street or hand over the legal affairs of one of the bigger joint stock companies. Who knows, he might have been some titled individual introducing a juicy, newsworthy and well-paying divorce. That thought used to keep us interviewing like prospectors for precious metal. I reached across to the door on the other side of my cubbyhole, which gave access to the human sardine container that served as a waiting room.

'Mr Cannon,' I said very professionally. No one stirred.

'Mr Cannon,' I repeated, slightly more firmly. Still no one moved, but the wee fellow in the corner furthest from me said: 'My name's Gunn. Is it me you're lookin' for?'

It turned out that he didn't want to buy either side of Argyle Street, nor did he have a title, but he did want a divorce. And what a divorce it was. He had lived with his wife for only five weeks and already he wanted to divorce her. In those days divorce was granted only on the basis of what the law viewed as a marital offence. In this case the alleged offence on the part of the wife was cruelty. The only physical cruelty involved was that she had attacked him three times with a spoon! However, when I tell you that he was five foot seven and more timid than any church mouse I ever encountered, perhaps that goes some way to explain how it was that he got his divorce.

We had inherited a fair amount of reparation business – accident claims – from the solicitor whose practice it had been. The bigger the claim, of course, the bigger the fee. Very few of our clients seemed to have injured themselves very seriously and in the main we seemed, despite the popular Glasgow song, to have a lot of grannies who had somehow fallen off a bus. There was the odd bright spot of whiplash injury, a broken arm, or, if we were really lucky, a broken leg. Whenever we were instructed in a new accident claim it was almost with a sense of disappointment that we discovered the fellow was perfectly all right now. In spite of the closest of questioning we seldom found any great continuing disability!

There was one bright star, however, in our little firmament. He was a docker whom we shall call John. He was continually hurting his back and every month or two, regular as a battery hen, in he came with his latest back injury. In each case, the fault for the injury lay with his current employers – or so he claimed. Medically, I imagine, these injuries are among the most difficult to detect and certainly the most difficult to see through and the consequence was that we had a great succession of claims on his behalf against practically every stevedoring company on the River Clyde in turn. They never seemed to exchange notes on those who suffered from 'compensationitis' or, I am sure, that fellow would have been prosecuted for fraud. In every case the insurers for the employers settled on the basis of a disability which would continue for several months and promptly disappear the moment he recovered damages.

I remember one Fair Friday, the day that the trades holidays begin in Glasgow, when he arrived at the office about eleven in the morning blind drunk. He was looking for a 'sub'. It was very common in those days for someone who had instructed a claim for damages to expect his lawyer to advance him sums of money until his claim was settled. These advances were known as subs, and Joe and I used to be besieged by requests. We always turned them down. Apart from any ethical consideration that might have been in the way, we never had the money to pay out.

However, here was our docker visiting the office, looking for his sub. We chased him. He got as far as the landing outside the office before he emptied the entire content of his stomach. We both rushed out and read the riot act to him. We made it perfectly clear that we never wanted to see him again – he was a filthy beast and a great deal more besides. He staggered down the stairs shamefaced and away he went, utterly disconsolate.

We went back in and then the great debate began. Who was going to clear up the mess? Obviously it was not a job for either of the girls that we employed and the lot had to fall upon one of us. I reckoned it was Joe's job – after all it was his client. Not really, said he. I was handling this particular claim and so he was my client. I pointed out that I had only taken on that particular claim because Joe had been busy at the time John came and so this really was my partner's case which I was only looking after for him. The client was his and of course I would never steal a client from my partner. This was going to be a difficult problem to determine. We concluded that the only way of settling it was by tossing a coin. That in itself presented difficulties. Who was to toss? Who was to call? The problem was taking on the appearance of being insuperable.

Soon, however, the solution came to our ears. We could hear someone making an unsteady way up the stairs to the landing outside the office door. The metallic clink of a bucket being laid down was unmistakable. The swish, swish, swish of a mop could be heard. A fairy godmother? An instant Mrs Mop? We ventured a look. There was the bold worthy complete with brand-new zinc bucket and mop cleaning up the mess! We quietly closed the door and fell about laughing! On the Tuesday following we got a letter from him, a difficult letter for him to write but any letter would have been difficult for him to write. Yet it was a lovely letter for us to receive. Not only was he apologising, but he asked if we would please carry on with his case. Rascal though he may have been, at least he had the grace to apologise. In due course our docker's claim was settled. The insurers did not include any sum for a zinc bucket or a mop!

On another occasion Joe asked me if I would see a new client who had arrived in the waiting room along with his mother. I brought them to my room. It turned out that they had been involved in a road accident and they wanted to pursue a claim for damages. The man did most of the talking and his mother remained silent. I got the details that I wanted from him and told him I would obtain a police report on the occurrence. There was only one thing I needed and that was his mother's full name. 'She's not my mother – she's my wife,' was the response. The one thing we did not have in our office was a big hole in the floor.

THE SPLIT PROFESSION

Early in a professional career in law in Scotland a decision has to be made. Do you go to the Bar and become an advocate? Or do you remain in general practice as a solicitor? I had no difficulty in 1957 in making up my mind. In those days if you wanted to go to the Bar you were required to do a period of 'devilling', which really means running around and acting as a kind of unpaid gofer to a practising advocate for about 12 months. Throughout this time the devil was not allowed to earn any money. To make matters worse (as though that were possible) it was necessary to pay an enormous sum to the Faculty of Advocates for the privilege of joining. In those days the sum ran into several hundreds of pounds. I could not even have paid several hundreds of pennies let alone pounds and so there was no real choice for me. In retrospect perhaps I'm glad there was no choice because it would have been a difficult one to make. I suppose I always fancied the idea of the horsehair covering my head. Now when I look in the mirror I fancy the idea even more!

Entry into the Faculty of Advocates is a great deal easier today than it was then. The conditions are much less demanding. The period of devilling is shorter and there are not quite the same enormous sums of money to be paid to join. If the newly qualified lawyer decides to remain in general practice as a solicitor, he has to make up his mind whether he wants to be involved in chamber work or in court work. Chamber work consists of conveyancing, executry, company work and generally all matters of human affairs which require legal advice. Court work on the other hand is different and, if I may borrow a phrase from elsewhere, *vive la différence*.

Our profession, as in England and in some of the other English-speaking parts of the world, is a split profession. We have the advocate (in England the equivalent is the barrister) and we have the solicitor. Solicitors have the right to appear (we call it the right of audience) in all courts and tribunals other than the Supreme Courts. In Scotland they are the High Court of Justiciary and the Court of Session. Originally only advocates had the right of audience in the Supreme Courts but since 1992 solicitors have been allowed to apply for the right of audience in those courts. That right is subject to their passing an exam, successfully completing a training course and doing the requisite number of 'sitting-in' days. When they are awarded the right of audience, they are called solicitor-advocates.

I had the great privilege of convening those training courses in respect of the criminal courts for a period of seven years and I found it all immensely satisfying. There had been a feeling in our branch of the profession that the members of Faculty and even the judges (who of course are all still members of Faculty) would resent the arrival at the Bar of mere solicitors who were not members of their club. I have to say that if there were any such feelings they were kept totally concealed and no solicitor-advocate to whom I spoke ever received such treatment. The advocate (who is a member of the Faculty of Advocates) is entitled to appear in every court in Scotland and in the House of Lords in England. There are other differences between the advocate and the solicitor. He must practice on his own and not in partnership. Except in some rare cases he may accept instructions only from a solicitor and not from a member of the public. He is subject to the discipline of the Dean of the Faculty of Advocates who is the Senior Advocate in Scotland and who by tradition is responsible for maintaining discipline in the Faculty. The Dean is the judge of matters of professional conduct and discipline on the part of members of the Faculty and his rulings are binding on members. He exercises a very summary jurisdiction over members of Faculty and he is always very quick to take steps against a member who has breached discipline, whether in his professional or his private life.

There is an enormous advantage in such a summary system because it means that these matters can be determined speedily and without any complex procedure lumbering into action. It is of course very much easier for the Faculty of Advocates to have this system because while there are now more than ever before, they still number only a few hundred.

On my own side of the profession, the solicitor branch, there are statutory rules and procedures for investigating and prosecuting any complaint. Accordingly the complaints procedure for the solicitor is much more complex, and (perhaps more importantly) much slower than for the advocate.

It is apparently a procedure that does not universally inspire confidence in the public. I was interested to read once in the Aberdeen *Press and Journal* of a comment by a witness. He was being cross-examined by the procurator fiscal depute and was asked why he had not reported a particular solicitor (who apparently had let him down) to the Law Society. Back came the reply: 'To report him to the Law Society would be like reporting Bill Sykes to the Amalgamated Society of Pickpockets.' One might be tempted to ask what the Dickens character Bill Sykes has to do with the Law Society!

Whether ours should be a unified profession with no distinction between advocate and solicitor (as in the United States for example) or whether there should be a right of audience before all of the courts on the part of every qualified lawyer are arguments which have gone on interminably and they will probably last as long as the split itself lasts. There are many arguments each way. Whatever faults there may be in the system as it is, there is this overwhelming advantage – it usually works. And I say that as a solicitor who has frequently sat beside some young and inexperienced counsel whom I have had to instruct in the High Court and many a time I have felt like saying, 'Oh, sit down and get out of my road.' For many years, though, I have taken the view that the split or the division runs the wrong way. The division ought not to be between advocates and solicitors but rather between chamber practitioners and pleaders, with the pleader given the right of audience in all of the courts of the country.

I chose to be a pleader rather than a chamberman. It is a decision that I renewed every working day of my life and it is a decision that I never regretted. I often wonder why and I have never yet come up with an answer totally satisfactory to me. Melvin Belli, the great American accident lawyer who was more responsible perhaps than any other individual for raising awards of damages in the American courts to the galactic figures that are frequently awarded over there, once said: 'Most trial lawyers are really married to the law. They work under a lot of stress and strain; they put in impossible hours. Most are pretty damned good guys. But no matter how hard they prepare, there is always the unexpected in that court room; that and the tensions of the battle keep them up on the high-wire.' There is a great deal of truth in that. In court, no matter what the outward appearance may be, the inner feelings are always of excitement and tension and of adrenaline coursing through the veins.

Another American, Dean William Crosser, said: 'Every good trial lawyer is to some extent an actor, be he artist or ham; and he is also a playwright and director, who prepares the script, sets the scene and stage manages the evidence.' I would not for a moment quarrel with that, and those comments perhaps hold the key, because to those of us who plead in the courts one of the things that matter (and it matters greatly to us) is how we perform. We are our own greatest critics. But those performances in court, like any performance on television, on film or on stage, are exhausting, mentally and physically. Perhaps the attraction of pleading is in the very exhaustion that follows.

I said our profession is split the wrong way. In my view the pleader should start off at the bottom with his right of audience restricted in his first year or two to the District Court, and thereafter by stages be admitted to have the right of audience in each court above. It is absurd that the day a young man qualifies he is entitled to take responsibility for the conduct and the pleading of the most important of cases. It is even more absurd that the young advocate freshly called and with no experience from general practice to draw upon, should have the right to plead in the High Court on a very grave criminal charge. The right of audience in any court is a privilege. It is a privilege not lightly to be bestowed and it is a privilege which should be worked for and merited.

For a solicitor, the alternative to a professional life of pleading is the life of chamber practice. Early on in my career I did my stint of chamber practice and I was glad when it was behind me. I found no great satisfaction in examining prior dispositions (titles to heritable property) to discover whether or not they formed a good title. I found even less satisfaction in helping draw up someone's will or in organising the restructuring of the authorised capital of any company. I would be the last to dispute that these are all valuable, useful and highly skilled operations. (For the sake of peace with those of my colleagues who daily indulge in these things I would have to say that in any event!) There is no question that chamber practice can be highly skilled, highly technical and highly rewarding (financially and psychologically) to those who are built that way. I am not. My body chemistry is different from that of the conveyancer and I would hate that chemistry to be interfered with in any way.

What gave me the kind of kick that I am sure only scheduled drugs could compete with was being there, on my feet, there in the thick of it all, there at the sharp end of a good going trial where facts are hotly disputed, where the law is seen in operation and where the law must be known. It did nothing at all for me to examine a proscriptive progress of titles, or to prepare an inventory of a deceased's estate so that the peering anonymous eyes in the bland faces of the civil servants locked away somewhere in Edinburgh might view it. But it did give me a kick to realise that a client's liberty or his future might very well depend upon my command of my native tongue, or the next question which I asked, or an instant decision which I made upon a line of evidence. That, I suppose, is what makes a trial lawyer tick; that and the *sine quibus non* of the pleader, a sense of drama, a sense of humanity, a sense of humility and a sense of humour.

HUMOUR

Humour can devastate a witness. It can also devastate an opponent and on occasion it can devastate the Bench.

I once represented a man who was charged with an assault with intent to rape. The victim was a downstairs neighbour. There was very little evidence against the accused other than that of the woman herself. It seemed to me that there was hardly any corroboration. My client's position was that the allegation she had made against him was a complete fabrication. The woman was well known in the area as being a bit odd and a liar into the bargain.

I had made representations to the procurator fiscal while my client was on remand that there was insufficient evidence against the accused and that accordingly the case should not proceed. All my eloquence and all my attempts at persuasion fell upon unsympathetic ears, however, and the prosecution went ahead. In the fullness of time an indictment was served which brought my client for trial before a sheriff and jury.

Even on the morning of the trial I spent some time with the procurator fiscal depute who was conducting the prosecution, Bill Morton, attempting to persuade him that the Crown should not proceed because in my view there was insufficient evidence. Bill, who was always a very able pleader, obviously had reservations about the sufficiency of the evidence but his attitude was a philosophical one. He said: 'Let the jury decide.'

The position as a matter of law was that if the jury believed the woman in question then they needed to find only a minimum of corroboration in the facts and circumstances. If they had doubts about the reliability of her evidence then that would be the end of the case. All would depend upon what the jury made of this rather unusual woman. I would have to persuade them that they could not view her as a credible and reliable witness.

In investigating the case my staff had discovered a lot of background information about the woman that might be useful for me. She was obviously not the full shilling. Indeed to carry that particular analogy a little further she could hardly make two and a half pence. She was distinctly and decidedly odd. For example, she regularly used to set a place at her table for her cat. She had many other eccentricities which delicacy compels me not to mention.

When she walked into court at the start of the trial to give evidence, her style of dress made her even less attractive than she was. It was a good start from my point of view. Her simplicity of mind was a kind of aggressive simplicity. While she was giving her evidence I got the distinct impression that she did not appear to impress the jury over much. The sensitive pleader is always looking for feedback while a witness is giving evidence. However, even though I reckoned she was not going down too well, her evidence on the crucial matters was crystal clear and pretty much to the point. She had described in fairly basic terms what my client had done to her in her ground-floor flat. If she were accurately reflecting what took place there could not have been much doubt about my client's intentions. If the jury believed the woman, and if they found corroboration in the other facts and circumstances, then there would be enough evidence to convict.

I started my cross-examination in a manner that was really kind and quite friendly towards her. I was anxious to appear to be making allowance for her simplicity: the jury, I hoped, would recognise what I was doing and would give me Brownie points for it.

Before long a little discrepancy appeared between an answer she gave me and an answer she had given in her examination-in-chief. I invited her to reconcile this little discrepancy, but she could not. I found an excuse for her. More Brownie points. A few minutes later another discrepancy appeared but this time I did not find any excuse.

My kindness was being slowly replaced by a kind of chilly politeness. The difference in tone did not go unnoticed by the jury. When she gave me an improbable answer I pressed her on it pretty hard and the improbability became even more apparent. I knew that I was making progress in my cross-examination; the jury must have been beginning to wonder what reliance they could place upon what this witness was telling them. In my mind's eye I had a picture of her in a boxing ring with me. My object in cross-examining was to push her, at first gently, towards a corner. When I had her in that corner I was going to deliver the knock-out blow and I was not going to miss. So I pushed and I could see her nearing that corner. I pushed some more and there she was in my mind, now in that corner, exposed and vulnerable. Now was the time for me to cast off all shade of kindness and courtesy and hit her with a thoroughly aggressive piece of cross-examination. I had no doubt that she would fall under that cross.

She stood on the other side of the court from me, alone in the witness box, while I was standing beside the jury as though I were one of them. Everything was going as I had planned. I could see her beginning to totter under the onslaught of my questions.

On the far side of the table from me Bill Morton was trying to attract my attention. He had a little note in his hand and he was gently waving that note back and forward. Immediately I saw it I reckoned that I knew what it would say. He was going to tell me not to bother asking any further questions, that he was going to drop the case.

I stopped my cross-examination, relieved that I did not have to go any further. I walked deliberately round the table that separated Bill Morton from me, took the note from his hands, still folded, and walked back across the floor of the court towards the jury. I stood immediately in front of the jury, facing them. I was going to open that note in their presence and I wanted to savour the last possible milligram of satisfaction. I wanted them to share with me that moment of denouement when the Crown was officially telling me they had decided not to proceed.

I took my time. I could relax now. I had destroyed the Crown case by the skill of my cross-examination. I felt very pleased with myself and I was making the most of the moment. Slowly, deliberately, and with a sense of the theatrical, I opened up that note. It contained one word – 'Knickers'.

My immediate reaction was nearly to convulse in mirth. The jury wondered what in heavens' name was going on to cause such a dramatic interruption of the proceedings. I crumpled the note as though it contained news not fit for decent eyes. Bill Morton had conned me. I had been a fool to allow myself to be interrupted. He was not dropping the case and I would have to go on.

I tried to disguise my feelings and get my mind back to the task on hand. I had to resume my cross-examination, get back into the frame of mind that I had been in before being stupid enough to allow myself to be distracted. I couldn't. I had fallen for one of the oldest forensic tricks in the book – a little bit of gamesmanship.

I was livid with myself for having been so stupid yet at the same time so full of admiration for Bill Morton's splendid tactics that my cross-examination totally disintegrated. The client was convicted and sentenced to two years' imprisonment. I often wonder what would have happened had I not allowed my curiosity to overcome me. It was Bill Morton's sense of humour and sense of timing which brought about that result and I never ever forgot the lesson I learned that day – don't ever be distracted when you are cross-examining an important witness.

Humour can also be useful in taking a pleader out of a difficult situation. A young solicitor friend of mine, whom we shall call Bob, was appearing in a trial in Dumbarton Sheriff Court. The evidence was finished and Bob was making his submissions to the sheriff, attempting to show why his client should be acquitted. His main submission was to the effect that the witnesses who had been called for the defence should be believed, and he was rash enough to say that the quality of their evidence was such that, if they had been Crown witnesses, they would have been believed. That was an ill-advised and quite improper comment to make because it reflected badly on the impartiality of the Bench. What he was really saying (though he did not mean it this way) was that the sheriff was more likely to believe a witness called by the Crown than one called by the defence. Since he was appearing before one of the best sheriffs in the country it really was a silly thing to say.

The sheriff pointed out that the remark was most improper. He pointed it out with no hostility but with a degree of firmness which made it clear he would not stand for such statements in his court. Bob looked at him with horror as he realised the enormity of what he had said. Most of us would have stuttered through some kind of inadequate apology and made mutterings about not having intended the comment as any kind of criticism and so on. Instead our Bob gazed up at the sheriff, grinned, and said: 'Rumpole of the Bailey would have said it.'

The sheriff dissolved in laughter and what might have been an unpleasant moment disappeared.

One of the more outstanding examples of the use of humour came in what for me was a truly memorable case. It lasted as I recall about eight judicial days. It was heard in a Sheriff and Jury Court in Glasgow. Each day when word got about, we played before packed public benches. It was said that some entrepreneur had come along and started issuing tickets.

The story was the kind of improbable one that only Glasgow could produce. I was representing a man with a lengthy criminal record. We shall call him Robert. In appearance, he was not likely to rival Apollo and he had a very obvious scar on one side of his face. He was not such a bad fellow in many ways and certainly he had always conducted himself impeccably in his dealings with me.

He was charged, along with a young married woman, with extortion. The story had begun about a year before when the young woman, the victim of an unhappy marriage, had left her husband and found a room in Oatlands, a district of Glasgow unlikely to receive many civic awards for its beauty. She had found a room in a house occupied by a 78-year-old man. In due course, the pair had gone the way of all flesh and the young lady in question had forgotten that obligation of fidelity so necessary in the bond of holy matrimony.

In time, however, true love prevailed: she left her septuagenarian lover and went back to the marital home. There, in an endeavour to start afresh, she confessed her infidelity. Her husband instantly forgave her and all was well again.

Unfortunately, the husband chose not to keep a discreet silence about the whole matter. He confided in his friend Robert. That might have been the end of it all, but unfortunately the husband also told Robert that the old man had several hundred pounds in the bank. Robert had a sense of loyalty to his friends and a sense of what was right in his eyes. Why should not the husband be compensated for having been deprived, however temporarily, of his wife's affection? A scheme, then, was hatched whereby the old man might be persuaded to part with some of his money rather than read about his virility in the tabloids.

The case was being conducted by one of the most eloquent and powerful prosecutors I have ever come across, the late Leonard S. Lovat, who became a sheriff in Hamilton before his retiral. On the bench was the redoubtable Sheriff James Irvine Smith. Not only did the public come in their droves but so also did a host of young depute fiscals, anxious to see what was regarded in many quarters as something of a Titanic clash.

When the septuagenarian was in the witness box the story unfolded of how Robert came to his door one night, announcing himself as the solicitor for the husband. Robert, according to the old man's account, told the old man that for seven hundred pounds the husband would not name him in the divorce action that was allegedly being raised. The old man, who perhaps did not wish to figure over large in the tabloids, agreed to pay over the money to the improbable-looking solicitor, and arrangements were made for the parties to meet in the city centre the following day. The rendezvous was kept. Robert turned up in an old lorry. That did not arouse the suspicions of the old man. It seemed in his mind at least that many a Glasgow solicitor ran about the city in pursuit of his professional affairs in a lorry and an old one at that. He went to his bank, withdrew the money, and handed it over to the lorry-driving solicitor.

When it was my turn to cross-examine him, I suggested to him a slightly different version, namely that my client had gone to him on behalf of the husband; he had explained, quite properly, that the old man would be liable for the expenses of the divorce action and all that was happening was that my client had been attempting to collect the expenses of the divorce case in advance. The old fellow, however, would not have it.

In any event, the case was not going half as badly as I had expected in spite of the valiant efforts of my good friend Leonard Lovat, who was prosecuting with all the fire and ability which were his trade marks.

The time came for my client to give evidence. As a witness, he was absolutely pathetic. The version that he had given me, and upon which I had built my entire defence and which I had been very careful to put in cross-examination, disappeared right out the door of the court as Robert altered his position. Not only did he move the goalposts – he moved the playing field as well as the stadium. The line that he was taking was now a denial that it had been he who was acting the part of the solicitor. His position was utterly untenable.

Disaster. I sat there livid when I had finished my examination of him and almost cheered when Leonard Lovat positively destroyed him in the witness box. Serve him damn well right. He had dropped me right in it and of course the jury might very well have been left wondering if the defence that I kept putting across in cross-examination was one which I had imagined and had no instructions to put forward. Anyway, I consoled myself, I could still go to the jury on the basis that they were entitled totally to disbelieve the accused yet still acquit him, depending of course upon how they viewed the rest of the evidence.

I could, that is, until the young errant wife, the co-accused, gave evidence. She realised that her time was up, that she was going down the drain, and her only hope was to make a clean breast of it in the hope that she would get away a great deal more lightly. She spilt the beans from beginning to end.

My client was well and truly scuppered. It was worse than spilling the beans. She had emptied the entire can! There was only one thing for me to do in my cross-examination and that was to pull on the tackety boots and have a real go at her.

I decided to open by being very clever, or so I thought at the time. Sensing that I could see some kind of biblical analogy in her treachery I opened by assuming my most arrogant voice and asking her very haughtily: 'Who was Delilah?'

She looked at me. After a long and noticeable pause she came away with one word: 'What?'

I repeated the question, the sarcasm in my voice ill concealed. The Bench was enraptured. This was the stuff to give her. The gold pencil invariably used by Sheriff Irvine Smith was scribbling furiously and rapidly, the tongue was characteristically darting in and out of the mouth, full of enthusiasm; a mutter from the Bench of: 'Go on' indicated that the Bench was as enthusiastic to pursue this line as I was.

Silence from the witness.

From the Bench: 'Did you hear the question?'

'Aye.'

'Do you understand what you're being asked?'

'Naw.'

She was excelling in the art of communication. I was anxious to be helpful so I persevered: 'With whom do you associate Delilah?'

Her solicitor was the very able Willie McGlynn. Willie was a very small man who had a quiet but effective style. He had played a minimal part throughout the preceding six and a half days and had kept a very low profile, head down and out of the line of fire. When I asked the question he was heard to mutter in a loud stage whisper that shattered the silence now upon the court: 'Tom Jones?'

The jury burst out laughing, the public burst out laughing, I nearly fell to the floor and the sheriff went almost apoplectic. The witness had been saved. I could not possibly resume such a cross-examination in that atmosphere. The formalities trundled on but the damage had been done and it was irretrievable. My man got nine months while the woman was placed on probation.

THE SHOES

In most television thrillers the focal point of the mystery is usually a single item that traps the perpetrator. I used to think it highly unlikely until one morning in 1959. I was 26 years of age, only two years qualified and I found myself ringing the bell of that brooding edifice, Barlinnie Prison in Glasgow. I had a client charged with murder, not only that but it was a capital murder. As I sat opposite my newly acquired client, James Watson, I suddenly realised that for the first time in my life I was looking at a man who could be hanged for his crime.

He had been referred to me by one of his friends who was on remand with him in the prison. Somewhere along the line I must have made an impression! James was fresh-faced and smiled a lot; and with great expertise told an extremely plausible tale, including the conclusion that he was, of course, not guilty. In those days I was young and inexperienced enough to form views on questions of innocence and guilt – something I would never do in my later years.

There was only one problem – money. No criminal Legal Aid was available in those days and if a person who was charged with a crime wanted a lawyer, then either he paid his own way or else he could be represented on the Poor's Roll. The Poor's Roll meant that no one who was in custody would go without a lawyer simply because he had no money. Those of us who were interested in criminal practice would spend a week in each year representing persons who appeared in the custody courts. If they were remanded in custody and could not afford a lawyer then we would take their case and it cost them nothing. It was our duty to give up a fee-paying case if it clashed with a Poor's Roll one.

For all of the work that came from that week on the Poor's Roll (and it might easily involve five or six trials) we were paid the sum of thirty pounds. Not thirty pounds a case, but thirty pounds in all.

However, my client Watson assured me there would be no problem about money. I quoted him £75, which was a huge fee in those days, and he assured me I would have it before the end of the week. I was so naïve that I had quoted him without even knowing how much work would be involved but experience would cure that.

Predictably the fee did not arrive at the end of that week nor the next one either and accordingly I told James that I was not representing him any further. To be frank, I was very disappointed. I suppose it was the dream of every young lawyer in those days to be instructed in a capital murder. Perhaps the adrenaline flowed much more in that type of case than in any other and that was the attraction. But it was not to be. I got on with the more humdrum crimes that gave me my daily interest and indeed my daily bread.

Months passed. I saw from the press that our Mr Watson was set for trial in Glasgow High Court. I could not help but wish that I had been instructed. It would have been nice to be in the big time! On the Monday that his trial was due to begin I was in the Sheriff Court waiting for a rather minor case in which I was instructed to get under way. The sheriff clerk himself, who was only inches away from the Almighty in my perception of things, came to me to tell me that my presence was urgently required in the High Court in connection with James's case. Such a command could only be bad news. What on earth had I done wrong? I had made my position clear. I was not instructed. I had not been paid. I had written to the man to say so. He had appeared at a pleading diet some ten days before represented by the Poor's Roll solicitor. A summons to our Supreme Court was not something I had ever had before and I did not like it.

My minor theft case was adjourned to let me go down to the High Court. The High Court building in Glasgow sits beside the River Clyde in the Saltmarket – on the north side of the river. Indeed it is situated not very far from Glasgow Cross, where convicted criminals were publicly hanged on a Friday a few hundred years earlier. It is an imposing building of granite or sandstone with neo-Grecian pillars on either side of its former main entrance. Inside there were two courts in those days – the North and the South. The corridors and both courts abound in wood panelling. In each of the courts the judge's bench sits at a height of about six feet higher than everything else. It used to look very imposing and was not for the faint of heart when the full ceremony of the day took place.

When I arrived, I went straight to see Donald Stevenson, the Clerk of Justiciary who ran the High Court. He told me to my astonishment that our James had just sacked his solicitor and counsel and had told Lord Russell, the presiding judge, that he wanted me to represent him. This was just the kind of situation that keeps heart physicians busy.

The trial should have started two hours ago. I knew nothing about the case. I had no counsel and what was perhaps more important I had no fee! A swift audience with Lord Russell followed and I was told that he would adjourn the case until the Wednesday morning at ten o'clock. Within that time I had to get instructions, prepare a defence, find counsel who were available and who would come into the case at that kind of notice. In addition, I would need money.

I went to see James in the cells and told him what I needed in the way of fees for myself and for counsel. He convinced me that money was now available and I should speak to his father. The fee was paid within the hour and I was instructed. The excitement of it all thrilled me as nothing else had done in my professional life so far. The adrenaline had taken over.

I telephoned the counsel of my choice, James Irvine Smith, and persuaded him to accept instructions. He nominated Alistair MacDonald as his Junior, and so the defence team was complete. We had only about 12 years' experience among us, but we had all the enthusiasm that callow youth can bring.

The Crown, who always prosecute in Scotland, could not have been more helpful. They gave us copies of their entire case, and my Counsel and I sat in a room in Justiciary Buildings and read. We read all that afternoon and most of the evening also. The Crown arranged that our client would be brought down the following morning from Barlinnie Prison so that we could confer with him. We spent most of Tuesday morning consulting with James, finding out his version of events and discussing the evidence that the Crown had. We went back upstairs and read again, and finally, in the late afternoon, we consulted with him again.

The killing was alleged to have taken place in the basement of a tenement in the Woodside district of Glasgow. The charge was that James Watson had assaulted a prostitute called Valerie Henshaw, beaten her with his fists and with a bottle, knocked her down, kicked her, tied a stocking and handkerchief round her neck, robbed her of a handbag, a watch, five pounds and a pair of shoes and 'did murder her'. The murder took place, according to the indictment, in the course or furtherance of the theft of these articles and so, in the terms of the Homicide Act of 1957, it was a capital murder. If convicted, young Watson would hang.

THE SHOES

In instructing the Counsel of my choice I had done something that had never been done before in Scotland – at least not in the twentieth century. I had instructed two junior counsel in a capital case. I had not instructed a Senior, a Queen's Counsel. Various tut-tuts were being expressed. This appalling mistake was being put down to my inexperience. A court official was quoted in the press as saying: 'It is most unusual that two advocates should be conducting the defence in a murder trial. Usually it is a Queen's Counsel who conducts the defence when the charge is of such a serious nature. Of course it is entirely up to the accused person whom he elects to defend him.' The thinly disguised criticism of what I had done did not escape my notice. My choice was a very deliberate one. Irvine Smith had only been at the Bar for about five years but he had already made an indelible mark as a pleader. He was more capable than any other that I had met before of captivating an audience. If ever a case required advocacy of the highest order then this was it because the case against Watson was absolutely overwhelming.

The Crown had the evidence of a taxi driver who spoke of picking up the deceased and the accused from a coffee stall in Glasgow city centre. He drove them to a point about 50 yards from where the woman was later found. When they got to their destination, according to the taxi driver, she wanted to go back into town. However, the accused pushed her along the very street where she was found and all this took place around the estimated time of death. In the taxi the woman had been in possession of a five-pound note, but when she was found there was no sign of money. When James Watson was arrested he had in his possession a five-pound note issued by the same Scottish bank.

When the woman's body was found her watch and shoes were missing. The shoes were later found in the possession of the accused's sister. She claimed they were hers but particles of dust and dirt taken from the soles of the shoes matched similar particles from around the spot where the body was recovered. In addition, Watson had been seen shortly after the murder washing blood from his clothing. As though that were not enough he had picked up another prostitute within an hour of the estimated time of death. In the course of his sojourn with her he had shown her a watch which could have been the property of the deceased. Worst of all, he had asked her to provide him with a false alibi covering the time of death. Would that be the final step to the scaffold?

On that Wednesday morning the trial began. The prosecutor was George Carmichael, advocate depute, who would die some years later in a tragic shooting accident. He was superbly articulate and a very able pleader. He could be relied upon to miss nothing.

As the trial unfolded it became obvious that George Carmichael had in fact missed nothing and the case was going as badly as we had thought it would. That scaffold was getting nearer as each day passed. The evidence finished on Friday morning and Carmichael addressed the jury after lunch. He was superb. His address was in the classic mould of the public prosecutor in Scotland, a mould that today often seems to have been cracked if not broken altogether. He did not demand a conviction from the jury like some Napoleonic prosecutor. Instead his approach was the coldly logical one, namely that if the jury were to accept the various pieces of evidence which the Crown had laid before them then a conviction was inevitable. Several times, however, he reminded them that the onus of proving the charge was on the Crown and if the jury felt that the Crown had failed to discharge that onus then it was their duty to acquit. He was the model of fairness. Not for him the modern approach of stressing the evidence against the accused and conveniently skipping over what is in his favour. He was the first to concede such weaknesses as there were in his case – though they were precious few.

I remember thinking as he was speaking that this really was a hopeless task and not even the powerful rhetoric of Irvine Smith would be able to save the life of our client.

In the North Court of Justiciary Buildings counsel for the accused used to sit with their back to the jury while counsel for the Crown used to face them. When George Carmichael finished, Irvine Smith rose to address the jury. He began his speech to the jury thus: 'Ladies and gentlemen. For three days now I have sat with my back to you and I turn now to face you for the first time.' With immaculate timing a female juror sitting at the end of the middle row collapsed in a dead faint!

His address was masterly. It must be one of the most powerful addresses ever made in any Scottish court and it was an example of forensic oratory at its highest. Even Lord Russell, a man economic with his praise, would describe it when he charged the jury as 'a performance of great ability'.

In his address Irvine Smith spoke of 'that dim half light on the fringe of society'. He spoke of the 'pitiful twilight world' in which both the accused and the deceased had lived and he spoke of a curtain having been drawn back on sordid scenes of this twilight world. Never have I heard an address so well received in any circumstance. A life was at stake. The public benches were packed. In spite of that not a body stirred, though I suspect that many a soul did.

When he was finished he sat down in total and complete silence. It occurred to me that if ever an advocate deserved a standing ovation then Irvine Smith did that Friday afternoon. I have been privileged over the years to hear all the great advocates of my day, but no performance I ever heard matched that one. 'Follow that' I thought challengingly to Lord Russell, who was now due to charge the jury. But instead of doing that, he decided to adjourn for the day. Had he gone on then to charge the jury I have no doubt that they would have acquitted James Watson, if only because they could not possibly have resisted the eloquence to which they had just been treated.

In those days, juries in capital cases were enclosed; in other words they were kept in a hotel at night until they had returned their verdict and they were afforded no access to the media. They were cocooned like a conclave of cardinals. In the normal event, even for a capital murder, the court would have reconvened on the Monday morning. However, the Scottish Motor Show was due to open in the Kelvin Hall on the Monday following and the Glasgow hotels were all booked up. For that improbable reason Lord Russell adjourned the case overnight and the court reconvened on the Saturday morning.

Lord Russell charged the jury, setting out the case fairly to them and they duly retired to consider their verdict. My Counsel and I went along the corridor to the gown room, and there we would await the verdict of the jury. Would James Watson hang?

Waiting for a jury's verdict is always an anxious experience. Waiting for the verdict of a jury in a capital case was like nothing else I had ever experienced.

We despatched the macer to buy a bottle of wine and he came back with two bottles of South African sherry! The three of us, Irvine Smith, Alistair MacDonald and I, sat around that large circular table in the gown room and we drank generously from those two bottles amidst nervous conversation. None of us had experienced this wait before, yet there seemed to be a reluctance to admit that this was all new ground to us.

In the middle of our wait I went down to the cells to see James. I suppose I went in an endeavour to relieve the nervous tension that we were all feeling. I spoke briefly to him but I doubt if my conversation made much sense. I do not think I had ever seen anyone as pale as he was. Gone was the confident air that he had exuded during the previous weeks.

I went back upstairs and along the corridor to the gown room. There was nothing we could do but await our summons back into the court when the jury had reached their verdict. A sharp jangle of the little bell high up on the wall of the gown room was the signal we had dreaded. Our taut nerves reacted to its first sound. The jury were coming back, 75 minutes after they had retired.

We got up nervously, each of us trying to persuade the other that we were really quite calm. If truth were told I felt quite sick and it had nothing to do with the South African sherry. We came out of the gown room, went down the passageway to the centre doors, swung into the judges' corridor and turned right into the North Court, Irvine Smith in front, Alistair MacDonald behind him, with myself bringing up the rear. When we got to the courtroom Donald Stevenson told us that the jury were coming back with their verdict, they were not back for further direction.

I remembered the words that Irvine Smith had used in that superlative address to the jury: 'If you convict the accused on account of those shoes, then they will be the dearest pair that any man has ever bought.' I wondered at that moment what price Watson was about to pay for those shoes.

There was no room inside that large panelled courtroom. The public gallery upstairs was packed. The press benches were packed. In those days Glasgow had two evening papers, the *Evening Times* and the *Evening Citizen*, and each had a reporter there on the press benches. I was conscious of their particular problem. It was whether they could catch the later editions with the verdict in this case or whether the fate of Rangers or Celtic that afternoon would be more important than the fate of that hapless creature who was just being brought from the cells to his place in the dock.

George Carmichael and his assistant were in their places at the left of the D-shaped table in the well of the court facing the jury box. Donald Stevenson was seated at his place. The two police officers who formed the dock escort brought the accused up the stairs from the cells and into the dock. Why was it, I wondered, that the two police officers had cushions to sit on, yet the accused, whom our law presumed to be innocent, had to sit on the wooden bench between them? Is that what the presumption of innocence means?

The macer brought in the jury. They all had a grim look about them. They looked neither at the accused nor me. I had read somewhere that a jury that will not look at the accused is a jury that has convicted him. I feared the worst.

The macer went for Lord Russell. He was taking an eternity to bring him. I thought: 'Hurry up. Let's get this charade over. Condemn him to death and then live with it on your consciences.' Where was Lord Russell? Why was he taking so long? The court was deathly still. What an adverb to use in these circumstances. How would James take it when the jury found him guilty and Lord Russell sentenced him to die? His sister was sitting there, the one who claimed the shoes were hers. Had she been telling the truth or was she being very loyal?

The shout went up: 'Court.' The macer always took about five seconds over that word. We all stood, I, at least, trembling. His Lordship bowed to the jury. They were not accustomed to this and they remained impassive. He bowed to the Bar and we bowed back. His macer helped him sit down. We all sat and everyone else in the court followed suit.

The clerk of court spoke first: 'Members of the jury, who speaks for you?' asked Donald Stevenson in that unique and unforgettable voice.

'I do.' The foreman was the one we expected, front row, second left.

'What is your verdict?'

'Guilty of murder, that is non-capital murder.' Someone had opened an escape hatch. A switch had been thrown and the coil of pent-up emotion sprang loose.

The accused was duly sentenced to life imprisonment. He almost skipped down the stairs to the cells in joyous relief to begin his sentence. We picked up our bundles of papers and walked disbelievingly out of the court and back to the gown room. Our feelings were of exhaustion, of relief and of incredulity. How on earth had they reached that verdict? There could only be one explanation – the shoes. The jury had not been satisfied that those shoes had belonged to the murdered woman. Personally I believe that that case provided another illustration of the reluctance of a jury to return a capital verdict. There was no other logical explanation.

The three of us made our way along the corridor and down the stairs to the cells to see the client. He was profusely grateful. He shook each one of us warmly by the hand. The script was fairly predictable. The only memorable feature was the last thing that James Watson said. Just as we were leaving he called to Irvine Smith and said 'Hey! You should have been a fucking minister.'

One thing is sure – if Irvine Smith had been a minister and not an advocate, Watson would have been sentenced to death. I have no doubt that it was the power of Irvine Smith's speech to the jury that saved James from the gallows.

When I got home I sat down and suddenly burst into tears. Emotion? I don't think I knew the meaning of the word until that Saturday.

There are two postscripts to the story. The first is that seven months later Watson tried to appeal even though he was many months out of time. I refused to do his appeal because I considered it was hopeless. The grounds of his appeal? That there had been insufficient evidence!

The second postscript is that ten years later he was placed on the Training for Freedom Scheme. This involved his working each day outside the prison. On one of those days he assaulted a 70-year-old woman, punched and kicked her repeatedly, knocked her unconscious and stole various articles from her. He admitted that assault and robbery and was sentenced to a further 12 years' imprisonment.

A SHORT TIME

In the old days Glasgow Sheriff and Jury Court had a wonderful institution. It was the morning tea break. It meant that every morning at about 11 o'clock the court adjourned for 10 or 15 minutes and a cup of tea was provided for the jury. The presiding sheriff always had one brought to him in his chambers, although those of us who practised in the court were not officially the recipients of any. Nonetheless we became adept scroungers.

The tea break was a splendid idea because it broke up the morning nicely. It also gave an opportunity to confer with the client and review the morning's evidence thus far. In addition it gave the prosecutor and the solicitor time for a quick smoke. Everyone would come back into court suitably refreshed and ready to resume the combat.

A SHORT TIME

The origins of the tea break in Glasgow Sheriff and Jury Court were shrouded in the mists of antiquity and far beyond the recall of most of us. There were, however, many who said that it had its origin in the fact that one of the Glasgow sheriffs of old had suffered from an ulcer and required to eat every two hours. Thus, according to the story, he could not sit from ten until one without a break. Others said that was rubbish and the tea break had been instituted by either the Medes or the Persians. Those of us whose knowledge of history was even worse than our knowledge of geography (or even of law) doubted if the Medes or the Persians had ever visited Glasgow Sheriff Court, at least while a sheriff and jury trial was going on. However, whenever or whyever it began, it was almost universally welcome. Indeed I remember only one sheriff who ignored the custom and sat all through the morning without a break. He was one of the most unpopular of sheriffs and I have no doubt that his attitude to the morning tea break contributed substantially to his unpopularity.

I found myself once defending a client in the Sheriff and Jury Court who was charged with living on immoral earnings. The allegation was that he controlled a team of prostitutes and that he shared the profit of their seedy business. The evidence against him came from a number of these ladies whose virtue could be overcome by the crinkle of pound notes. The main thrust of their evidence was broadly that they were in the business of selling sex and my client had an interest in how much they earned. Put another way, according to them, he was their pimp.

The jury had obviously known little of these things and were fascinated at this glimpse into an alien world. In particular they were fascinated to learn that these ladies sold their wares by a measure that was unusual in the world of commerce, namely a measure of time. The longer the customer wanted to dally with the ladies then the more expensive it all became. Not surprisingly perhaps, the jury learnt that the most popular request was for 'a short time'.

Throughout the first day of the trial we heard from a number of these ladies who told how they had met up with a customer, usually in the Blythswood Square area of the city. So it was that the evidence was peppered with expressions like 'My friend and I went round the back for a short time.'

There were moments of humour liberally sprinkled throughout the evidence. Much of it was behind-the-hand humour and much of it approached the indelicate but everyone seemed to a greater or lesser extent to enjoy it – everyone that is except his Lordship, who sat there with a face like stone throughout. Not once did we see even the merest ghost of a smile. We used to say that he could see a joke only if it made an appointment. Her Majesty's courts of justice were no place for levity!

On the second day of the trial the Crown called another 'business lady' as a witness. I was surprised, incidentally, how many of them preferred that title. We heard from her how she earned her living; how she met up with her 'friends'; how the most popular request of her was for a short time and how most importantly of all she gave over a share of her earnings to my client. When it was my turn to cross-examine her I am sure that I made little impression. My instructions from my client were that these women were liars and he never took any share of their profit. Accordingly I had to suggest to this witness that she was lying when she said that my client had any share of her income. She would have none of it and when I had finished my cross-examination and sat down I had the distinct feeling that I had scarcely made a dent in her evidence.

I looked over my shoulder at the clock at the back of the court. Two minutes past eleven. Good. It was near time for tea; time to marshal my thoughts; time to concentrate. The procurator fiscal paused. He would have called his next witness but he too had noticed the time and so he sat looking expectantly at the sheriff. The sheriff, realising our eyes were on him, looked at the clock. Time to let the jury have their tea.

'Ladies and gentlemen,' said he with what I could have sworn was a twinkle in his eye, 'I think we'll all adjourn for a short time.'

THE LAMPPOST

Pomposity on the part of the pleader must surely be one of the cardinal sins. You know the kind of thing I mean. Lawyers so much in love with themselves and the sound of their own voice that they forget why they are there in court and they turn the occasion into another exercise in self-adulation. It is the sign of a good judge that he does not allow this to happen, and equally it is the sign of a bad judge when it does. I have for long thought that a judge should carry on to the bench not just his notebook and any textbooks he wants but he should also have a large-sized pin to deflate the egos that seem to abound these days.

We had a gorgeous illustration of the well-merited put down in Glasgow Sheriff Court some years ago. A solicitor thought he was God's gift not just to the profession but indeed to the whole of humanity. (And our profession seems to breed that type on occasion.) He was representing an individual accused of an assault which had taken place in Duke Street in the east end of Glasgow, just outside one of those public houses which kept Glasgow Sheriff Court busy for all the wrong reasons. An off-duty bus conductor had been walking along on the other side of the road on his way to Parkhead Garage to take up duty when the assault took place right beside a lamp standard, and he had given his account of what he had seen under the streetlight.

Our self-opinionated friend (we shall call him Mr Swan) was cross-examining the conductor. The cross-examination was longwinded and wearisome. But what was much worse and much less forgivable was the objectionably condescending tone in which it was being conducted. The sheriff before whom the trial was taking place was not one to suffer fools gladly and we had expected some kind of judicial interruption. We had not expected the judicial comment that did come.

In that superior tone which he had adopted, our cross-examining friend told the witness that he wanted to try and get the picture which the witness had been trying to paint. He wanted the witness to imagine that the floor of the court was Duke Street; the witness was standing in the position he was occupying that night and he invited the witness to imagine that he (Mr Swan) was the lamp standard. He said something like: 'I would like you to imagine all this even although I'm not as tall as the streetlight.' We heard from the presiding sheriff for the first time with the withering comment, *sotto voce* but loud enough to be heard all over the court: 'And not as bright either it would appear!'

One could almost hear escaping wind with the deflation of our Mr Swan.

THE SOLDIER

I often say that the courts are places of emotion. They frequently deal with emotional matters and accordingly it is near impossible to be a pleader without a soul that can experience and understand emotion.

In no case do emotions run higher than in a case involving the taking of a life. One such case was that of a young man whom we shall call Michael Reilly. Michael was a young soldier of 20. He was utterly devoted to his girlfriend Linda but when I first met him he was charged with murdering her.

This took place in July 1965, a year after the introduction of Legal Aid in criminal cases. I was the Legal Aid duty solicitor that week, meaning that I was required to be available for anyone charged with murder or culpable homicide. The chances of that happening in Glasgow in any week are always high.

The case began for me one morning at about 3.15 a.m. when the telephone rang with the unrivalled persistence that only telephones have at that time in the morning. I picked it up, eventually, and was sufficiently conscious at least to mutter my number. The booming voice of Bob Brown, then the Detective Chief Inspector of Maryhill CID, was at the other end and he immediately and needlessly introduced himself. I say needlessly because as soon as I heard his voice I recognised it.

What he had to say brought me wide awake. He told me that a young man called Michael Reilly was in custody charged with murdering his girlfriend and had asked for my services. Bob asked me if I would come to Maryhill Police Station, where the young man was being held.

I dressed excitedly and pretty swiftly (for such a call always excited me in those days) and I was at the police station in Maryhill a very short time later.

I saw Bob Brown before seeing the client. I wanted to know what it was all about. We sat in Bob's room, he unshaven and obviously desperately tired; I, by this time, was wide awake, full of adrenaline and desperately interested in learning as much as I possibly could about the case.

Over a cup of tea and a couple of cigarettes he told me the story and I was struck by the pathos of it all. The accused was a boy of 20 with no criminal record at all. He came from a decent, hard-working, God-fearing family and he was overwhelmed by what had happened. The murder had taken place six or seven hours before in the strangest of circumstances. The accused lad and his girlfriend had been babysitting for friends of theirs. There had been a quarrel between them and in the course of that quarrel Michael grabbed his girlfriend by the throat and the next thing he knew she was dead at his feet. He had stayed by her body until their friends returned and then he telephoned the police. He had told them all about it and now he was in custody charged with her murder.

I had known Bob Brown since I had qualified and I had endless regard for the man. He had an insatiable appetite for work and he was the kind of police officer who was utterly dedicated to the job. For all his tough and gruff exterior he had a soft heart when the occasion merited it and this was such an occasion. He was moved by the whole affair and he wanted to ensure that everything that could be done for that heartbroken lad would be done.

I went along to the cell area in the crumbling office that in those days served the Maryhill Division of the City of Glasgow Police. The Victorian conditions under which police officers in those days were expected to work never failed to amaze me. To describe the conditions as appalling was as inadequate as saying that Jacqueline Onassis was the widow of a Greek merchant seaman.

The door of Michael's cell was unlocked for me and I went in. The boy was on his knees on the stone floor of that cell, praying. He looked at me in a disinterested kind of way when I introduced myself.

The cells in those police stations could not have changed much over a period of 100 years or more. The cell in which Michael was being held had a metal door that always had finality in its slam. The walls were concrete, the floor was stone, and the light was allowed in, grudgingly, where the wall met the ceiling. It was almost as though God's daylight was an unwelcome guest in those cells.

This particular cell was probably about ten feet by eight feet, and most of the back wall, underneath what passed for a window, was taken up by a raised layer of concrete on which rested an uninviting Dunlopillo, a sponge rubber mattress. There was a ceramic toilet bowl in the opposite corner, seatless and lidless. A blanket on top of the Dunlopillo completed the inhospitable picture.

Our conversation was not easy. The youngster was deeply shocked. He gave me his account but it came in a way that was disjointed, disinterested. I told him I would see him later that day at court and left. By the time his cell door was slammed again, with me thankful to be on the outside, he was back on his knees resuming his interrupted prayer.

I wondered about his mental condition. Was it only shock or was it perhaps an impairment of reason? Bob Brown had been ahead of me and had already had the divisional casualty surgeon out to see the lad. The doctor had formed the view that he was sane and fit to plead. I could pass no opinion but what I did know is that never in my life had I met anyone so deeply shocked as Michael Reilly. I saw him later that day when he appeared in court charged with murder and his condition was not much better.

A few days later I saw him at Barlinnie. By this time he had been seen by the customary two Crown psychiatrists. They were satisfied, as was everyone else involved, that Michael was sane and fit to plead; but they were equally satisfied that there had been a tremendous traumatic reaction to the whole affair.

Over the next few weeks I had various talks with the procurator fiscal, with the accused and with the police officers concerned in the case. I met his parents and that was a tough meeting. His mother was broken by it all and the poor woman was clearly on the verge of complete mental breakdown. His father was doing his best to be brave but was obviously taking it all very badly.

After very full discussions with Michael, I offered the Crown a plea of guilty to the lesser charge of culpable homicide, or manslaughter as it is known in some other criminal systems. The Crown readily agreed. There had been a special feature in the death. The girl had been menstruating at the time and for some physiological reason that I did not understand, this had involved a narrowing of the throat. The pathologists reckoned that the chances of death resulting from the degree of compression which Michael had applied to Linda's throat must have been a thousand to one or more. Nonetheless his unlawful act had taken a life and a lengthy period of imprisonment was the likely result.

THE SOLDIER

I gave the Crown formal notice of my client's intention to plead guilty to a charge of culpable homicide and all that I could do now was await service of the indictment. It came a few days later. Michael was cited to appear in court for sentence on 5 August 1965. I went up to Barlinnie and saw him again. I met with him and, separately, with his parents. I needed information on the entire background and I was able to obtain it at those meetings. I chatted with a pathologist friend of mine and my preparation for Michael's case was complete.

In those days, cases on indictment in Glasgow were often heard in Justiciary Buildings in Saltmarket Street. I loved those courts because they were courts that lent themselves to a pleader.

The day before Michael was due to appear I enquired which sheriff would hear our case and I discovered that it was James Forsyth, QC, a sheriff before whom I liked to appear. He was not the most popular because he had a fairly short fuse but he was a first-class lawyer and the best kind of judge – the kind who would always listen and respond. There is nothing more soul-destroying for a pleader than to be before a judge who shows no reaction to what is being said. I reckoned then that we were in with a chance of doing something for Michael.

In those days a sheriff could imprison for only two years and if that were not enough then he could remit to the High Court for sentence. I began to wonder if I could persuade James Forsyth to deal with Michael and not remit him for sentence. A life had been taken but in spite of that there were a number of mitigating factors: the circumstances of the case; the devastating effect of the whole affair upon Michael and his family; and the immeasurable punishment he had already suffered. But the most important factor was the sheriff who would preside and how he viewed the matter.

I remember sitting up late at home the night before, preparing what I was going to say the following morning. It would be an emotional plea but I say that utterly without apology because it was an emotional case.

On 5 August, the morning that Michael's case was to be heard, I went down to Justiciary Buildings long before I needed to be there. I wanted to ensure that there would be no rush and I wanted now to compose myself for what I knew would be an emotional ordeal. I sat down alone in the solicitor's room and felt that tightness in the stomach that I always experienced before an important case. I needed that tightness. It indicated to me how the adrenaline was flowing. I did not go down to see Michael. I did not want any more interruption of my thought process than was necessary. I went over what I had prepared and I added one or two other thoughts.

I took my place in the North Court a few minutes before 10 a.m. I now knew pretty well what I was going to say. I sat down. Michael had already been brought up from the cells below the court and he was seated in the dock, flanked by a police officer on either side. I mouthed the question to him: 'Are you all right?' and he nodded. His appearance belied his answer. I looked beyond him and there in the public benches was his mother. There was a lady beside her, a lady I did not know. He looked round for the first time at his mother and the lady concerned and turned back to me saying, disbelievingly, 'That's Linda's mother.'

I went back to the public benches to speak to her and I was still in conversation with the lady when Sheriff Forsyth came on to the bench. The introductory formalities were gone through. I indicated that I was appearing and that Michael was tendering a plea of guilty. The sheriff clerk dutifully wrote out his minute, which indicated that a plea of guilty was being tendered to the charge on the indictment. Michael signed that minute and now it was the moment for the Crown to submit their summary of facts.

Henry Herron was the procurator fiscal of Glasgow at the time and he had come down to Justiciary Buildings from his office in Ingram Street to present this case himself. He was a big man in every way. He was very tall, always immaculately turned out and he had the kind of presence in court that few before or after him have ever had. He was an outstanding pleader, an excellent prosecutor and scrupulously fair. He rose to his feet in that commanding way that he had. He narrated the facts, reading from a prepared summary. As I anticipated, the summary was scrupulously accurate and utterly fair. On occasions such as this Henry Herron always displayed that impassive objectivity which is the hallmark of the distinguished prosecutor in Scotland, a hallmark that seems to become more rare as the years pass. He moved for sentence and sat down. It was my turn.

The news reporters' benches were fairly busy and it was obviously the kind of case that had caught their interest. I remember feeling uncommonly nervous when I got up on to my feet. There was a total silence, the kind of silence that one could almost hear. In honesty I doubt if I could now have recalled much of what I said, but one of my friends in the press was so moved by it all that the following week he sent me a transcript of my plea in mitigation. I still have it. I have changed only the names. There is no point in opening old sores. I began:

> Michael Reilly, my Lord, was born on 3 July 1945. Three days before the tragic event which altered so many lives he became 20.

I wanted to paint a pretty detailed background, but I had to keep the attention of our sheriff throughout.

> He first met Elizabeth, Linda as her friends called her, in November 1961. Ironically, if irony can ever have any part in a tragedy such as this, they spent their first evening together babysitting. Thereafter there grew up between them a very deep and a very real affection one for the other, affection soon to blossom and to ripen into a love deeper than either had ever known. They were very young then, 17, and there was no thought of marriage. That thought was first expressed by them in the summer of last year when Michael Reilly joined the army. In the intervening two years they had been utterly faithful to each other and neither had enjoyed the company of any other member of the opposite sex. He had been an apprentice painter and he joined the army to better himself, for his sake and for hers . . .

The court was totally hushed; I had the sheriff's total attention so I could continue on along this line.

> In October 1964 they decided to become engaged on her birthday the following February. Their marriage they would celebrate in the summer of 1966. At Christmas they decided to advance the wedding and they then arranged to marry on the 21st of this month, 16 days hence. While he was away from home they wrote to each other three and four times a week and clearly their thoughts were almost exclusively for one another. On 24 May of this year Michael Reilly came home on leave so that he might undergo plastic surgery to his nose. Some two years before he was in a fall and he broke his nose,

fractured a cheekbone and suffered various other injuries. As a result of constant difficulties and recurring pain with his nose it had been decided that surgery was the only solution. He was therefore admitted to the Western Infirmary on 25 May where his nose was broken, deliberately, and reset. He was detained for a week. He reported back to his Unit on 17 June.

In the interim, on Sunday, 13 June, Linda told him she wanted to postpone the wedding. He accepted her wish without question. On the Wednesday she suggested that until they were both ready to marry they would be better off parted. The following day he returned to his Unit and his world, which revolved around this girl to whom he was so devoted, began to crumble. On 25 June he came back from Hampshire, where he was stationed, to see her. In the intervening eight days he had known a depth of despair and despondency which he had never before experienced.

I knew that Sheriff Forsyth was an emotional man, and clearly he was being moved by the story. My voice was the only sound in that court, and the dreadful realisation of my responsibility came home to me. I was being caught up by the emotion of it all. I paused, really to steady myself. A quick sip of water and I continued.

On the Saturday, he telephoned her. She agreed at first to meet him, but before the conversation ended, she had refused. His misery was complete. He went to see a film that evening but what it was and what it was about he does not know. By the time he had reached home he had already decided that if Linda was not for him then nothing else in life was worth having and he took aspirin. How many he took is a matter for speculation but he took them until his throat was so swollen that he could take no more. His mother's suspicions soon gave way to certainty and an ambulance was sent for. The agonies of his mother as she watched him slip into the sleep from which he would never waken can be but imagined. In the event the Infirmary was gained on time and Michael was revived. Two days later he was discharged. On Thursday, 1 July, while on sick leave, he met Linda by accident. It was a meeting which embarrassed them both, and neither could hide their feelings, one for the other.

She told him, when the trivia of their conversation came to its embarrassed end, that she still loved him. He asked her out and she accepted. Linda never knew during the remainder of her life of Michael Reilly's attempt at killing himself.

I felt a quiver in my voice when I referred to his attempt at suicide. I paused. The silence in that large courtroom was total, and I realised that everyone's attention was on this pathetic story. I wished that someone could take over the narrative from me. It was becoming more and more difficult for me to continue.

On the Friday evening they went together to the home of friends of theirs in Maryhill. On the Saturday, his birthday, the Sunday and the Monday they met again, though Linda's mother and Michael's parents knew nothing of this. Their secret trysts were known only to their friends in Maryhill. They arranged to meet, in the event for the last time, at the friend's home the following evening. During the first few days of July, the last of Linda's life, they both knew again the joys which their devotion to each other had brought. There was no longer any talk of their being parted or their not marrying or even of the marriage being postponed. Their happiness was now again complete.

On the Tuesday evening they were babysitting and they spent the evening watching television. In the course of the evening they quarrelled. The result of that quarrel was so enormous that it has blotted out the cause from his mind.

They sat opposite each other and they did not speak. Linda rose, crossed over and made to slap him on the face. He turned his head and as he did so the slap intended for that cheek struck him on the nose. That nose which so soon before had caused him such pain. He got up and they struggled and when the struggle was over Linda lay quite still on the floor, dead.

His first thought in her death, like his first thought in her life, was for her. He took a cup of water and he administered to her the Sacrament of Baptism according to his faith, that Sacrament which is to him the *sine qua non* of eternal life and which she had not received. And he prayed. He prayed, my Lord, not for himself but for her and for those who had believed in him and whom he had wronged by his act. He kept vigil by the body of that girl until his friends returned and he did not leave her. He stayed in that kitchen alone, alone my Lord, with his thoughts, with his fears, with his prayers and with his love dead at his feet.

At this point I could not continue. There was a lump in my throat that was as big as any I had ever known. Swallow, you fool, I commanded myself. I swallowed. It was to little avail. I couldn't say any more. I looked up at the Bench wondering how I could tell a sheriff that I was too overcome by emotion to continue.

I was amazed to see tears running down his cheek as he sat noting what I was saying. I knew then that I had achieved what I had wanted, to project an understanding of that young man's emotional hell. There wasn't a sound in that court except for sobbing from somewhere behind me in the public benches. I took a drink of water. I realised that I had to continue and so I did.

That night a torment began for Michael Reilly, a torment which will never end. No matter what punishment your Lordship might impose upon him, no punishment can ever equal the one which he has brought on himself. Since then his parents and Linda's mother have found solace in the cross which the other has to bear. There has grown up between them a friendship deep and true, cemented by their sorrows. Linda's mother has already forgiven the accused. She realises that this act was not prompted by malice nor by jealousy nor by evil. There is no wish for vengeance in her heart. This is a crime, my Lord, which cries out, not for vengeance but for clemency. Michael Reilly is one of a family of three, a family to whom trouble is anathema. Clearly the offence itself could never be repeated. The feelings of Linda's family are feelings of charity and feelings of compassion. The feelings of the accused are feelings of very profound remorse and very sincere contrition. In brief, there is present every possible circumstance to justify your Lordship in dealing with this offence with the utmost leniency.

A sip of water. Another look at the sheriff. He was still badly upset by it all.

Henry Herron was sitting opposite me, noting what I was saying in case Michael was being remitted for sentence to the High Court and he would require to complete a report to Crown Office. He was always the professional. I remember thinking, 'You'll not need your notes, Henry.'

I had been on my feet long enough. I had the sheriff totally with me. Quit while you're ahead. A few sentences more, you'll manage them. I tried.

> This is a very human case and a very tragic case and a very pathetic case. The persons involved are all very human and very pathetic. Linda, who is now dead. Her mother, whose courage and whose character have been amply demonstrated by her forgiveness and by her presence here in this court today. The parents of the accused and the accused himself. An ordinary young man from ordinary surroundings but caught up in a maelstrom of emotion. Your Lordship has heard how his feelings ran from their zenith to their nadir so many times in so few weeks. On 6 July of this year, my Lord, time ceased to have any meaning for Michael Reilly. It still has a meaning for those to whom he is near and to whom he is dear. It is for this reason and for their sake that I beg your Lordship's clemency.

I remember sitting down feeling utterly drained and totally overcome by the tragedy of the whole affair. I was emotionally exhausted. Henry Herron passed a little note over to me that was highly complimentary. A compliment from him was one to be treasured.

Sheriff Forsyth was showing greater signs of emotion than I have ever seen from any judge. I did not think that he would pass sentence because he was too upset. I thought he would rise for 10 or 15 minutes to regain his composure then consider his sentence. But he did not. He placed Michael on probation for three years, and immediately rose and walked off the bench, tears still very visible on his cheek.

It was a disposal far better than we could have hoped for and certainly far better than I had anticipated. The press had a field day and the coverage was almost spectacular. The following day the leader writers were pontificating in their sanctimonious way about the scandal of 'a killer' being placed on probation. Not one of those leader writers had been in court. Not one of them had heard the background or the facts as presented by the Crown. Yet each of them was prepared to pass judgement without that knowledge.

I often wondered how they felt, those leader writers, when they read the following week that Michael Reilly had tried again to commit suicide.

FRANZ MÜLLER

Picture the scene in Court 5 of the old Sheriff Court in Glasgow. A courtroom that was not terribly big; perhaps about 35 feet long by 20 feet wide. There were some benches at the back where the public could sit, but the public were seldom sufficiently interested in what was going on in Court 5 and usually it was only friends or relatives of the accused (camp followers we called them) who occupied the public benches. On that morning Thomas Smith was on trial. He was charged with having assaulted a German sailor by name of Franz Müller.

The clerk of the court called the case. Ian Cullen, solicitor of Glasgow, was representing Mr Smith.

'I appear my Lord. Mr Smith is pleading not guilty.'

'Thank you Mr Cullen,' said the sheriff in a way that was uncharacteristically amiable for him. 'Mr Fiscal are you ready to go to trial?'

'I am my Lord. My first witness is Franz Müller.'

At that the court officer whose duties included bringing the witnesses into the court did a smart about turn and walked out the door calling 'Franz Müller' to summon the witness from the witness room perhaps 30 paces away. Moments later he threw the door of the court open calling out 'Franz Müller, my Lord' as though the sheriff might have forgotten the name of the witness already. He directed Müller, who was close behind him, towards the witness box. The sheriff rose with his right hand raised. He said to the witness: 'Raise your right hand and repeat after me: "I swear by Almighty God . . ."'

The witness, tall, blond and in his mid-20s stared back blankly.

'I said raise your right hand,' said the sheriff this time more deliberately. Franz stood impassively, almost as though he had not heard a word. The sheriff slowly lowered his hand as a look of incredulity crossed his face.

'Do you speak English?' he asked.

From the witness box came the words that the sheriff did not want to hear: '*Ich verstehe Sie nicht.*'

The sheriff sat down wearily and turned to the prosecutor:

'Mr Fiscal, this man does not understand a word of English. Where is your interpreter?'

Bill Brown, who was the fiscal in court, had only been in the Procurator Fiscal Service for two weeks and he did not like such crises especially before this particular sheriff. He was well known as one of the more intolerant people, who seemed to enjoy acting the bully, especially with the less experienced.

'If your Lordship will give me a few moments,' said Bill, looking furiously through his papers as though he would find the answer to the question among them.

'I don't imagine you will find an interpreter there,' said the sheriff, pleased with himself for having thought of such a clever thing to say.

'Perhaps not, but I might find some information on what steps my office has taken about getting one,' said young Mr Brown. The testiness in his voice was not concealed. And from the Bench came, 'Huh, I doubt if you will.' Our sheriff had something to complain about now. That should cheer him up.

'Tell me, Mr Fiscal, do you speak German?'

'No, I don't, my Lord, but even if I did I could not see myself as being competent to act as interpreter this morning,' said young Mr Brown agreeably enough.

'No, I doubt if you would be competent enough.' There was no attempt to conceal the nastiness in that remark.

'Mr Cullen, what do you have to say about this?' said our sheriff, hoping to involve the solicitor as well.

'Nothing at all, your Lordship. It's not my affair.' Ian Cullen had far too much experience of this sheriff to be anxious to help. The Bench was not best pleased with him but Mr Cullen was right. It had nothing to do with him and he quite rightly was not going to be dragged into this.

'Tell me, Mr Fiscal. Two questions. Did your office know this witness could not speak English and if they did what steps if any did they take to ensure the attendance of an interpreter?' The ill humour was apparent to everyone who heard.

'At the moment I do not know the answer to either of those questions, my Lord, but I shall take steps to find out,' said young Mr Brown, sticking manfully to the task.

'That's all very well but it is simply not good enough. Am I supposed to sit here twiddling my thumbs while you try and find out information which should have been in your possession before you came into my court?'

'Yes, I appreciate the difficulties this has caused and I'm sorry that it should have arisen.'

'I wondered when you would get round to apologising. I shall adjourn just now and I shall come back on to the bench when you send word to me that you have someone who can act as interpreter to this court.'

The judicial face was red; the voice was several decibels higher than it should have been and, sad to relate, the sheriff's composure was going right out the window.

'Excuse me, your Honour.' The voice came from the front row of the public benches. 'Ah speak German.'

He was a small man in his mid-50s and his raised right hand held his rolled-up bunnet.

'Do you?' said a surprised sheriff.

'Ah do,' said our man. 'Ah spent four years with the Eighth Army, Sir,' he added by way of explanation.

'Really? Do you know that I might have been one of your officers? I was a major in the Eighth Army, you know.'

Yawn, yawn. How often had we heard that? Only the rank and the regiment changed at each telling.

'And tell me,' enquired the sheriff, 'would you be willing to act as interpreter for this witness?'

'A great pleasure,' said the ex-Eighth Army man, already coming forward.

'Well, first of all tell me your name and address,' said his Lordship.

'Robert Davidson and Ah stay at 35 Aberdalgie Road, Easterhouse.' (A district in Glasgow not usually noted for its contribution to the city's linguistic achievements.)

'Mr Davidson, if you are willing to act as interpreter I shall be very grateful. You must translate everything word for word, question and answer and please do not add or omit anything. Do you understand?'

'Ah do indeed, Sir,' said our Robert, clearly delighted at having a hand in the judicial process.

'Gentlemen do you have any objection if I use Mr Davidson here as interpreter?'

'I have none, my Lord,' said Mr Brown, who saw the appearance of wee Mr Davidson as a panacea for this morning's problems.

'What about you, Mr Cullen?'

'I have no view on the matter,' said Ian Cullen. Our sheriff was getting no change from him this morning.

'Very well. Mr Davidson if you raise your right hand I shall swear you in.'

Robert Davidson did as he had been told. The interpreter's oath was administered. Robert swore that he would well and truly discharge the office of interpreter to the court. He was now the official interpreter and the pride he felt in his newly found position was obvious to all.

'I think Mr Davidson it might help if you were first to ask the witness his name.'

'Very good, Sir,' said Robert, by now revelling in the importance of his post and responding to a command from one who might have been his CO. He marched as though still in uniform across the floor of the court until he stood just below the witness box. He fixed the German sailor with a commanding stare and yelled at him:

'*Vot iss your name?*

The effect was dramatic. Confusion reigned. A hoot of laughter erupted from the public benches. A gasp of astonishment came from Fiscal Bill Brown and a chortle of glee came from Ian Cullen. Meanwhile the sheriff exploded in anger. I fled the court stuffing a handkerchief in my mouth. Twenty minutes later, wee Bobby Davidson of Aberdalgie Road, Easterhouse, emerged from Court 5 and almost skipped along the corridor. He had just been fined fifty pounds for contempt of court but what was that compared with the joy of taking the mickey out of a bad-tempered Glasgow sheriff?

THE WARRANT

One bright sunny June afternoon I noticed that a new client was due to come to see me. Her name was Margaret Smith. The name meant nothing to me and my secretary told me that the lady had telephoned on the recommendation of another client of mine. She had been involved in a road accident and she wanted to instruct me to pursue a claim for damages arising out of the accident. She was due to see me at 3.15 p.m.

When the time came she was shown into my room. She was a rather frail old soul and she walked with a stick on which she was leaning rather a lot. It took her a considerable time to be seated. I remembered what Mother had taught me, got to my feet, seated her comfortably in the chair on the other side of the desk from mine, went back round the desk and sat down. I then took details from her and I noted that she was aged 77. The road accident in which she had been involved had taken place on Easter Monday. She had been crossing Scotland Street, a pretty broad street in Kinning Park, on the south side of Glasgow, when she was struck, knocked down and fairly badly injured by a car, which on her description had been travelling too fast. She had sustained various injuries including a broken ankle, and shock. She had recovered from her injuries but the shock of her experience was obviously still with her. I took the information that I needed and told her that I would apply to the police for a report on the accident and thereafter I would write to the driver concerned to intimate a claim for damage to him.

She was a gentle old lady and one to whom I took an immediate liking. She belonged in many ways to an age that was gone, and I was anxious to do all that I could for her. I told her that she should not put herself to the trouble of coming into town again. Next time she wanted to see me or wanted to give me information then she should either telephone my secretary or drop me a note and I would arrange for myself or even a member of my staff to go and see her. I did not want her to be put to more trouble than was necessary.

When the interview was over she shook hands with me, bade me 'Good afternoon' and left. She was the sort who made you feel better after you had seen her. I was determined that I would do all that I could for her and I wrote off for a police report that same afternoon. This was a case on which I would keep a special eye.

Some weeks later I noticed Mrs Margaret Smith in my diary for an appointment. I wondered what on earth she was doing coming into town to see me at the office when I had made it perfectly clear to her that there was no need for her to trail into town. When she was announced by reception as having arrived for her appointment I went out to the waiting room to bring her in to my room. I saw immediately that it was not the old lady at all but another Margaret Smith. This one was a woman in her early 40s. She had been charged with theft of certain items from her husband's home after they had both had a massive row and had parted. She had pled not guilty and wanted me to accept instructions for her trial and so I did. I discussed the matter with her and I told her how much it would cost and she agreed to the fee.

In due course I prepared for her trial. I wrote to her reminding her of the date and she came in to see me to have a pre-trial consultation. I had done all that I required to do and we were ready to go to trial. It was due to take place the following week.

On the morning of the trial I went to Govan Police Court on time and ready for action. To my dismay and my anger I found that she had not bothered to turn up. When the case was called the court granted a warrant for her arrest. I must say that I felt like the harpist who had brought his harp all the way to the party but was never asked to play a tune.

By the time I got back to the office I was really feeling quite furious about her failure to appear. If she had decided not to turn up then the least she could have done was to phone me in advance and tell me. I picked up my tape recorder and barked instructions into it to my secretary to write to Margaret Smith and tell her that because she failed to appear at her trial this morning the procurator fiscal had taken a warrant for her arrest. If she wanted to do anything about it then she had better come to see me urgently with her explanation for her absence. The letter frankly reflected my mood: thoroughly ill tempered.

It was the following morning first thing when my receptionist rang me through to say: 'Mrs Margaret Smith is in the hall and wonders if you could spare her two minutes.'

'Send her in,' said I, ready to tell her in two minutes or even less what I thought of clients who did this kind of thing to me. Imagine my feelings when gentle old Mrs Margaret Smith of Kinning Park came unsteadily in, clutching my letter of yesterday, looking like death and asked me what this was all about. Had I laid hands on my secretary who had sent the letter to the wrong Margaret Smith there would have been a strangulation!

THE IDENTIFICATION PARADE

It was one of those rare moments. Sitting at home with my feet up reading the newspapers. Saturday morning and all was well with the world . . . until the call from Partick Police Station in Glasgow. A regular client of mine had been charged with murder; he was to be placed on an identification parade and would like me to be present. I was surprised that Danny Pollock should be in custody on a murder charge. He had several convictions but they were for dishonesty. Murder was not his territory.

The crime had made headlines the previous week. A horrified city had read how a 16-year-old boy who had never been in trouble in his life was making his way home late one evening. He was attacked and stabbed in Byres Road, a busy thoroughfare in the west end of the city. He had run away from his assailant and sat down on a wall a few hundred yards away. Minutes later he died from what turned out to be a vicious knife wound to the stomach.

A cruel and motiveless attack, it had taken place just when the pubs and cinemas were emptying. Hundreds of people must have been in the vicinity when it happened yet a week later the police were still appealing for witnesses to come forward. Arthur Steward was the Detective Chief Inspector in charge of the enquiry. He gave me a brief run down on the case and on Danny's arrest.

Pollock had protested his innocence strongly and had given details of an alibi that was being checked out. In the meantime he was going to be placed in an identification parade. Two witnesses had come forward. Their description of the murderer fitted Danny and they would now be given the chance of seeing if they could identify the killer. I went along the corridor to the room where he was being held.

A young, powerfully built six-footer, he had thick black curly hair which was long according to the fashion of the day. His dark eyes filled with tears the minute he began speaking to me. He could not believe it! He had nothing to do with this murder and he knew nothing about it. He was at his auntie's that night with his sister. They would remember. I asked him about his evening at his aunt's. I wanted to know who else were there or who else might have seen him. It turned out that only his aunt and sister were there and so only they could provide an alibi. This disappointed me. There are always problems about alibis provided by close relatives.

DCI Steward and myself had a cup of tea and chatted about the case. The witnesses had not yet arrived and the police had gone out to look for stand-ins for the parade. It might be a little while yet before the parade got underway. As we chatted it became clear that DCI Steward had been impressed with the strength of Danny Pollock's denial. Fifteen minutes later we were told that the witnesses had arrived and the stand-ins had been found. The identification parade could start. We would soon see if Danny had been telling me the truth this time.

I entered the room where the parade was going to be held. We could object to any of the stand-ins if we wanted so we had a look at them with that in mind. They were a fairly motley crowd. Most of them had been in a local bookmaker's and they had been persuaded to take part by the promise of fifty pence or whatever was the going rate at the time. One advantage of a city as large as Glasgow is that there is always a bookmaker's shop near a police station and they are marvellous places for providing stand-ins for identification parades. There were five stand-ins for our parade and they were all approximately Danny's height and build. We had no objections to any of them and so the ID parade got under way.

In those days, though not now, the witnesses were brought into the room where the parade was being held so they were in effect brought face to face with the person whom they might be accusing of committing a very serious crime. That was not a good idea but it was normal at the time. A uniformed inspector was in charge of the parade.

The first witness brought in was a man in his late 20s. He was told by the inspector that he was about to be shown a parade of men and if he saw the person to whom he had referred in his statement then he should point to him and give the number at his feet. The witness meantime was staring at Danny and almost as soon as the inspector paused to draw breath he walked straight up to Danny, pointed to him and said, 'Number five'. There had been no hesitation and the identification had been made with obvious confidence.

'Number five, what is your name?' It was the Inspector who asked the question.

'Danny Pollock,' came the somewhat surprised reply. There was no mistaking the quiver in the voice.

'He gives the name Danny Pollock. Will you remember that?' asked the Inspector. The witness nodded and was shown out of the far door of the room so that he could not meet up with the other witness who was still to view the parade.

The Inspector told Danny that he could change his position in the line-up if he wanted. Danny did not and he kept his eyes firmly on the floor steadfastly avoiding my gaze.

'Bring in the next witness.'

In came a schoolteacher in her early 20s. The Inspector went through the formalities and then let her walk over to the parade.

She walked to the end of the line-up and turned round. She stood opposite Danny and stared at him accusingly.

'Number five,' she said almost defiantly. The voice was firm and the identification certain.

'Number five, what is your name?'

'Danny Pollock.' The weakness in the voice was noticeable.

'He gives the name Danny Pollock.' The witness nodded, curtly turned and walked briskly from the room. She was in no doubt that she had just come face to face with the murderer.

I looked at Danny but he still kept his eyes on the floor and refused to meet my gaze. The two identifications could not have been more positive. This was a murder which had taken place when there were hundreds of people in the vicinity. Many must have seen both victim and assailant, yet only two had come forward. Why on earth?

The stand-ins were taken out of the room to get their fifty pence or whatever and then away to the pub to tell their mates how they had been standing in a line-up next to a murderer. That little piece of tittle-tattle would be almost as important as the football results. Danny was taken by the jacket cuffs by two CID officers and led out back along the corridor to the Detective Chief Inspector's room. I followed at the rear of the little party. Nothing was said until we were in and the door was closed.

DCI Steward spoke: 'Daniel Pollock, I am about to prefer a serious charge against you. I want you to listen carefully. You need not make any reply to the charge but anything you say will be noted and may be used in evidence. Do you understand?' Danny nodded.

Mr Steward then went on to charge Pollock with the murder and he detailed in the charge the specific acts of violence that were alleged. When he reached the end of the charge he said: 'First of all do you understand the charge?' Again, a nod was the only reply.

'Now, do you wish to say anything in reply?' The voice was firm without being hostile. Danny's reply was immediate: 'Honest to Christ I know nothing about it. Get my sister. She'll tell you where I was.' DCI Steward and the two detective officers who were with him scribbled furiously. Their notes of the reply were important. We all trooped down to the charge bar of the office and similar formalities were gone through in presence of the officer on duty. In those days he had to write the full detail of the charge into what we knew as the blotter, the popular term for the detention book. It took some minutes. Once that had been done the officer on duty read the charge out to Danny and cautioned him in similar terms about any reply.

'I have already told this gentleman I know nothing about that murder. I was never near Byres Road that night,' replied Danny.

The officer on duty wrote that reply in the detention book and then said to Danny: 'You will now be detained and you will be taken to the Sheriff Court on Monday.'

Danny was searched. His tie, his belt and his shoelaces were removed and he was taken through to the cell block. A few seconds later a cell door slammed shut and Daniel Pollock was in custody for a murder that he claimed he did not commit. Two witnesses had positively and firmly identified him as being the person responsible. The question was were they right?

I asked the officer on duty if I might see my client. I did not want him brought out of his cell and I was quite happy to see him in there. A uniformed officer took me along to the cell and unlocked the door for me.

Danny Pollock was squatted in a corner, head on his arms and sobbing helplessly. I tried to think of some words of comfort but I could not. I told him I would come and see him the following day.

DCI Steward was uneasy. The identifications had been good and had been given without hesitation. At the same time he felt there was something not quite right. Good detective officers often go by gut feeling and Arthur Steward was a good detective officer. The search for the accomplice was in full swing. He had been wearing a piece of rather distinctive headgear and that might make the search for him a little bit easier. Other officers were looking for Danny's sister and his aunt to check out the alibi.

I had been home for something less than two hours when DCI Steward phoned me. He had spoken to Danny's sister and aunt and had taken statements from them. He had seen them separately. Not only did they back Pollock in what he claimed they also had persuaded DCI Steward that they might be telling the truth. Could both eyewitnesses be wrong?

It was about half past eleven on the Sunday morning when DCI Steward telephoned me again. The accomplice had been caught and he was about to be put on an identification parade but he had asked if I would represent him. I made my way down to Partick and back to the police station there.

Peter Brown was a different type altogether from Danny. He was a few years older and much smaller. He had a squeaky, high-pitched voice. He had been there he told me. He saw the stabbing.

He was with the person who did it but he had nothing to do with it and was so horrified by the attack that he had been in hiding ever since. He did not mention who his friend was but I desperately had to know. I was not just being curious, though God knows I was that too. If he was blaming Pollock then obviously I could not represent him.

'Who was your friend?' I asked, almost fearful of the answer.

'Billy Collins.' I felt a great sense of relief. Perhaps Danny had been telling the truth. Peter had not made any statement to the police. He wanted to talk to me about it first but he would give them a full statement after the parade. The witnesses and stand-ins for the identification parade were there already and everyone was waiting. We went into the same room as the day before and the parade assembled.

The same two witnesses were brought in. They identified Peter without hesitation. Peter was taken from the parade room to the DCI's room and there charged with the murder. His reply was forceful and immediate: 'It was Billy Collins that stabbed the boy. Ah was there but Ah'd nothin' tae dae wi' it,' he said. He was anxious to make it clear that he was not acting along with Collins in the murder. He wanted to tell the police all that he knew of the incident and so an officer from another division was sent for. Voluntary statements (statements from a person already charged with the crime in question) need to be taken by an officer who has had no connection with the enquiry. That officer duly arrived and the three of us, he, Peter and I, all sat down in another room while Peter's statement was taken. He told all about the events of the evening of the murder. It took about 50 minutes to write down verbatim what he had to say. He read over the statement and signed it. If he were telling the truth then not only was Danny Pollock innocent but those two witnesses had identified the wrong man as a murderer!

Peter was put into a cell. I went to see Danny to report to him on the rather extraordinary events while DCI Steward led his team in the search for Collins. Within the hour Collins was in custody. I saw him come in. He bore no more than a passing resemblance to Danny Pollock. Another parade was rather swiftly organised. Those same two witnesses who had identified Pollock the day before came along and identified Billy Collins as the murderer with just as much confidence. The case was reported to the procurator fiscal on the Monday morning and he ordered Pollock's release. Danny walked out of Glasgow Sheriff Court that morning intensely relieved and forever grateful to a detective officer who responded to a gut feeling. It had been quite a weekend.

Billy Collins admitted the murder and the Crown did not proceed against Peter. That experience served as yet another reminder of the danger of visual identification. It was to me a particularly frightening example because those two witnesses had been within a few feet of the killer yet each independently of the other had picked out the wrong man. To convict on visual identification alone is highly dangerous. Our judges and sheriffs constantly remind juries of the dangers. In the early part of this century Oscar Slater learnt of those dangers. In latter days so did Peter Hain and Patrick Meehan, both victims of wrongful visual identification. One Saturday afternoon in a police station in Partick Danny Pollock learned the same lesson.

THE WEE HAPPY BUS

There is still a single-decker bus route in my native city that is uncommonly popular. It is free, but that is not the cause of its popularity. It runs regularly every afternoon from Monday to Friday. Its popularity has never waned even in these days of cutbacks and recessions. It has a surprisingly high seat-occupancy rate, the envy of Stagecoach and probably every other bus operator anywhere in the country. Indeed, I am told that it is so busy that sometimes it is difficult to get a seat for the short journey which it makes from the Gorbals to Riddrie. The way things are going I am told that it is likely to be a busy service for many years to come. I refer of course to the prison bus operated by Strathclyde Police which conveys prisoners from Glasgow Sheriff Court and Glasgow High Court to Barlinnie Prison.

On the particular afternoon with which we are concerned, the police escorts who travel in the bus had, unusually, taken a rather elderly man into the front cabin with them. This was unusual because there was room in the passenger section of the bus; there were empty seats and there was no apparent reason for taking somebody into the front. He did not fit the usual pattern of passenger. He was clean, tidy, well groomed and he had all the appearances of a man unused to such surroundings.

Suspicions were immediately aroused amongst the other passengers. Why was this preferential treatment being afforded? Who was this individual and why should he be treated in this special way? The shouted efforts of the prisoners to the escorts to find answers to these questions were met with total silence. The escorting police officers were obviously determined not to say anything about their passenger or why he was being accorded a seat amongst them.

Within moments a conclusion was reached among the passengers. This must be a sex offender. That's why he's being kept apart. Sex offenders are pariahs amongst other prisoners and they are frequently segregated for their own good. That must be why this one is being kept apart. A growing sense of anger at the individual was almost palpable. The unrest was evident. An angry shout went up: 'He's a dirty beast.' Others who indicated what they would do to the hapless individual when the bus reached Barlinnie took up the theme. None of it sounded particularly welcoming.

One of the escorting officers in the front, sensing perhaps that things had gone far enough and anxious to set the record straight and thus avoid any trouble turned round to the passengers and shouted: 'Cut it out. He's no' a dirty beast. He's no' a sex offender at all. He murdered his wife. Alright?'

The startling news took its captive audience totally by surprise. The brutal revelation had been as sudden as it had been unexpected. There was a moment or two of silence then a small voice was heard from the back of the bus:

'Hey, Mac, dae ye dae homers?'

NEVADA II

There are many shipwrecks dotted around the Hebridean islands. Sir Compton MacKenzie amused us with his tales of these islands and their inhabitants in *Whisky Galore!*, which centred round the sinking of a ship. Both the novel and film gave us a taste of the wonderful simplicity and deviousness of the islanders.

Another ship, the *Nevada II*, went down off the island of Coll in similar circumstances – but the prize was not that precious amber nectar. In 1942 the *Nevada II* had sailed from Tilbury Docks in London to join a convoy assembling in the Sound of Kerrera near Oban. It was headed for Lagos in West Africa. The cargo of *Nevada II* consisted of gun carriages, tea, tools, asbestos, cloth, cigarettes and, most importantly, currency, West African twenty-shilling notes to be precise, and, reputedly, amounting to £75,000.

The Second World War was at its height. Germany had overrun France, Belgium and Holland. The obvious and the shortest route for any ship sailing from Tilbury Docks to West Africa was through the English Channel and down across the Bay of Biscay. The entire continental shore of the Channel, however, was occupied territory and the Channel itself had become a favourite hunting ground for German U-boats. It was too dangerous for merchant shipping. Accordingly, the *Nevada II* was directed to join the convoy which was gathering off the west coast and which would be escorted by destroyers. Ironically, while the *Nevada II* dodged the torpedoes of the German U-boats, it was unable to avoid the fierce fogs of the west coast of Scotland and while trying to navigate through one of those fogs, it ran aground on the rocky beach of Struan Bay on the Island of Coll. It was only a mile from the Coll Lighthouse but the fog was so dense that no one on the ship could see the light. Mercifully the entire crew of 60 were saved. The islanders helped the crew to safety and some said they helped themselves to the cargo as well.

After the appropriate surveys of the ship had taken place, the *Nevada II* was declared a wreck and Philip Bauer, a diver from London who had turned to salvage as a result of the number of wartime sinkings, was awarded the salvage contract. Bauer got on with the salvage and there the matter rested . . . until February 1960. In that month some of the West African Currency Board pound notes which had been carried in the strongroom of the *Nevada II* began to turn up. They no longer had any face value because they had been cancelled following the wreck of the *Nevada*. However, some had been exchanged for money and accordingly those concerned had lost out. The trail of these notes led back to Zurich and to a money dealer called Theodor Arnold. It transpired that he had bought them in 1960 from an Englishman by the name of Philip Bauer, the same person who had carried out the salvage of the ship all those years before.

Interpol were alerted and Argyllshire Police were placed in charge of the enquiry, for, if a theft had been committed, it had been committed in their jurisdiction.

In due course Philip Bauer was arrested and charged with having stolen 19,749 twenty-shilling notes belonging to the West African Currency Board from the *Nevada II* while she was ashore in Struan Bay on the island of Coll between 1 September 1942 and 30 September 1944. He appeared in Oban Sheriff Court, was originally refused bail and remanded in custody. A local solicitor in Oban, Jim Graham, recommended that Bauer instruct me.

He was being held in Barlinnie Prison and so I went to Barlinnie to see him. He was not at all a typical Barlinnie inmate. He was intelligent, well educated and he had never been in bother in his life. He did not take kindly to being remanded in custody. I was instructed by him to appeal the refusal of bail to the High Court. I did that but the High Court refused his appeal. The Crown alleged that if Bauer were released, they were afraid that he might jump bail and not turn up for his trial. With the refusal of his bail appeal it looked as though Bauer would be required to remain in custody until his trial.

In those days an untried prisoner was allowed to have his own food sent in from outside the prison, a practice discontinued due to fears of prisoners' food being laced with drugs. Philip Bauer decided to avail himself of that privilege and gave me instructions accordingly. I had a client called Henryk Grunwald. Henryk was a Polish ex-serviceman who had settled in Glasgow and had opened a restaurant in Hope Street. The food was good and the restaurant was one of our favourite watering holes in those days. Henryk was delighted to supply lunch to Bauer. So every day that Philip Bauer was in custody a taxi arrived at Barlinnie Prison with his lunch from the Grunwald Restaurant. There were always three courses and a flask of coffee. It was long after Bauer's release on bail that Henryk told me how he used to lace the coffee with a very large Courvoisier! No wonder Philip Bauer raved about the quality of the catering!

The Crown, however, eventually relented on the question of bail because they would not have been ready to bring the case to trial and complete it (as they had to do in those days) within the statutory 110 days. Accordingly I got a telephone call from the then deputy crown agent, Stanley Bowen, telling me that if we appealed to a bench of three judges the Crown would agree bail of £5,000. This, incidentally, did not involve the English idea of sureties. It meant the physical handing over of the cash to the sheriff clerk concerned – in this case in Oban.

I instructed Manuel Kissen QC (later to become Lord Kissen) for the bail appeal, together with Irvine Smith as his junior, and they went in before Lord Clyde and two of his colleagues. The Crown indicated to the court that they were now in a position to agree bail of £5,000. That was not good enough for Lord Clyde. Notwithstanding the attitude of the Crown, who obviously knew more about the case than he did, he increased the figure of bail to £7,500! How much is that worth today?

This meant that Philip Bauer would get out but not until the cash had actually been lodged with the sheriff clerk in Oban. He in turn would issue a liberation warrant that would need to be taken to Barlinnie Prison in order for Bauer to be released.

After much to-ing and fro-ing we managed that. It involved bringing a certified copy of the Appeal Court's interlocutor back to Glasgow, picking up £7,500 in cash from my firm's bank, driving to the sheriff clerk's office in Oban and consigning the money there. He then issued me with the liberation warrant which I had to take to Barlinnie. Eventually, at about ten o'clock at night, Philip Bauer was released.

Our preparations for the trial got underway and I found it all fascinating. I learnt about ships and salvaging and diving. The only ships which I had come across up to that time were those which carried passengers up and down the River Clyde, so this was a whole new world to me. I got to travel not just to Edinburgh, which was about the horizon of my world at that time, but to London and Antwerp and Brussels and, of course, to Zurich.

It was in Zurich that the whole matter had begun with the exchanging of the notes and it was there that the key to the whole case lay.

Bauer was convinced that the two bankers from Zurich with whom he was alleged to have negotiated the exchange would not come over to Scotland to give evidence, for that would be a breach of confidence on their part. The entire ethos of international banking in Switzerland was confidentiality and Philip Bauer could not contemplate those bankers making any statement. Without them the Crown clearly would have no case for they were the only witnesses who could speak to the fact that the notes were ever in the possession of Philip Bauer.

So I had to go to Zurich. I would have to interview them to find out whether they were coming over to give evidence at the trial and if so what that evidence would be.

I went first to Brussels to interview one of the Crown witnesses. His evidence was fairly inconsequential and did not take the case very much farther forward. I had arranged to fly on to Antwerp (my first ever helicopter journey) and thence to Zurich. I arrived in Zurich at about 5 p.m. and booked into an excellent little hotel which was very centrally placed and just around the corner from the offices of the banker with whom I had arranged a meeting. I speak no German and when I realised that that was the very first occasion I had been in a country where I was not able to speak the language I really felt quite vulnerable.

Not having any German immediately proved disadvantageous. I wanted a wash when I arrived but I could not see any soap in my bathroom. I telephoned reception and asked if I could have some soap please. A rather surprised receptionist explained to me in her best but slightly broken English that I would need to wait until seven o'clock when they served dinner to get my soap.

I had arranged to see the first of the bankers, Theodor Arnold, that very night. He was still in his office and working away when I went there around 9.00 p.m. It was a very difficult interview for me to conduct because the man was much more interested in what information was coming continuously into his office on one of those infernal ticker-tape machines. Every time it started to click (and that was about every two minutes) he would jump up and run through to the office next door where the machine was situated. He scanned the tapes anxiously before he came back in and let me try to resume my interview.

In the event Bauer's optimism was quite unwarranted. Herr Arnold had every intention of coming over to give evidence. He felt that Bauer had betrayed and defrauded him when he exchanged the notes. Bauer must have known perfectly well that they were worthless. That was reason enough for Theodor Arnold to come to Scotland and give evidence. Confidentiality was not an issue when dishonesty was involved. The following day I saw the other banker who had been involved with Arnold and his attitude was exactly the same.

It was with some disappointment that I reported to my client when I got back to Glasgow on what the Zurich bankers had told me. I am sure that it was with even more disappointment that he heard my news.

The rest of the preparation for the case went according to plan. There was something of a problem on a professional level. I had instructed Manuel Kissen QC for the bail appeal to the three judges although I did not want him for the trial. I wanted Irvine Smith to lead because Irvine was a far better jury lawyer than Manuel Kissen. Manuel was a bit of an intellectual genius but he was not right for a jury. Irvine Smith would make a far better job of it. The problem, however, was that Manuel had taken charge of the preparation on the basis that he was now instructed! I did not have the courage to tell him that I did not really want him for the trial. After all it was not for a boy who was only five years qualified to speak that way to one of the country's leading Queen's Counsel.

The case was heard in the old Court 3 of the Parliament House in Edinburgh. It really is a magnificent old court. It positively reeks of history and tradition. Some of the most celebrated cases in our legal history have been heard there. It was in that very court that John Inglis (later to become Lord Inglis) led the defence in one of Scotland's most celebrated murder trials – that of Madeleine Smith. I can never enter that court without being conscious of the history involved. It was on 12 November 1962 that our trial got underway. The presiding judge was Lord Cameron, one of the country's most respected judges and an old sailor himself. Rumour had it that he had asked for the case to be put in front of him. Manuel Kissen QC appeared for Philip Bauer and J. Irvine Smith assisted him.

We had many a laugh with the evidence in the case as it unfolded. Clearly the locals had helped themselves to the cargo of the *Nevada II* but not surprisingly no one was prepared to say so. There was evidence that the strong room was breached, that money was scattered about the foreshore, that some was missing and never accounted for, but not one of the locals had seen any of this. There was no accounting for their temporary blindness!

One of the witnesses who lived on the island, James Mackinnon by name, told of how he had found bundles of notes in the sand near the wreck and how he had handed them into the coastguard. Very admirable, thought everyone, but it was only in cross-examination that he admitted that he had first taken them to a bank in Oban to see if they were worth anything! Manuel Kissen asked at one point: 'Did the islanders go aboard the ship?'

Mr Mackinnon hesitated and then replied: 'I don't know about that.' He must have been the only islander who didn't know.

Manuel Kissen then asked: 'Did they go over your land?'

'Och yes, they did that, but I don't know whether they were going to the *Nevada*.'

Perhaps he thought they were going for a swim. When Mr Kissen pressed the witness by suggesting that they didn't just disappear into the sea Mr Mackinnon had no answer.

Another of the islanders who was called to give evidence said only: 'Ah canna hear' when he got into the witness box. Even when the presiding judge, Lord Cameron, came right along the bench to administer the oath and stood no more than a couple of feet away from him he claimed that he could hear nothing. Perhaps he was fortunate. He would not need to answer any questions and so he was sent away. I wondered that others had not thought of that!

Notwithstanding our best efforts Philip Bauer was found guilty on 14 November 1962 after a three-day trial. In his plea in mitigation Manuel Kissen asked Lord Cameron, who was no soft mark when it came to sentencing, to impose a fine because in his submission Bauer had stolen 19,749 worthless pieces of paper. Lord Cameron did not accede to Manuel's request but he gave Bauer only nine months, which was remarkably lenient.

At the end of the case I discovered that the majority on the jury for guilty was only 8–7. I was left wondering what might have happened if Irvine Smith, one of the greatest jury pleaders I have ever heard, had led the defence as I had wanted. I was totally convinced that Irvine would have persuaded at least one more juror.

A souvenir of a case is sometimes a nice thing to have and so immediately after the trial I approached one of the court officials who now had care of the twenty-shilling notes. Looking him straight in the eye, I told him that when I counted those old bank notes there were only 19,748.

His reply was memorable: 'Mr Murray, when I counted them there were only 19,747.' We both had a souvenir!

The day after the trial the *Daily Express* carried an article about me and my travels. It described me as a 'One Man Interpol'. Even though it was highly complimentary, I was horrified by it and I promptly wrote to the Law Society to distance myself from it and to point out that I had nothing to do with its appearance. In those days there was a total ban on any kind of advertising or self-promotion. I received an acknowledgement that was rather aloof and which made it clear that that kind of publicity was deplored. The tone was that if I said I had nothing to do with the article then they would believe me, but really I had to be careful with these journalists!

How attitudes have changed. Nobody today would give it a second thought. Indeed today many of the members of my profession seem to me to go about their daily affairs actively seeking that kind of publicity.

JAMES IRVINE SMITH QC

I often complain that the Scottish Bar seems to do its very best to discourage characters. In my day there have been many: Lionel Daiches, Frank Duffy, Irvine Smith. All these were characters in their own right with their own personality and their own charisma.

Of those great pleaders that I have mentioned it was Irvine Smith that I knew best. I am of course referring to James Irvine Smith QC. He was an advocate who was appointed a sheriff in Glasgow in 1963 while he was at the peak of his career at the junior Bar. He remained in Glasgow until he moved to Greenock in 1982. He retired in 1992 and is sadly missed.

I first met Irvine Smith in 1954, through the auspices of my then apprentice master, the late Willie McRae. I was just beginning my professional apprenticeship while he had just been called to the Bar and was thus just setting out on his career. I am proud to say that I have been a friend of his ever since. He was truly a character on the bench and I doubt whether in my lifetime we shall see his like again.

I have described earlier in this book how he delivered the best jury speech I have ever heard while he was defending a capital murder trial in the High Court in Glasgow. It was the first capital murder case in which I was ever involved and he did a superb job. The client was convicted of non-capital murder and I am in no doubt that it was only his powerful oratory that saved the man from being hanged.

However, apart from being one of the most persuasive of advocates that I have ever heard in my years in the profession, he was truly a very colourful character. He has a great command of language and he brought to the position of sheriff not just an ability which very few of his colleagues possessed but a splash of colour to an otherwise grey landscape. If there was a grain of humour in a situation then Irvine Smith would find it, let there be no doubt. He never allowed the intrusion of humour to cloud his approach nor did he permit it to affect his judgement. What he did, however, was to attempt to preserve the sanity of those practising before him by the injection of judicious and judicial humour. Whether he was successful in his efforts may not be for me to judge, but I am in no doubt that he was.

He used to delight in telling how he was possessed of divine qualities. He illustrated this by telling how, on his return to duty following a heart attack, two accused persons had been brought up the stairs from the cells in Glasgow Sheriff and Jury Court where he was presiding. When they saw who was on the bench one muttered to the other: 'It's him, Jesus Christ.'

The story goes on to narrate that the second was heard to exclaim: 'I thought that wee bastard was deid.'

Not only did Sheriff Irvine Smith illustrate that he was not deid but by the subsequent sentence which he imposed he also illustrated that he was still a wee bastard!

His humour was legendary. Two homosexuals appeared before him in the days when that practice was still subject to public condemnation. They pled guilty to having indulged in some homosexual practice or other. Irvine Smith took some moments to consider his disposal and then announced that he was going to defer sentence on them in order that they could pull themselves together.

He was forthright in his language. After a particular trial when he thought that the young man who was the accused had been less than truthful he called him 'a fecund liar'. Most of us know that that adjective comes from the noun 'fecundity' and that it indicates a degree of fertility. The young accused however clearly did not know the word and mistook it for some other of Anglo-Saxon derivation which is much less polite. The ensuing confusion was memorable!

A client of mine was one day making his way down one of the corridors on the first floor of the old Glasgow Sheriff Court in Ingram Street looking for Court 6. He thought that he was going in the right direction but was unsure. A small dapper man appeared from a room to his left. He seemed vaguely familiar to that gentleman. The familiar look also encouraged him to ask: 'Is Court 6 doon here, Jimmy?' (Everyone whose name is unknown to a Glaswegian is called Jimmy.)

The familiar face paused, and looking him up and down for a moment or two said: 'Just round the corner on the left.'

At the sound of the helpful voice the worthy realised why the face was vaguely familiar. It was the dreaded Irvine Smith, gownless and wigless. Time for a sharp exit, as the television advert would say. The man turned to his wife: 'Come oan.'

Half a dozen steps down the corridor and it was safe to speak. The client turned to his wife and said: 'That's the first time that wee bastard has spoken to me without sayin' six months.'

On one celebrated occasion he took ill while sitting on the bench in Glasgow. Because of his history of coronary problems an ambulance was summoned and it came to the Sheriff Court with blue lights flashing and klaxons blaring. Its crew rushed up the stairs to the chambers where his Lordship was sitting and whipped him away to the Intensive Care Unit of Glasgow Royal Infirmary. That did not prevent posterity from recording that as he was being stretchered downstairs he was heard to exclaim those words which used to come so readily to his lips: 'You'll be remanded in custody and there'll be no bail!' Mercifully, he survived.

Humour in his courts was not always caused by him. After he went to Greenock one of the regulars of that town appeared before him. When Irvine Smith saw who it was he exclaimed: 'Oh God! Not you again!'

Said the worthy Greenockian: 'Who did you expect? [Greenockians are not all noted for their ability to distinguish between the nominative and the objective cases in personal pronouns] Joan Crawford?'

THE PLEADER

He was one of the most feared sheriffs in the country; feared, that is, not by the pleaders in his court, for he was always the soul of courtesy to them, but feared by those who appeared in the dock of his court. No one could ever accuse him of being a liberal when it came to sentencing. Notwithstanding that, I can truthfully say that I preferred to appear before Irvine Smith than any other sheriff in the country. I was not alone in that view.

He was often described by police officers, who incidentally had a great affection for him, as the Hammer of the neds. Not for him the softly-softly approach so often favoured today and so often a failure. He had the old-fashioned idea that is apparently more and more unpopular these days: that those who do wrong deserve to be punished. When the offence was bad enough society had to be protected and if that protection could only be brought about by removing the wrong-doer from society and placing him where he could do no harm then so be it.

In my view, by accepting judicial appointment when he was still in his 30s he deprived the country of one of the finest pleaders it ever had. That was bad enough but in doing so he also deprived the profession of one of its sharpest intellects – an intellect that was wasted on the shrieval bench. He would undoubtedly have risen to the very top had he remained at the Bar and there is no telling where eventually he might have ended.

THE TEA LEAF

Glasgow pubs are notorious places for picking up bargains. It would appear that in my native city there are innumerable vehicles which go around with their load insecure and many an object seems to fall from those vehicles. A surprisingly large number find their way into the public houses of Glasgow, where they are often made available at bargain prices.

The doctrine of wilful blindness in the crime of reset is neither obtuse nor difficult to understand. Broadly, it means that if you are offered a thieves' bargain you should be on your guard, and if you decide to go ahead without further enquiry, then you could be in trouble. It will come as no surprise to hear that there are those who prefer to turn the proverbial Nelson's eye to such bargains, frequently for commercial profit. When they are caught, they usually face a charge of reset.

One such accused was representing himself in the old Marine Police Court of Glasgow. The Police Courts have long since gone but they were rich in little cameos of life in Glasgow. The District Courts that replaced them are, like many another creature of Statute, a long way short of what they sought to replace. The trial with which we are concerned was taking place before one of the great characters of the legal scene in Glasgow, Stipendiary Magistrate James Robertson. Jimmy had been the procurator fiscal of the Police Courts of Glasgow and in due course he was appointed to the position of Stipendiary Magistrate. In those days Glasgow had only one stipendiary, and Jimmy Robertson was appointed to succeed the legendary James Langmuir when the latter retired. James Robertson, like his predecessor, may not have been a giant in the world of criminal jurisprudence, but he was a lovely, caring man.

The charge was one of reset. Reset consists, according to the textbooks, of knowingly being privy to the retention of stolen goods from their true owner. It is often difficult to prove knowledge and for that reason the courts are interested in the circumstances in which the accused came into possession of the goods in question. The English use a different term: they speak of receiving but the concept is the same.

The accused in the case with which we are concerned had bought a record-player at what could only be described as a bargain price. He had not bought it from any of the recognised retail outlets in 'the Dear Green Place', but he had bought it from a man in the pub. He did not know the name of the man, nor where the man stayed. He had seen him before, but funnily enough he had not seen the man since. A receipt, needless to say, was neither sought nor offered.

When the accused in our case was giving evidence on his own behalf, he maintained, predictably enough, that he had no idea that the record-player was stolen, otherwise he would not have bought it. When he had finished giving evidence, the stipendiary magistrate asked him if he had not considered that the record-player was so cheap that it must have been stolen. William, for that is what we shall call the accused, had not considered this at all. An analogy occurred to his Honour and the subsequent exchange went like this:

'But did you not think, Mr Brown, when you heard that the price was only two pounds, that this article might be stolen?'

'Ah never gave it a thought, your Honour,' said our William, with all that feigned sincerity which accused persons often profess when they are giving evidence.

'But supposing somebody came to you and offered you a new Jaguar for a hundred pounds, would you take it?' asked Jimmy.

'No, I would not, your Honour,' said William.

'Aye, exactly,' said his Honour, sitting back in some triumph, thinking that he had made the point with his improbable analogy. And the note of triumph came through in his voice when he asked, almost rhetorically: 'And tell me, why would you not take it?'

He was not prepared for the answer: 'Cos it wouldnae fit in ma garage.'

LAURENCE DOWDALL – THE GREAT MAN

One cannot talk about pleading in the Scottish courts without mention of Laurence Dowdall. Laurence died a few years ago but he was one of the greatest pleaders in the criminal courts that I ever heard. In the mind of many he was the finest of his time.

He was a remarkable man. Whenever he walked into a court he seemed to take command and the entire court seemed to respond to what he was doing or what he was saying. I confess that I hero-worshipped him from my schoolboy days. As an apprentice and as a young solicitor I spent a lot of time listening to him, watching him and studying his little mannerisms. It was impossible to see him in action without coming away deeply impressed.

Laurence had a charismatic presence no other pleader possessed. He had a marvellous command of English yet the language he used was always simple. He brought a freshness to every case in which he was involved and could hold the attention of his audience, be it sheriff or jury, for as long as necessary. He was the perfect pleader. His achievements in his professional lifetime undoubtedly bore this out. He looked the part. He was quite tall and always comported himself very well. He was invariably turned out immaculately and was as straight-backed as any guardsman, although he had been below decks in the Royal Navy during the war.

For two generations the cry of the criminal fraternity in and about Glasgow and far beyond when they were in bother was always: 'Send for Dowdall.' To see him in action was to understand why. One of the earliest occasions on which I saw him was when he was defending in a sheriff and jury trial. His client was charged with assault by stabbing following upon a scuffle in a side street in Glasgow.

The Crown called a young woman to give evidence. She told of how she was on her way home one night when she witnessed the incident in question. She had just got off the bus and was walking along towards her home when she heard the sound of a scuffle. The witness looked over to the other side of the street and saw a man falling to the ground and another running away. She identified the man in the dock as being the one who ran away. Apart from the victim of the assault the young woman was the only witness who could identify the accused as having been at the scene of the crime and so her evidence was crucial. If the jury believed her in what she said then undoubtedly they would convict.

When it was time for Laurence Dowdall to cross-examine the woman he began in his usual charming way, almost chatting with her. He found out that the young woman was on her way home from the dancing and he joked with her about it. She had been at the Albert Dance Hall in Glasgow. Laurence told her he knew the Albert well and he and his wife had often been there. A good move. He won bonus points from the jury for they liked this nice man. More importantly the witness was beginning to relax. She probably did not realise that it is easier to destroy a witness who has her guard down than one who has her guard up. Laurence was still at his most charming when he got her to tell him that she had not really noticed anything until the sound of the scuffle. It was only then that she saw the accused running away and she was able to identify him only because he had passed under one of the tall streetlights. She agreed with Laurence that her identification of his client was based upon a sighting that could have lasted for no more than about two or three seconds as he ran under that streetlight.

Laurence turned away from her towards the jury so that she was no longer able to see his face. He said: 'You saw my client for at most about three seconds. You have been watching me for about four and a half minutes I think.'

His voice was clipped as always, but now it was not relaxed: now it contained a sense of urgency. Still facing the jury, he pushed his papers up in front of his mouth and up to the bottom of his nose. He turned slowly, deliberately, till he was facing her and asked a simple question: 'Have I got a moustache?'

The witness gazed at him, helplessly, hopelessly. A look of horror came across her face. Laurence stared back steadily at her across a court that was totally hushed by the drama of it all.

'Well?' said he.

The jury could hardly hear her answer.

'I don't know.'

He lowered his papers, shrugged his shoulders to the jury, walked across the floor of the court and sat down. The accused was acquitted.

It was a remarkable question. It broke every rule of cross-examination. He was asking a material question without knowing the answer. He had no idea, on his information, how this witness would answer that question. Had she immediately answered the question correctly then her evidence of identification would have been reinforced and there would have been no way back for Laurence's client. He sensed, I am convinced, that she would not know the answer to his question and so he had the temerity to ask it. Few of us would ever have dreamt of taking such a risk. He took it and it paid off.

At the same time his humour and his appreciation of the realities of any situation never failed to pay dividends. I remember once, when I was still a young fellow and still trying to learn my trade, Laurence was conducting the defence in a pretty straightforward drink and driving charge. It was in the days before the advent of the breathalyser when the charge was of driving while unfit through drink or drugs. The evidence was in its usual predictable form. One could always write the script for police evidence in those days. The officers invariably spoke of having seen the car in question weaving from side to side; they stopped it and had detected a strong smell of alcohol from the breath of the accused. The script would continue and we would hear that the accused's eyes were glazed, he was unsteady on his feet, and his speech was slurred. The officers formed the view that he was unfit to be driving. Evidence in that kind of case in those days was as unchanging as any litany or as time itself.

Laurence got to the attack straight away. He had the first officer in the witness box – a young man of limited experience who was trying his level but inadequate best. Laurence wanted to know when they first detected that the man's speech was slurred. The officer could not remember. Who had spoken first? That was something else that the constable could not remember. What was it the accused had said that made the witness think his speech was slurred? The officer was not sure. Who opened the conversation? They did by asking him to get out of the car. They? Well no, not they, but his colleague told the accused to get out of the car. And then? They had probably asked him was this his car? They? No, his colleague. What did he mean by probably? Did they ask him or did they not? Yes, he thought they had. What did the accused say to that? He probably said yes. The constable was taken to task again over his use of the word 'probably'.

This was good stuff. The witness did not like to be pushed in this way and he was not standing up to the attack terribly well. Had he no recollection of anything the accused said? No, he had not. Well then, asked Laurence, did he remember anything about the accused's voice? Did he have any speech impediment or any accent? Not that the officer could remember.

Then came the dash of humour in the middle of all this hostility: 'Tell me, Constable, did my client not say to you, "This is a helluva way to treat a man from Lewis"?' When this quotation was inserted, Laurence affected the accent of a man from that island. The question brought a burst of laughter from the Bench. The witness was nonplussed. His script did not cater for such an unexpected question, especially when it was put in such an unexpected way, nor did it cater for such a reaction from the Bench. From then on the outcome was never in doubt. Yes, the formalities continued but once the witness was bewildered and the sheriff was won over the result was a foregone conclusion.

On another occasion, and even more dramatically, I heard him lead a witness right up the garden path (if you will forgive the expression) and I don't think the witness realised what was happening. The charge was a simple one of theft of coal from a garden bunker. The complainer, the woman whose coal was allegedly stolen, identified pieces of coal which were produced in court by the prosecutor as having come from her bunker, though how she was able to do this escaped the understanding of most of those who heard it.

Laurence had a briefcase on the table, and in that briefcase he had half a dozen pieces of coal which he had taken from his own coal bunker that very morning. He pulled these out, one by one and he showed them to the witness and asked was she able to identify these pieces also? Yes, she was. They also were pieces of her coal and had come from her bunker. And as each of these pieces of coal was produced from the depths of his briefcase, so the witness without a second's hesitation identified these varying and varied bits of coal as being hers! The prosecutor wisely abandoned his case there and then.

There was even an occasion in Stornoway Sheriff Court when he had a witness chewing pieces of timber to ascertain whether they had ever been in the sea. He called it a pine tasting and the presiding sheriff asked if there was any cheese!

Early in my professional career I had the good fortune to be appearing for the first-named accused in a case where Laurence was appearing for the second-named. I felt terribly inadequate at being in the same court let alone in the same case as 'The Great Man' but he made me very welcome. At lunchtime on the first day of the trial he took me along to the Carrick, the former RNVR Club which was then moored on the River Clyde only three or four hundred yards from Justiciary Buildings, and bought me lunch. I soon directed the conversation towards St Mungo's Academy, the Glasgow school which both he and I had attended, though a generation apart, and I asked him about a particular mathematics teacher. Laurence remembered that teacher well. He told me a lot about him and especially how he had nearly belted the hide off Laurence. Yet at the end of the day Laurence had the greatest regard and admiration for him. The teacher concerned was my father and I told Laurence so.

From then on I could do no wrong. He nursed me through that trial, tugging gently at my gown when it was time for me to sit down, scribbling notes and sticking them in front of me and encouraging me in every conceivable way either to pursue or to abandon particular lines of cross-examination. That trial lasted some three days yet my wish was that it had lasted a month. For in those three days I am sure that I learned more about the craft and tactics of pleading than I had learned in my first five or ten years in the profession.

A classic illustration of his tactics in court arose when he was conducting a sheriff and jury trial in Glasgow with all the presence that he could command. One of the witnesses was a detective officer who had the reputation of always listening at the door of a court before he gave evidence to hear what was being said. He particularly did this when any of his colleagues were giving evidence. He would then, he thought, know what to expect.

Laurence was examining the man's colleague. He was doing it superbly well and holding the jury enraptured. Suspecting that our detective officer friend was up to his usual tricks, he asked a question from the middle of the floor of the court then, while waiting for the answer, tiptoed to the door. He put his hand on the handle of the door and called out rather dramatically: 'Come in, Mister Grant,' as he yanked the door open. The jury had the unbelievable sight of Grant falling in through the open doorway and ending up on the floor, highly embarrassed at being caught out. No one but Laurence would have thought of doing it. The importance of it was that immediately it made the jury suspicious of the evidence given by Grant and his colleague, and Laurence was then halfway home in his task.

It was Laurence who introduced a new phrase in the English language when appearing for a fairly celebrated holder of judicial office who had pled guilty to a charge of driving while unfit through the influence of drink. He described his client's intake of alcohol as being 'a sensible modicum'. Had it been possible for him to take out a copyright on that phrase then he would have done well. He wrote a book some years ago and it came out round about the time of my youngest son's 16th birthday. I bought a copy and telephoned Laurence at his home in Helensburgh. I asked him if he would autograph it and when he heard the reason for my purchase he insisted, despite my protests, that he travel up from Helensburgh to Glasgow that very day to autograph the book and this he did. He wrote a little dedication on the frontispiece of Derek's book. It read: 'To Derek Murray, son of my friend and illustrious colleague Leonard, and grandson of my *quondam* mathematics teacher – who with justification was wont to knock the hell out of me – on the occasion of his 16th birthday,' and he signed it. Derek treasures that book.

When Laurence Dowdall retired from active practice many years ago he took with him all the respect, regard and affection of those of us who were privileged to know him. Many have followed him but in my estimation none has ever filled his place.

THE CARDINAL

On the morning of Sunday, 17 June 2001 the Catholic and indeed the Christian community of Scotland was shocked to learn of the death of Thomas Joseph Cardinal Winning, Archbishop of Glasgow and leader of the Roman Catholic Church in Scotland. He was 76. He had taken a heart attack some days before and had been rushed to Glasgow's Victoria Infirmary. He had been hospitalised for a week and then been sent home to recuperate. This made it seem that he was on the road to recovery and thus it was that news of his death from a second and bigger heart attack had been all the more shocking.

He was surely the most charismatic of men, but he was also a man of conscience, a man of courage and totally fearless. He would take on king or commoner; politician or primate; rank mattered not to him. He would speak out fearlessly denouncing what he thought was wrong regardless of who might be involved.

I was privileged to know him. In 1982 when Pope John Paul II visited Scotland, a visit that would never have taken place had it not been for the Archbishop, as he then was, I was appointed Deputy Chief Steward Scotland for the visit. In that capacity I worked closely not just with Archbishop Winning but with many others concerned with the organisation of the visit and, in particular, its stewarding.

I must say that the work of the Scottish police forces with whom I came into contact, namely Lothian & Borders and Strathclyde, was absolutely splendid. They emerged with huge credit for the success of the visit. Untold man-hours were devoted by the forces concerned and there was never any hesitation in what they would do. They gave of their time, their energy and their expertise unstintingly and unwaveringly.

His Holiness arrived in Scotland on 31 May 1982 and went first to Murrayfield Stadium in Edinburgh and then on to St Mary's Cathedral. He stayed overnight with the late Cardinal Gray in Edinburgh and the following morning he visited St Joseph's in Dalkeith before setting off by helicopter for St Andrew's College, Bearsden. From there he went to Bellahouston Park in Glasgow for an open-air Mass and the climax to the visit.

After His Holiness left on his helicopter at the end of the day, the Hierarchy of Scotland left Bellahouston Park by coach for Edinburgh. In addition to all the bishops of Scotland, other than Cardinal Gray who was still in Edinburgh, the coach also carried the late Cardinal Basil Hume – a very ascetic man who kept to himself on the journey back to Edinburgh – Hugh Farmer who had been the press officer for the visit, Buchan Chalmers who was Chief Steward Scotland for the visit and myself. It was a scorching day. The Archbishop and the bishops were all in their heavy soutanes and their Roman collars. Not unnaturally they loosened these things as we all relaxed in the coach at the end of a fabulously successful visit.

As we neared Edinburgh it was time to smarten up. The Archbishop, who was sitting opposite me, asked for my assistance in dressing. I commented that acting as temporary unpaid valet to a mere Archbishop was small beer for a man who had just shaken hands with the Pope. He enjoyed the joke but he capped it when he told me that an Archbishop had got stoned in Edinburgh some 400 years before and there was a very distinct possibility that another Archbishop would get stoned that night in 1982!

In 1996 he did me the enormous order of recommending to Rome that I be admitted to the Equestrian Order of the Knights of the Holy Sepulchre of Jerusalem, one of the oldest orders of chivalry in Christendom and he, as Prior of the Order, conducted the admission ceremony in September of that year. In May 1998 both he and I attended a Requiem Mass for a member of the Order. The Cardinal presided and the members of the Order attended in their ceremonial cloaks and bonnets.

At the end of the Mass I was at the boot of my car putting my cloak, hat and gloves away when I heard His Eminence shout my name. I turned and saw him, still vested as for Mass, standing on the steps of the church concerned. He beckoned me over. Thinking that he wanted my view on some weighty matter of Archdiocesan importance I hurried over to where he was standing: 'Yes, Eminence?' I enquired obediently.

'Len, is Wim Jansen going to stay?'

For those readers unfamiliar with the affairs of Scottish football, Wim Jansen was a Dutchman who was manager of Celtic and he had just led them to the Championship of the Scottish Premier League days before.

Controversy was raging as to whether he would stay at Celtic Park or quit. The Cardinal loved his football.

On Friday, 22 June 2001 I was speaking at a dinner at Glasgow University at which he should have delivered the main speech. I finished my own speech, which was the closing speech of the evening, with my own brief tribute to His Eminence. This is what I said:

> A last word. It would be so inappropriate for me to speak here on this wonderful occasion without reference to that enormous loss which we are all feeling. An era has ended; the mould has been broken. A great leader has been taken from us and none of us has as yet come to terms with the shock and the enormity of our loss. In addition to being our spiritual leader the Cardinal was the voice of conscience, not just the Catholic conscience but the conscience surely of every God-fearing Scot of whatever denomination. And no one else had ever filled that role.
>
> The Preface of the Requiem Mass contains that seminal sentence: 'Lord for your faithful people life is changed, not ended.' With the death of our beloved Cardinal, life *is* changed, not just for the Catholic Church in Scotland and abroad, but for all of us whose lives had been touched by this fearless yet lovely man. Every single one of us who had the privilege of knowing him is the better and the richer for the experience.
>
> We read in the Gospel of St Matthew: 'Well done, good and faithful servant; come and share the joy of your lord.' On Sunday of this week Thomas Joseph Cardinal Winning was given that invitation. May he now be blessed with eternal peace.

His funeral took place in Glasgow the following Monday, 25 June 2001 in St Andrew's Cathedral. It was attended by representatives of all the churches in Scotland both Christian and non-Christian, and by Prince Edward representing Her Majesty the Queen, by the Lord Provost of Glasgow, the Secretary of State for Scotland representing the Prime Minister, many other politicians of all parties, and most importantly of all by the Cardinal's people.

The greatest honour ever bestowed upon me, and one of which I am intensely proud, was the invitation given to me to do the second reading at

ABOVE: Civil defence workers search the ruins of Clydebank after the two nights of bombing raids by the *Luftwaffe*.

BELOW: Glasgow University seen from the Queen's Park on Glasgow's south side. Picture by George Wilkie.

RIGHT: My graduation from
Glasgow University in 1957.

LEFT: The late Lord John
Wheatley, who sat in
judgment in many benchmark
Scottish trials, including that
of Tony Miller and James
Denovan in 1960.
Picture courtsey of *The Herald*.

LEFT: The late Lord Clyde, Lord Justice General, one of the Appeal judges in the case of Tony Miller. Picture courtesy of *The Herald*.

BELOW: With my wife Elizabeth and sons Brian, Kenneth and Derek in 1963.

RIGHT: Laurence Dowdall in the 1960s during his heyday as a Glasgow lawyer. Picture courtesy of the *Evening Times*.

BELOW: Sheriff James Irvine Smith (left) and Laurence Dowdall in 1991. Picture courtesy of the *Evening Times*.

ABOVE: Sir Paul McCartney and his late wife Linda.

BELOW: Baron McCluskey of Churchhill. Picture by George Wilkie.

RIGHT: Solicitor Willie McRae with the ever-present cigarette and mug of tea. Picture courtesy of *The Herald*.

BELOW: The sending-off incident at the 1987 Old Firm game after which Butcher, Woods and McAvennie were charged by the police. Picture courtesy of the *Evening Times*.

LEFT: Archive portrait of Antanas Gecas in his uniform and wearing his Iron Cross.

RIGHT: The ancient city of Vilnius where war criminal Antanas Gecas plied his evil trade during the Second World War.
Picture courtesy of the Lithuanian Tourist Board.

RIGHT: Antanas Gecas during the court case in Edinburgh against Scottish Television.
Picture by George Wilkie.

BELOW: The author at Glasgow's Suspension Bridge in 2002.
Picture by George Wilkie.

his funeral. The reading I was given was from the Letter of St Paul to the Romans, 14:7–12: 'The life and death of each of us has its influence on others . . .' I could think of no reading more appropriate, for surely no one in recent times has had greater influence on the lives of others than Cardinal Tom Winning, one of the greatest men I have had the privilege of knowing. May he rest in peace.

THE DODGER

There was once a sheriff (he has now retired) who might well have been nicknamed 'The Dodger' as he was so superb at dodging work. He was very fond of his golf and while he was a sheriff in Dundee he was much more likely to be found on the golf course than sitting on the bench.

On the occasion in which we are interested he had arranged a golf match for a date a few weeks ahead. He had no idea of what his judicial commitments were going to be for that week but he was sure that as always he could probably get out of them one way or another. Thus arrangements were made and the venue was set – a Tuesday, one o'clock on the first tee at Carnoustie.

The week before the match was due to take place Dodger learnt from the court administration what his duties would be for the following week. Disaster. There it was in his diary for the Tuesday, unmistakable and indelible, a criminal jury trial. How could he possibly make the first tee at Carnoustie for one o'clock when he was due to preside over a criminal jury trial? To make matters worse the case was down for three days!

Those in the know chuckled. Dodger could not get out of this one. He was landed with it. He would have to call off the golf match. It had never happened to him before but it was bound to happen some time.

By Monday afternoon poor Dodger was sick with worry. There was no sign of the trial going off. Would he have to scratch? He sent for the sheriff clerk to find out if there was any news. The sheriff clerk was able to tell him that he had been speaking with the procurator fiscal just ten minutes before coming in to see the sheriff. As far as the Crown were concerned the trial was still going on.

This was bad news. There had always been the hope that for one reason or other the Crown would have been seeking an adjournment. Was there any word from the defence? No, said the sheriff clerk, none at all. Now there was a possibility, thought Dodger. Phone the solicitor, he told the sheriff clerk, and find out if perhaps they wanted an adjournment. The sheriff clerk should let them know that if they did want one the sheriff would not prove difficult about granting it.

Back came the sheriff clerk ten minutes later with bad news. He had spoken to Ken Pritchard, the solicitor concerned. Mr Pritchard did not want an adjournment and the trial was definitely going on. What was worse, much worse, Mr Pritchard anticipated that the case would last for three or four days. The charge was one of theft by housebreaking from a shop in Broughty Ferry and there would be lengthy debate on quite a number of issues in the evidence. Mr Pritchard had also told the sheriff clerk that he would love to tender a plea of guilty but the client's record put that out of the question. If the client were to be found guilty then the sheriff would be bound to give him a substantial prison sentence. Indeed, the sheriff might even be thinking of a remit for sentence to the High Court. Mr Pritchard had added that from his own point of view he was not keen to go to trial but the client was insisting. What the sheriff clerk did not tell Dodger was that Mr Pritchard knew of the sheriff's plight and was determined to make the most of it!

The following morning, the morning of the trial, a small knot of solicitors had gathered just inside the front entrance to the court building. Mr Pritchard was there, resplendent in black jacket and pinstripes, as was the custom in Dundee in those days.

In came Sheriff Dodger, bounding up the steps. He was clad in plus fours! Had he taken leave of his senses? Had he forgotten what he was doing that day? No sheriff ever wore plus fours on the bench, especially not in front of a jury. It was an occasion for best bib and tucker. What was Dodger thinking of? He saw Ken Pritchard in the group. Three long strides and he was alongside.

'Good morning, Mr Pritchard.'

'Good morning, Sheriff.'

'*Fine* day, Mr Pritchard,' said Sheriff Dodger.

'Indeed it is,' said Ken Pritchard and promptly went off in search of his client.

Willie Reid, Ken Pritchard's client, was sitting on the bench in the corridor beside Court 1. He was wearing a suit that made recognition more difficult. Mr Pritchard could hardly remember ever seeing Willie in a suit before. What's more it almost fitted him.

'Willie, come on with me,' said Ken Pritchard, leading the way to a corner of the building that afforded them some privacy. He turned and faced Willie who had followed obediently behind him.

'Well, Willie, how are you today?' he asked with that charming smile that characterised him.

'A bit nervous,' said Willie.

'No need to be, Willie. It doesn't help any of us. I'll tell you what I think we should do. I think we should tender a plea of guilty.'

Willie was dumbstruck. A plea of guilty was the last thing on his mind.

'Plead guilty? What would Ah want tae dae that for? Mr Pritchard, just last week you told me you thought Ah'd a wee chance of gettin' aff. Ah want tae take that chance. If Ah plead guilty Ah've got nae chance. What's goin' on?'

'There's nothing going on, Willie. It's just that I've got a feeling that if we tender a plea of guilty we are in with a far better chance of keeping you out the jail than if we go to trial,' said the solicitor.

'Keep me out the jail? Ah've had the jail every time Ah've been convicted in the last 20 years. Mind when you and me were talkin' last week you said eh might even get a remit to the High Court? Mr Pritchard Ah don't want a remit. As a matter of fact Ah don't much fancy the jail at all.'

It was beginning to look as if Willie was not very keen on the idea of pleading guilty!

Then came the psychological trump card from Ken Pritchard, drawing on all of his professional experience: 'Willie, have I ever let you down? When I tell you that I've got a feeling that we can do something today then you just have to trust me as you have always done. All right?'

How could Willie say no?

'Ah want tae go and see the wife and tell her. Ah'll be back in a couple of minutes. Will Ah get you here?'

'Yes, but don't be too long, Willie. We'll need to be getting into court.'

A few minutes later Willie reappeared.

'All right,' he said, sounding as though he were not entirely convinced, 'Ah'll plead tae it, but you'll do your best?'

'Do you think I'd ever do anything less?' grinned Ken.

A few minutes later they went into the court. Willie took his place in the dock flanked by two police officers wearing their ceremonial white gloves that looked as though they had just come out of a bleach vat. Ken Pritchard took his seat at the oblong table in the well of the court, opposite the procurator fiscal.

They all stood as Sheriff Dodger came on the bench. Even he remained standing while the Court was 'fenced'. The bar officer, the man who carried the sheriff's notebook for him (amongst his other duties) called out that command which, alas, is heard no more: 'In Her Majesty's name and authority and in name and authority of the Honourable Sheriff Dodger, I hereby lawfully prohibit and forbid all persons from troubling or molesting this Court by speaking one to the other without leave being first asked and obtained under pains of law.' All who heard were suitably impressed as they sat down.

The sheriff clerk took over. 'Call the diet Her Majesty's Advocate against William Reid. Are you William Reid?'

'Yes, Sir,' replied Willie. The tremor in the voice was audible. Ken Pritchard rose:

'I appear for Mr Reid, my Lord. He instructs me to tender a plea of guilty.' Mr Pritchard raced through those two sentences as though afraid that Willie would change his mind. Sheriff Dodger beamed amiably at Mr Pritchard.

Both Willie and the sheriff signed the court minute which recorded his plea of guilty. Some ten minutes later after a brief summary of the case from the procurator fiscal and an even briefer plea in mitigation from his solicitor, an incredulous Willie Reid walked out of the court having been fined £100.

Ken Pritchard walked out a few minutes later. An intensely grateful client came over to him holding out a congratulatory hand. 'That was magic, Mr Pritchard. But tell me what made you think Ah might get a fine?' Ken Pritchard grinned and pushed Willie gently to one side as Sheriff Dodger, already off the bench and changed out of his wig and gown, came striding past. The sheriff nodded amiably to the lawyer and his client as he made his way out the front door and down the steps on to West Bell Street. It was 10.20 a.m. He would make the first tee at Carnoustie for one o'clock after all.

How did Ken Pritchard know that Willie would not be going to jail if he pled guilty? Well, the Sheriff had said that it was a *fine* day, had he not?

WILLIE GLEN

In my day one of the great characters of the legal profession (regrettably long since gone) was Willie Glen. I always had a great affection for him. He was one of the most popular of all the court lawyers and I never heard anyone speak an ill word of him. Willie had been in the army during the Second World War and had been demobbed with the rank of major. He set up his own practice in an office in Bath Street, Glasgow, and he soon became one of the well-known figures of the profession. In addition to his interest in law he was also deeply committed to the Tory cause and indeed year after year he would stand for that cause in Townhead at the local elections. A Tory in Townhead had as much chance of being elected as the proverbial Orangeman in the Vatican. But Willie was never daunted. He was never elected either. His persistence for the cause he was hired to champion was an attribute which he brought into his professional practice and it came to the surface whenever Willie was in court.

Prior to the passing of the Legal Aid Act of 1986, applications for criminal Legal Aid in a Summary Court (that is a court where the judge sits alone without a jury) were made to that court. In other words a person charged on summary complaint in the Sheriff Court would apply for Legal Aid to the sheriff and not as now to the Scottish Legal Aid Board. This was never satisfactory because individual prejudices and jealousies became apparent. There were no financial limits and no guidelines. Whether an application was granted depended upon the whim of the individual sheriff who heard the application. The worst feature of all was that there was no right of appeal or review as there is now.

The consequence was that the whole question of criminal Legal Aid was scandalously unsatisfactory and many sheriffs were notorious for their extreme reluctance for one reason or another to grant Legal Aid in summary criminal matters. There was no particular statutory way of dealing with a Legal Aid application. The practice for a time in Glasgow

Sheriff Court was to put the applications out for public hearing and each day the Diet Court in Glasgow was crowded with applicants who had been cited to appear at the court to show cause why they should be granted Legal Aid. The solicitors concerned were given a note of when their clients' applications were to be heard. Many of them would turn up to argue the application on behalf of the client but many more would not bother. They took the view that they were not instructed until a Legal Aid Certificate had been issued. Willie Glen did not subscribe to that view and he was a regular attender at the Legal Aid court to help his clients with their applications.

On the afternoon with which we are concerned, Willie had four clients whose applications were due to be considered. Unfortunately for him, he was before one of those sheriffs who did not believe in Legal Aid (probably because it was not available when he was at the Bar) and who did everything in his power to ensure that Legal Aid applications were not granted. That kind of thing would never daunt Willie and he approached his plea for Legal Aid in each case as though he passionately believed in the justice of it.

His first application was called. Willie jumped to his feet: 'I appear for this applicant, my Lord.'

His Lordship acknowledged him and asked: 'What's the defence, Mr Glen?'

'He was drunk at the time and has little recollection of the incident. However, he knows he would not assault anyone in the circumstances set out in the charge,' said Willie with all that confidence which he could muster for occasions like this.

'Has he a record?' enquired the sheriff as though that were relevant.

'He has, my Lord,' said Willie, just as confidently as before.

'Has he previous convictions for assault?'

'He has two, my Lord.'

'Legal Aid refused,' said the sheriff. Clearly people with any previous convictions had no right to expect Legal Aid – at least not from this sheriff. Willie turned to his client who had not been asked to contribute to this rather bizarre scenario and who was standing there astonished by it all.

'Your application has been refused. You'll need to pay for your defence. Here's my card. Fifty pounds for a trial if you're pleading not guilty; ten pounds for a plea if you're pleading guilty.' Willie had no inhibitions about the delicacies of discussing fees in public. Off went applicant number one to ponder on the quality of justice that had been handed out to him that afternoon.

The next application in which Willie had an interest was called. He told the sheriff he was appearing.

The sheriff looked at the client: 'Do you smoke?' This sheriff was hot on relevancy.

The applicant nodded. 'Uh-huh.'

'How many?'

'About 15 a day.'

'Give up smoking and you'll be able to afford to pay for a lawyer. Legal Aid refused.'

Willie turned to the client and putting his hand into his pocket produced another business card.

'Your application has been refused. You'll need to pay for your defence. Here's my card. Fifty pounds for a trial if you're pleading not guilty; ten pounds for a plea if you're pleading guilty.'

Off went applicant number two. Even if he could give up smoking how long would it take him to save up for a lawyer?

The next application was called. Not only did that applicant smoke he drank as well. His application was given the same amount of objective judicial consideration (and about the same amount of time) as the preceding two. Willie went through the by now familiar ritual of handing over his card with a quotation of his terms.

His last application was called. The client came forward with considerable apprehension. He had watched not just Willie's three previous applications but indeed a whole series of them before that and they had all been refused for one reason or another.

'Do you appear for this applicant, Mr Glen?'

'I do, my Lord.'

'Tell me about the defence.'

'He pleads alibi. He wasn't there at the time the crime was committed.'

'Who are his witnesses?'

'Two members of his family.'

The sheriff was not impressed.

'Mr Glen,' said he, 'give him your card.'

THE JURY

Presently the jury system is undergoing a raft of new proposals in England. Whether the outcome will be sustainable, legally safe and fair, only time will tell. In Scotland, as in many civilised systems of criminal law, juries decide questions of innocence or guilt in serious cases. For reasons obscured in the mist of legal history, the Scottish jury uniquely comprises of 15 folk. That is probably a statement of the obvious to most Scots, but not all.

Some years ago four lovely jury courts were built within that outsize public toilet that served as Glasgow Sheriff Court until 1986. It was only when they were finished that those who observed them realised that neither the Scottish architects nor the Scottish contractors nor even Scottish Courts Administration, who had approved the plans, were apparently aware that Scottish juries were not made up of 12 people. For there were the jury boxes, nice and neat, and modern and comfortable – and with only 12 seats!

We have always had majority verdicts in Scotland, which is probably why our juries number 15. After all it's easier to calculate the majority out of 15 than the majority out of 12. It is well within my recollection that the English imported the concept of the majority verdict and now an English jury may return a verdict of guilty by majority when either 10 or more out of the 12 are in favour of that verdict.

The majority of 15 is 8. That may appear to be a self-evident statement, but not universally in Scotland. Some years ago up in Aberdeenshire, a man was convicted by a majority when six jurors were in favour of guilty, five were in favour of not proven and four were in favour of not guilty. Thank God somebody found out and the Appeal Court set the matter right. But that case demonstrated as no other could, how important it is to ensure that a jury, or at least its foreperson, can count up to eight. Now every Scottish jury is charged that they cannot convict unless at least eight of their number are in favour of a verdict of guilty. In England it is not competent to convict an accused person by a simple majority, but that is only competent, as I understand it, when at least ten jurors are in favour of such a verdict.

Heaven and English lawyers alone know what it must have been like when all 12 had to agree!

Juries are cited either to the High Court or to the Sheriff Courts in their droves. The local Sheriff Clerk's Office, in accordance with a formula laid down about 100 years ago and still in vogue today, selects them. They turn up at the courts not quite knowing what to expect. They appear in the main in their Sunday best and always arrive a good half-hour before they need to. They have a puzzled and unfamiliar look about them as though they are about to embark upon some mission unknown. They are about to be thrown into what may be the white-hot heat of an arena and asked to return a verdict on facts where two parties are pulling from totally opposite directions. They sit in the court nervous, apprehensive and utterly unfamiliar with what is about to go on. Along with their citation they are sent a little booklet which tells them something about being a juror. The clerk of court usually addresses them en masse before the court convenes and tells them roughly what is liable to happen.

Until 1980, an accused was entitled to five peremptory objections to prospective jurors without any cause being shown, and thereafter he could object to as many as he wanted on cause shown. In that year the number of peremptory objections was reduced to three but there still existed the right of an accused to object to a prospective juror without showing any cause. I never understood the logic of that position. Now things are different. If an accused wants to object to a prospective juror he must show cause why that person should not be empanelled on the jury and that is as it should be.

Little slips with their names, their occupations, and their addresses are all cast into a glass jar. When the court convenes and the first case for trial is called, the ballot takes place. The clerk delves into the glass jar and produces one slip at a time. He mutters first the number of the juror concerned for the benefit of the prosecutor and the defence and then calls out audibly the number and the name. In my day we would look furiously at the copy jury list in front of us and see if that was a name or an occupation that we did or did not fancy. If we did not fancy it we muttered to the sheriff clerk that that person need not come. Thus it was we often had a situation that went something like this:

Clerk of Court quietly to prosecutor and defence: 'Number 62.' We would look furiously to see his name, his address, and his occupation – don't fancy that.

The clerk would call out audibly: 'Number 62, Joseph Brown.'

We would mutter to the clerk: 'He needn't come.'

The next thing that Mr Brown would hear was the clerk saying: 'You needn't come, Mr Brown. Please resume your seat.'

The poor chap, clothed in self-centred embarrassment, would wonder: do we not like his aftershave? Do we think he has body odour or have we found out about that dirty weekend he had in some romantic place like Rochdale 17 years ago? In fact all that happened was that we had noticed from the list that Mr Brown was a schoolteacher. Poor Mr Brown would sit down, wondering what the reason was for this mystifying rejection. The reason was that schoolteachers are undesirable people on a jury because they are accustomed to dictating to their class; thus, ran the theory, they would dictate to that jury and their dictation would necessarily be prejudicial to the accused. Not only was there the view that teachers cast a spell on juries, but so did accountants and upper level management, whereas artisans and other people who earn their wage as a result of physical rather than mental endeavour had no such power! I don't know which clown in our profession first propounded that theory but it was one which never appealed to me.

I recall one occasion when I had a jury with three schoolteachers and one university lecturer in it. The accused was acquitted by a unanimous verdict and ever since then I discarded the idea altogether. I was always inclined, subject to a few exceptions, to allow a jury to be balloted just as it came out of the clerk's glass jar. I am not aware of any client having been prejudiced.

Today in Scotland there are now no peremptory objections available to each accused. He may, however, object to as many as he wants if he can show cause why the person whose name has been drawn should not be part of the jury. What would be a cause shown? There obviously can be no definitive exposition but a relationship to or with the injured party or the accused might be adequate cause. A person having personal knowledge of the event, or a person living so close to the event as to be affected by popular talk in the neighbourhood – that might be enough. If it could be shown that a person had already expressed a view on the matter going to trial, that might well be cause shown.

Prior to 1980 when each accused person had five peremptory objections you could well imagine a situation where there were five accused in the dock. There could be a possible twenty-five objections – a clerk of court's nightmare!

Once all 15 are seated in their places the clerk reads the indictment, setting forth the charge against the accused to the jurors. The oath is then administered. They are required to swear that they will well and truly try the accused and give a true verdict in accordance with the evidence. That style of oath is a recent innovation. I always preferred the old style where they swore that they would truth say and no truth conceal in so far as they were to pass upon that assize.

Today the presiding judge or sheriff generally then takes a few minutes to tell the jury about the procedure that they are about to witness and to tell them roughly what their job is to be, after that we go straight into the evidence without opening speeches.

I remember a Glasgow jury once being totally startled by one of our sheriffs. In his opening remarks in a case involving an indecent assault, he told the jury he would adjourn the court for ten minutes before beginning the more serious business of the evidence in order that they might retire to the jury room and take their clothes off! I am reliably advised that before he presides over a jury trial now he writes down in large letters in his notebook the phrase, 'Take your COATS off.'

A jury trial to my mind is the occasion for the practice of a pleader's greatest skill. The art and the psychology of a trial before a sheriff or justice on his own is totally different from that which obtains before a jury, and the approach of the pleader has to be absolutely right in everything he does. The profession is literally under the public gaze in a jury trial as it is in no other exercise. Fifteen people are going to take away from that court a lasting impression not just of our profession but indeed of our whole system of law. There lies upon the pleader a far greater professional onus in a criminal jury trial than in any other exercise of his professional skill. The responsibility of a jury trial is very considerable.

Juries in my experience generally return results which we would be entitled to call the right results. Their reasoning and their approach may be unusual but by and large most of us would agree, if we were asked, with the majority of verdicts that Scottish juries return. Wool cannot really be pulled over the eyes of the average citizen, particularly when that average is the average of 15 citizens. I confess though that there have been occasions when I have been puzzled by a jury's verdict or perhaps more correctly by the reasoning behind it.

I remember many years ago being instructed by a lady who was charged with performing an abortion on a 15-year-old girl. It seems that the young lassie, who came from Drumchapel, one of those vast sprawling soulless housing estates on the outskirts of the city for which our town planners must continue to accept moral blame for generations to come, missed a menstrual period. She went to my client in the hope that menstruation could be induced. My client alleged that she had no idea that the girl was pregnant. She resolutely denied any attempt or any intent to procure an abortion. The case went to trial.

The abortion was proved by medical evidence and proved beyond a peradventure. Notwithstanding that, the jury came back with a majority verdict that the accused lady was guilty of an attempted abortion. I have no idea how, in the light of the medical evidence, they could have reached the view that the abortion was only attempted. Even greater cause for wonderment was to follow. They then unanimously recommended clemency. That recommendation was quite startling in the circumstances because it was much more appropriate in capital cases, that is where the result of a finding of guilt would be a sentence of death. However, the recommendation was acceded to by the presiding sheriff who fined the lady some fairly modest sum. I was overcome by curiosity. Accordingly, as we were all leaving the building, I caught hold of the foreman of the jury and asked him what the majority was, an act which incidentally is now illegal, though it was perfectly permissible in those days.

His voice conveyed that he came from somewhere north of Maryhill. If truth be told his origins were clearly somewhere north of Fort William and he replied in that lovely Hebridean lilt which I always find so attractive no matter who the speaker: 'There was 12 for guilty,' and here his brain was clearly being taxed. I saw him mentally count the number of people on the jury one by one and deduct from the resultant 15 the number 12, 'And there was 3 for even more so.' I advised that there be no appeal in that case!

Juries have impossible tasks in our courts. They are to sit there exercising a judicial function; a task for which by training and experience they are singularly ill equipped. They are to concentrate intently for hours on end and often for days on end and they are to give a decision on a matter of grave importance, and all this without ever asking a question. Which of us in being asked to make a decision on a matter of importance in our own affairs would not set about immediately asking questions of this one and that one until our curiosity had been satisfied? Not so with a jury. They must sit in silence. They are, however, as I have said before, usually right and frequently very discerning. We may question their reasoning but what matters is the result not their method of achieving it.

Some years ago in Dundee a jury convicted an accused person in circumstances where it seemed unlikely that the accused would be convicted. Indeed, it seemed much more probable that he would get off. The sheriff clerk subsequently asked one of the jurors what had led them to their verdict and was told to his amazement by the juror that she had noticed that the shoes of the solicitor for the accused were dirty. She had learnt never to trust a man with dirty shoes and so she was in favour of conviction. A strange approach, an unfair approach but an approach which led, I am told, to the right result in that particular case.

Every good pleader should be conscious of a jury. They are the people who matter. They are the people who are going to return a verdict and consequently they are the people whose impression of the evidence matters.

In Scotland we have the hallowed institution of a verdict of not proven. It is a verdict of acquittal and the result of it, whatever it may mean in the eyes of the man in the street, is that the accused is discharged, is forever free of any blame and he can never be tried again. There are those who say that a not proven verdict means we know you did it but it cannot be proved so do not do it again, but in law it is an acquittal. Presiding judges are nowadays usually at some pains to point this out to a jury.

There is absolutely no justification in my mind for retaining the verdict. It is totally contrary to logic. We have a system where an accused is presumed in law to be innocent and that presumption lasts until the guilt of the accused is shown beyond reasonable doubt. If guilt is not shown, then the presumption must still apply and the accused is innocent. Why then should he not be found not guilty? Ours is the only legal system, so far as I am aware, where such a verdict exists.

Many years ago I was involved in a trial in Glasgow where the accused was charged with fraud. He was accused of ordering many items for his business without paying and without intending to pay for them. His defence basically was that he himself had been deceived and he was as great a victim of the fraud as those who had complained to the police. At the end of the day the charge of fraud was found not proven. The police officer who had been in charge of a very long, hard slog of an inquiry asked one of the jurors why they had found the charge not proven. He was told to his astonishment that they simply found the charge not proven so that when the police caught the other fraudster then my client could go back into the dock with him and this time the jury would convict them both! The ingenuousness of such an approach was, if nothing else, at least refreshing, however misguided.

It is, of course, essential that a pleader should be in control of every situation. He has to be in control of his examination or his cross-examination and above all else he has to be in control of himself. When he is not in full control there can be some disastrous results. The story is told of a young advocate who had not previously appeared in court and who was retained to represent an accused person who was for trial in the High Court on circuit in one of the provincial towns in Scotland. He came into court shortly before his case was due to be called with his pristine white wig on his head and exuding an apparent air of self-confidence. He sat down at the table, still with apparent confidence. Moments later the macer preceded the judge on to the bench, calling out 'Court'. Everyone present, including our newly called young friend, stood up. The judge bowed to the Bar and the Bar bowed back and they all sat down.

Our young friend suddenly became conscious of the importance of it all. In but a moment or two when the indictment against his client was called, he would have to stand up for the first time as a member of the Faculty of Advocates in the High Court of Justiciary and conduct a trial. Would he cope? The colony of butterflies breeding in his stomach seemed to have multiplied ten times since he walked into that courtroom.

The clerk of court called out 'Her Majesty's Advocate against William McDonald.' Our young advocate shot up, pushing his chair backwards and out of the road as he did so. He started to say 'My Lord, I appear . . .' and was interrupted in the middle of it all. In thrusting himself upwards and in pushing the chair backwards he had not legislated adequately for that highly polished linoleum floor under his brand-new leather-soled feet. The result was disastrous. His heels, which had been resting on the cross bar of his chair only a fraction of a second ago, kept going forward as he thrust himself to his feet. The consequence was that he disappeared right under the table, a victim of his own anxiety to get to his feet.

To that boy's eternal credit a by now convulsed waiting public heard from below the table: 'My Lord, I did appear for . . .'

That particular Counsel is doing very well now. He only wears rubber-soled shoes.

THE JURY

A young advocate was conducting a trial in the South Court of Justiciary Buildings in Glasgow. In that court there was a small radiator, probably about 18 inches in height, and it was near enough the jury and far enough away from the witness box to be conveniently placed for the pleader to rest a weary foot on it when conducting a cross-examination. There are some of us who regularly used it for that purpose. The idea was to put the right foot on top of it and lean on top of that resting right leg in a kind of relaxed manner when conducting the examination. Like every mannerism, however, it has to be natural and not artificial because if it is artificial it is quite unacceptable.

At any rate our young friend, who had obviously seen some of the more experienced pleaders do this, thought that was obviously a mannerism that he must adopt. When it was his turn to cross-examine, he got straight up from the table, went over to the radiator and very obviously raised his foot until it was resting on top of the radiator. From there he began a somewhat laborious, tortuous and obviously inexperienced cross-examination. Twenty minutes later he decided that he had asked all the questions necessary and it was now time to resume his seat. The dynamics and the physics of that move were comparatively easy. He would take his weight off the reclining leg that was perched on top of the radiator, transfer his weight to the other leg, lift his right foot and the rest would be simple. He put these moves into action.

The next few seconds were seconds that all his life he will want to forget. He discovered to his horror when he tried to lift his right foot that the heat of the radiator had welded the sole of his shoe to it. There he was, in the gaze of the jury and an unbelieving public, swaying about with his right foot trapped and hopping around on the left to regain his balance. He had to slip his foot out of his right shoe and thereafter tug the shoe free, blushing furiously all the time.

That, incidentally, was the last time that fellow ever wore composition soles in court.

TEDDY

We used to have some right characters on the shrieval bench, especially in Glasgow. One of them was Edwyn Oswald Inglis, alias Teddy Inglis.

When I came on the scene in the late 1950s Teddy used to preside in Room 59 of the old Sheriff Court in Glasgow. Like most other sheriffs he did his turn of other duties and he moved around the building when the occasion required. He may not have been the best of lawyers but he was an excellent sheriff and it was always a delight to appear before him. He had a pawky sense of humour which was never far below the surface.

In all matters that came before him Teddy was very fair but he could also be very hard when the occasion required and he would not hesitate to imprison when he thought it right. He was a very gentle man and he abhorred violence.

On one occasion he was presiding over the custody court in Glasgow. In those days most of those appearing from custody had already spent four days in prison. They would appear first in the old Police Court (now the District Court) and from there be remitted to the Sheriff Court and be remanded in custody to Barlinnie Prison for four days. So much for the presumption of innocence. However, I digress.

On this particular day that delightful kenspeckle character Willie Glen was on duty as the solicitor for the poor. That meant that Willie would appear for everyone who was in custody and who did not have his own solicitor. On the particular day in question, one of those for whom Willie appeared was a seaman and he was charged with an assault by striking a man in a public house with his fist and breaking his victim's jaw. Teddy was usually hard on crimes of violence and even though the accused had no record (at least so far as was known) there was still a fair chance that Teddy would send the seaman to jail. The First Offender's Act had not even been thought of then.

Willie indicated that his client was pleading guilty. The procurator fiscal depute gave a brief narrative. The accused and the victim had apparently been drinking together in a public house the previous Friday evening when suddenly and for no apparent reason the accused had lashed out at his companion and struck him a blow on the jaw. The victim had been conveyed by ambulance to Glasgow Royal Infirmary where an X-ray revealed a fracture. The accused had been arrested almost immediately and when he was cautioned and charged with the offence now before the court he said, 'He was asking for it.'

When the fiscal sat down the sheriff turned to Willie Glen: 'Mr Glen?'

Willie rose to address the bench in mitigation. He told the sheriff that the accused was 54 years of age. He had never offended before. He was a seaman and had been a seaman all his working life. He was married, though with no children. He much regretted the incident, which had been caused by a loss of temper after drink had been taken. He and the victim, another seaman, had been drinking together and the other man had said something derogatory about a ship that the accused used to serve on. An argument began and the accused had lost his temper and struck out in anger. There was only one punch thrown. This act was absolutely out of character for the accused. He had spent four days in custody over this and Willie invited the sheriff to exercise leniency.

'What did the victim say about your client's former ship?' asked Teddy.

'My Lord I understand that the two had been speaking of ships on which each had served. My client spoke of this particular one and the complainer called it "a filthy old tub". My client objected and in a flash of blind temper he struck out,' explained Willie.

'What ship was he referring to?' asked Teddy.

Before Willie could answer for him, the accused answered the sheriff himself. '*The Kenilworth*, Sir,' said he, naming one of the Clyde's more popular steamers.

'*The Kenilworth?*' mused Teddy. 'She was built by Inglis of Pointhouse in 1898, was she not?'

'She was indeed, Sir,' said the accused.

Teddy thought for a moment. 'You are admonished,' he said.

'Thank you very much, Sir,' said a surprised and much relieved accused, who clearly had been expecting something much worse. He was taken back upstairs to the cells to get his property before being released.

We were all astonished rather than admonished at the leniency shown. No one would have predicted that outcome. It was some years later that I learnt that Teddy was a descendant of the original Inglis of Pointhouse.

THE EXTRA QUESTION

It has been said that the zenith of the art of oratory is to know when to sit down and the zenith of the art of cross-examination is to know when to stay down.

The answer to every question asked is potentially deadly. In cases where the evidence against an accused is thin, more convictions have resulted from bad cross-examination than from any other single cause. The extra question, the one that should never have been asked, is the dreaded curse for a pleader. Many a story is used to illustrate the point. The one I remember best came from a sheriff and jury trial in Falkirk. The case was one of assault and one of the eyewitnesses to the assault was a little ten-year-old girl. Her evidence was crucial.

When she gave that evidence it was crystal clear. She had seen the assault and it was the man in the dock who committed it. The solicitor concerned rose to cross-examine. He was no tyro. Indeed he was one of the most experienced and most able men of his time.

'Susan,' said he amiably enough, 'your daddy is a policeman, isn't he?'

'Yes sir,' said she very politely. Charles Black (for that is what we shall call him) looked over knowingly at the jury. They had taken the point.

'Indeed, he's not just a policeman – he's a detective, isn't he?'

Again a polite 'Yes, sir.' Another look at the jury from the lawyer. They had taken the point.

'And I dare say you and your daddy have spoken about what you saw that day, have you?'

'Yes, sir.'

The jury were now beginning to wonder about Susan's evidence.

'And, Susan, has your daddy told you what to say?'

'Yes, sir.'

The child's innocence was leading her into who-knows-what trap. The jury by now were thoroughly sceptical of what reliance they could put upon the evidence of the ten-year-old child of a detective who has been coached by her daddy on her evidence.

This was the time to sit down, to leave it, to back off. But no, the extra question came.

'And tell me, Susan, what did your daddy tell you to say?'

'He told me to stand up, speak up and tell the truth.'

The jury believed her and convicted the accused. No amount of subsequent cross-examination could make up for the terrible blunder of that extra question.

The other case that I believe illustrates the deadly danger of staying on your feet too long was one that I witnessed in Glasgow Sheriff Court. My trial was next in line and so I sat through the one that was in progress. A young man was charged with a handbag snatch in Renfield Street in Glasgow. He had been chased and caught by two policemen. The defence was that in the busy thoroughfare they had grabbed the wrong man. The first constable was in the witness box and he had identified the accused as the person who committed the assault and as the one whom he had chased and caught.

The cross-examination went something like this:

'You said that it was my client who assaulted John Craig.' (That sounded to me more like a statement than a question and I did not see the point of it.) Constable Macleod was not put off by such a consideration and he was not prepared to dispute that assertion.

'Yes,' said he.

'Are you sure it was him?'

(Did the questioner really expect Constable Macleod to say, 'No, I'm not. I just grabbed the first guy I saw and locked him up'?)

'I am very sure.'

Warning bells should have been ringing in the mind of the questioner. If they were, he ignored them for he blundered on:

'How can you be so very sure?'

'Because I was born in the same street as your client. I went to school with him and we played in the same Boys' Brigade football team.'

Had there been a hole in the floor of that court there would have been someone diving in. The episode illustrated the golden rule for any advocate, namely that you must never ask a material question unless you know the answer.

LOCHMADDY

In my time I appeared in just about every Sheriff Court in Scotland, from Dornoch to Dumfries, and from Dunoon to Dunbar. I enjoyed my appearances in them all but my favourite was Lochmaddy. Lochmaddy, incidentally, is the principal town of North Uist in the Outer Hebrides. Come to think of it, it is the only town. To the west, as Compton MacKenzie once said, there is nothing – but America. North Uist, as its inhabitants will tell you, is the home of all Celtic civilisation and it has retained its Celtic culture notwithstanding its proximity to that lesser island of Great Britain.

The court there used to begin at 2.30 p.m. and would sit on continuously until eight or nine or ten at night. It could not begin before 2.30 in the afternoon because the plane landed in Benbecula at 1.30 p.m. and it took nearly an hour to drive north from Benbecula over the causeway and up the coast of North Uist to Lochmaddy. The plane would leave again about 10.30 the following morning so the idea was to sit as late as might be necessary to conclude court business so that it was possible to get back to the mainland the next day. If you did not catch that plane there was not another for a couple of days. There was then every possible incentive for getting on with your case!

The procurator fiscal of Lochmaddy is now a full-time civil servant who also holds the post of procurator fiscal at Stornoway, where he has jurisdiction over Lewis and Harris. The post, however, used to be part time and the holder in my day, David Thaw, was also the local grocer. His shop was situated across the road from the Sheriff Court and when it was time for the court to convene he would slip on his gown, lock up the shop (or get a member of his staff to hold the fort) and come over the road to prosecute. He usually did not bother to change out of the slippers that he wore in the shop. David was a delightful character and if ever a solicitor had the good fortune to be instructed in a prosecution to take place in Lochmaddy Sheriff Court then the procurator fiscal would phone him up and tell him all about the case. Matters were done in a highly civilised way in those days.

My first trial in Lochmaddy arose out of an incident on the Isle of Barra – the island that was immortalised by Compton Mackenzie in *Whisky Galore!*. A local family had a difference of opinion with the local constabulary, one of whom was English and always assumed an air of arrogance in dealing with an islander. The difference of opinion on the occasion with which we are concerned became not just heated but violent. Blows were exchanged and as a result a whole variety of charges was preferred against a father and his two sons. All three instructed me. It seemed to me, after I had had a fairly lengthy chat on the telephone with the procurator fiscal, that the case against the father was quite different from the case against the sons and indeed his interests were quite different from those of his sons. Clearly the father required to be represented by another lawyer. Accordingly I telephoned my good friend Laurence Dowdall and asked him if he would represent the father. Laurence agreed and I was delighted. Apart from the fact that Laurence was a good friend of mine I knew that he was familiar with Lochmaddy and indeed with all the islands. His local knowledge then was something which I valued and something which I reckoned would do us in good stead.

My everlasting recollection of the trial (which began at the appointed hour of 2.30 p.m.) was of the sheriff interrupting proceedings at 8.25 p.m. when he whispered something to the sheriff clerk. I had no idea what he had said but it did not particularly trouble me.

The sheriff clerk promptly scurried out of the court. I had no idea where he had gone but a few minutes later when I was still cross-examining a witness he came back into the court and pushed a dinner menu from the Lochmaddy Hotel in front of me. He handed one up to the sheriff and one to Laurence Dowdall and in the background to my cross-examination I could hear the sheriff and Laurence discussing the relative merits of the grilled trout that the hotel served. Nothing like this had ever happened to me before.

Picture the scene:

Murray in disparaging tone to police officer: 'What do you mean, Constable, when you say "I required to defend myself"?'

Sheriff to Dowdall *sotto voce*: 'I don't agree, Laurence. I think we would be better with a Chardonnay.'

It was slightly off-putting, so I decided to leave the witness's explanation until after His Lordship and Laurence had chosen the wine. In the event (though I obviously did not know it at the time) last orders for dinner at the hotel had to be in for 8.30 p.m. and our sheriff was very conscious of the things that really mattered. Meanwhile the sheriff clerk acted as head waiter, noted our orders and nipped in next door to place them with the chef!

We finished the trial about 9.30 that night. The result didn't greatly matter but it was no forensic triumph for me. We adjourned to eat, sheriff, sheriff clerk, Laurence Dowdall and myself, and a splendid meal was served, liberally washed down with a couple of bottles of Chardonnay. The following morning Laurence and I set off on the return journey to Benbecula Airport. We had hired what was probably the only self-drive hire car on the Uists and I was driving. As it happened there was another resident in the hotel who was going to the airport and we gave him a lift.

Unbelievably enough I got lost on that journey. That really was an achievement. Not even the sheep get lost in North Uist. I was journeying up the east coast of the island (and I am sure well within the Arctic Circle) before I realised that by that time I should have been travelling south down the west coast of the island. Panic.

'My God, Laurence,' said I, 'I've taken the wrong road. We're in trouble now.' I was by now convinced that we were going to be stuck out in the Outer Hebrides for the next two days and the prospect did not really appeal. From the back seat we heard the very welcome words, 'Don't worry. I'm the air traffic controller at Benbecula Airport. The plane can't take off without me!'

That was the last time I ever hired a car in the Outer Hebrides.

MULL OF KINTYRE

Let me say from the outset that I have never been a member of the pop culture. I have never been on anyone's A-list; I have never been ushered through the golden ropes of a nightclub as I tumbled from a stretch limo. The paparazzi have never chased me along the street at 3 a.m. after an evening's carousing.

No, my musical taste, although reasonably catholic, leans more to the classical. I do admit that on more than one occasion I did manage through the first verse of 'Blowing in the Wind'. I can still recall the words of 'Guantanamera' and I do admit, in common with other parents, to singing a nightly version of 'Puff the Magic Dragon'. Happily, however, not for many years did I realise the hidden meanings in the lyrics!

I suppose that it was due to my reasonably catholic tastes that in the 1960s and '70s I had an admiration for The Beatles. Their rebellious attitude to the establishment was refreshing in those heady days and many a person would hum the ever-present hits that they continually produced.

One of them, Paul McCartney, bought a farmhouse near Machrihanish on the Mull of Kintyre, where he and his then wife Linda McCartney would often visit. That area is absolutely gorgeous. The land, the sea, the colours are all spectacular. No wonder he eventually produced the hit 'Mull of Kintyre'.

However, the call I received that rainy afternoon in Glasgow was from a London solicitor who wished me to represent his client in the Scottish courts. The client was a well-known celebrity and total confidentiality was required.

You can well imagine my surprise on learning that the client was Paul McCartney, who was being prosecuted in Campbeltown Sheriff Court.

Following a tip-off, the police had mounted a raid on the farmhouse. They had found cannabis plants growing and as a result Paul had been charged with some contraventions of the Misuse of Drugs Act. If you cast your mind back to that decade, cannabis was probably the hardest drug available and still viewed seriously in law.

I was asked to retain counsel and I chose a man who would go on to have a very illustrious career at the Scottish bar. His name was John McCluskey QC. He later became Solicitor General for Scotland and was subsequently appointed a life peer with the title Baron McCluskey of Churchhill. He was then appointed to the bench of Scotland's Supreme Courts. He would also be appointed – and in the eyes of many this was much more important – to chair the Scottish Football League Compensation Tribunal.

John McCluskey had been an advocate depute, a Crown Prosecutor in the High Court, for some years and it was in that capacity that I had first met him. I had been most impressed. He was a prosecutor to be feared, with a great presence, a good delivery and he always knew his case. His preparation was legendary. This would be the first time I had instructed him but it would be the first of many celebrated cases that he would handle for me. Indeed, until his elevation to the Bench, John McCluskey was thereafter to become my first choice of counsel in any important case. I used to tell my trainees to take every opportunity to see John McCluskey in action. He was a superb pleader and a role model for every young man who wished to make advocacy his career.

The papers that I received from London gave me all the information that I needed at that stage. I had sufficient information to enable me to tender a plea of not guilty. In spite of the veil of secrecy that I drew over the case – I would not allow the file to be taken out of my room – word soon got about. When the case was first called in the Sheriff Court in Campbeltown the place was mobbed with media expecting Paul McCartney to appear in person. They were bitterly disappointed to learn from the sheriff clerk that the plea of not guilty was being tendered by letter.

A date was fixed for the trial, in March 1973. It was now my job to begin our preparations. This involved interviewing the various witnesses whom the Crown intended to call to give evidence to discover what they would be saying. We could then form a view as to the strength of the Crown case.

John McCluskey and I consulted, and at one of our consultations he told me rather excitedly that he doubted the competency of one of the charges. We decided to go and see the procurator fiscal in Campbeltown to discuss the whole matter.

Alistair Iain Balfour Stewart – his name sounded like that of a Scottish rugby full-back – was among the last of the part-time procurators fiscal in Scotland. Now they are all full-time civil servants, but not in those days. Iain Stewart, as he was generally known, was a solicitor in practice in Campbeltown and he had the part-time job of being prosecutor in the local Sheriff Court. He was a lovely man and very highly regarded. A solicitor from the old school, it was always a pleasure to deal with him.

By the time I had investigated the case, and John McCluskey and I had finished our preparations, he had spotted what we both considered to be fatal flaws in two of the three charges. We had arranged to see Iain Stewart in his office the evening before the case would be heard. He made us very welcome and our discussions began.

John McCluskey quietly but quite forcibly put our arguments forward. There was no answer to them. What we maintained was obviously right and two of the charges had to go.

I remember Iain leaning back in that great big chair of his and telling us that he had been a prosecutor for 30-odd years; the world had generally ignored him and had allowed him to get on with his work. Now, when the eyes of the world were upon him for the first time in his life, he had managed to make a mess of the charges. (Those are not the words he used, but that was the meaning!)

We told him that we would recommend to our client that he plead guilty to the one remaining charge (which the Crown could prove anyway) and the meeting came to an end. I really felt so sorry for Iain Stewart that night, but sympathy was no bedfellow for our professional duty to our client.

The following morning Paul and Linda McCartney flew into Machrihanish airfield in their private jet. We sat and talked to the chap. He was a pleasant young man fashionably dressed with longish hair. His wife, Linda, sat quietly sipping an orange juice. We pointed out that only one charge remained and our advice was to plead guilty. He sat for a few moments, looked at the ceiling and said with a trace of a Liverpool accent: 'Yes. Let's go with that and get it over with.'

When we arrived at court we were astounded to see the number of newspaper and television people already there.

The case was called and John McCluskey pled guilty on Paul's behalf to the one charge which now remained. There was no spectacular plea in mitigation, just a request from Counsel for a commonsense approach to the plea. Sheriff Douglas Donald fined the former Beatle £100 and the case was over within a few minutes.

As was usual we asked for a month in which to pay the fine, much to the amusement of the Bench and the media. Paul, aware of the seriousness of the situation, still tried to hide a smile.

We decided to hold a press conference after the case and dozens of journalists and photographers crammed in to the Solicitors' Library of Campbeltown Sheriff Court. Paul was in great humour and answered a lot of their questions at length. A great laugh went up when it was suggested from a reporter that perhaps the cannabis seeds could have been blown in the wind on to his land. No, he replied, he would leave 'Blowing in the Wind' to Bob Dylan. The singer and his good lady posed for the photographers and then left. I was amazed to see how cooperative they both were with the media. No hassle, no minders.

I remember Martyn Lewis was then ITN correspondent for Scotland and he asked me why I requested a month to pay. I said 'because it sounded better than fifty pence per week'. Martyn did not report that answer but others did. I learnt then to be more careful – not every reporter shared my sense of humour.

CHOW MEIN

Sheriff Lionel Daiches QC sat as a sheriff in Glasgow and found the whole job a great big bore. He was supposed to sit there day after day listening to all that was being said and try and keep his mouth shut. He never did because he never could. His problem was one that so many would have had in his position – he was listening to pleaders who were not fit to lace his shoes. He had been one of the most eloquent of all pleaders and it was difficult for him to listen to those who appeared in his court and who could never be anywhere near his equal.

In truth we did not want him to keep his mouth shut simply because it always was a joy to listen to him. When he came on the bench it was as though a window had been opened and a breeze both pleasant and refreshing came in wafting away ahead of it the musty, dull, uninteresting smell of so much that goes on in our courts.

The monotony of some pleaders, their very dullness, their inability to be interesting and their painfully slow pace, were all things that used to frustrate him no end. If truth be told (and that may not be often in the courts) most of the time none of us could or did blame him for his frustration. Our profession has always seemed to me to attract more than its fair share of people who were incapable of doing the job for which they were being paid; or people who had a love affair with the sound of their own voice. Lionel Daiches on occasion found it all too much to take.

One fine June day the sheriff was listening to a case of careless driving. The accused was a Chinese restaurateur and the allegation was that on a particular occasion he had been driving his car without due care and attention and had caused a pretty minor road accident. Ling (for that was his name) denied it and insisted that the accident was due to the fault of the other driver. On that basis battle commenced.

The other driver concerned had been driving his car eastwards along Sauchiehall Street in Glasgow towards the city centre. He was just approaching North Claremont Street, which is a street joining Sauchiehall Street on the north side, when he noticed a car sitting at the mouth of that street waiting to turn left into Sauchiehall Street to go in the same direction as he. Just as he got within a few yards of the vehicle it turned into Sauchiehall Street right in front of him and the inevitable collision took place. The driver of that vehicle was Mr Ling.

Fortunately no one was hurt but two police officers were standing at the opposite corner. They would infinitely have preferred not to have been there because they had been on the point of going off duty but they could hardly walk away as though they had seen nothing. Thus they became involved; they had to submit a report on the occurrence and to their surprise a prosecution ensued.

Today, since there was no injury, the insurers would be left to fight it out. However, Sheriff Daiches found himself sitting in judgement on the question of whether Mr Ling had been lacking in care and attention on that occasion when he had come out on to Sauchiehall Street into the path of the other driver's vehicle. It was not the greatest intellectual challenge he would have to face in his judicial career.

The day was a hot one. The court was stuffy and uncomfortable. The prosecutor and the solicitor for the accused were approaching the case as though it were one of murder. The procurator fiscal depute was calling a succession of witnesses who were adding little to his case. Even two bystanders who were fully preoccupied with their conversation and thus paying very little attention to what passing traffic might have been doing were called to give evidence. They did not even look up until after the impact. Nonetheless the fiscal concerned regarded it as his duty to call them to give evidence. The case was so trivial that one could not help but wonder what on earth something like this was doing in the courts.

Making matters worse, each witness was being cross-examined with astonishing vigour by Mr Ling's solicitor. The defence (such as it was) was that the left indicator of the other vehicle was blinking as he approached the junction of North Claremont Street and because of that Mr Ling thought that the other driver was going to turn left. That might have been relevant in mitigation of the offence but it could scarcely be enough to avoid conviction. Even although there was an argument that the case should never have been brought, in reality it was there and so it should have resulted in a plea of guilty. Patently Ling should not have assumed that the other driver was going to turn the corner. Having said that, the case was the proverbial bag of peanuts and here were these two would-be pleaders converting it into a banquet.

At the end of the evidence the sheriff not surprisingly convicted Mr Ling. There was ample evidence that either he had not been paying sufficient heed or alternatively he had jumped to a wrong conclusion. On either view he was driving without care and attention. Other than produce the statutory Notice of Penalty the fiscal had nothing more to say and it was now for Ling's solicitor to make his plea in mitigation.

Iain Macdonald had been admitted as a solicitor all of three weeks before. It showed. He did not realise that what was required was either to say nothing or alternatively to make a swift plea in mitigation which would occupy but moments. Instead he chuntered on and on. After three or four minutes when there was still no sign of an end to his plea the sheriff interrupted:

'A moment, please,' said he with that consummate courtesy which characterised him.

'Yes, my Lord?' said young Mr Macdonald expectantly and enthusiastically.

From the Bench: 'How much does your client charge for a plate of chow mein?'

'I'm sorry, my Lord?'

'How much does your client charge for a plate of chow mein?' repeated his Lordship.

'I really have no idea, my Lord,' said an astonished Mr Macdonald.

'Well, Mr Macdonald, I should be deeply obliged if *ad iuvandum hoc forum* [he loved his Latin tags] you would take the time and the trouble to ascertain from your client the answer to my question.'

'Certainly, my Lord.' A whispered conversation between solicitor and client ensued. Meanwhile the rest of us who were sitting in the court wondered what would come next from this delightful man on the bench. We would not have long to wait.

But first it was Mr Macdonald: 'I understand, my Lord, that Mr Ling charges fifteen shillings.' (These were those heady pre-decimal days.)

'Very well, I am deeply grateful to you, Mr Macdonald. Mr Ling, as a measure of how gravely I regard this breach of your obligations under the Road Traffic Act I shall fine you the sum of fifteen shillings.'

There was only one thing to expect of Sheriff Lionel Daiches and that was the unexpected.

WILLIE McRAE

Solicitor Willie McRae died a horrible death on 6 April 1985 at the age of 61. Assassination or suicide – the arguments still rage on.

Found slumped in his Volvo just off the A87 with a bullet wound to his right temple, he was rushed to Raigmore Hospital in Inverness and then on to Aberdeen Infirmary. He died without regaining consciousness and his death left a mystery to rival any thriller novel ever written.

Many Scottish Nationalists insisted that he had been assassinated. They maintained that MI5 had killed him because of his political views. Willie McRae believed passionately in the Nationalist cause. He had been a vice-president of the Scottish National Party, but his was an extreme brand of nationalism which was not universally popular within the party. The extremists amongst the nationalists made him a martyr. They formed the Willie McRae Society and erected a cairn to his memory near the spot where he was found.

There has never been an official verdict on Willie McRae's mysterious death because there was never any official public inquiry. His supporters vocally insisted that the security services or the national intelligence forces had been involved in his death and they campaigned long and hard to try and persuade the Lord Advocate to hold a fatal accident inquiry. The Lord Advocate, who canvassed the views of Willie's family, decided not to hold one. I imagine that that was in accordance with the wishes of his family. As a result the rather emotional idea that Willie was murdered by the secret service was given credence and never finally dispelled.

I do not understand how such a conclusion could be reached upon so little information. Any that is there within the public domain is the result of gossip, rumour or speculation. The report on the post-mortem conducted on his body was never made public. That report would have contained vital information about, amongst other things, the wounds that Willie sustained. In the absence of details about this vital aspect it is impossible in my view to reach any informed conclusion. We have no idea if there was bruising or soot or tattooing around the wound or any of the tell-tale signs of close-range entry. Indeed, so far as I am aware there is no relevant information on the wounds at all.

A handgun that fired the fatal shot was found near the body. The precise spot where that was found could also shed light on what caused Willie's death. If the gun were found beyond perhaps a distance of about one metre from the body then that would tend (I put it no higher than that) to indicate something other than suicide.

He had a lot of professional and personal worry at the time of his death and he was so supercharged with emotion that he was very liable to succumb to the pressure of it all and take his own life. That is what I believe happened. That, however, is something between Willie and his Creator, a Creator, incidentally, in whom he always passionately believed.

I also have difficulty with what I call the 'Liquidator Theory'. If officialdom were behind Willie McRae's death then why leave doubt about it? It would be a matter of unbridled astonishment to me if it were seriously suggested that a killing could not be dressed up to look like suicide. Instead he was killed, according to the proponents of the 'Liquidator Theory', in such a way that there is apparently room for some doubt as to the cause of death. Besides why on earth should a liquidator leave the weapon (if it were the murder weapon) near the body at all?

In my naivety I have difficulty in believing that in this country we have any official liquidators who get rid of people with unacceptable political views. Why should Willie McRae be singled out? What was so unique about his political views that he alone of all politicians in recent years has met such a fate? Those who believe in the liquidator can point to no other politician in recent years who may have been killed off in this way. It may be that Willie was murdered for some reason other than his politics but no one has ever suggested any other. Personally and sadly I tend to believe that Willie died at his own hands.

Friends tell me that there had been a mysterious fire at his Queen's Park flat on that Good Friday morning. At 7.45 a.m. the emergency services that attended found him suffering from smoke inhalation and in a 'confused state'. He refused to take the advice of the ambulance crew and his neighbours who had rescued him and go to hospital. Later that day he drove north to his death.

I probably knew Willie McRae better than most. I first met him in 1954 when the headmaster of my former school introduced me to him and I became Willie's apprentice at Levy & McRae. When my apprenticeship finished I was his assistant for several months. As I have mentioned, in 1958 I went into partnership with Joe Friel. We then amalgamated our business with Levy & McRae, of which Willie McRae was the only remaining partner, following the retiral of Abraham Levy on 30 June 1959. The three of us went into partnership together with effect from 1 July 1959. He and I remained in partnership for 22 years until he left the firm in 1981. After his death I was often asked by the media to comment on some aspect or other of what they were reporting about Willie and I always refused.

Let no one criticise or judge him over the matter of his death. If he did take his own life, then when it comes to the Final Accounting, there will be very many credits on the balance sheet of his life, credits which are likely far to outweigh any debit brought about by his peccadilloes or by the manner of his death.

Willie McRae was huge in every way. A big man and a generous man. He held court over his old oak desk wearing his favourite blue pinstripe suit. His eccentricity showed itself as he constantly wore a knitted pullover beneath the waistcoat. That garment had been the victim of many stray fallouts of egg yolk and sundry foodstuffs. A gentle snowstorm of dandruff settled permanently on his shoulders. His huge hands, fingers stained brown with nicotine, constantly searched on the top of his desk amongst a mass of files, papers, cigarette lighters and ashtrays for his never extinguished cigarette. Comfortable in his surroundings, his booming laugh would reverberate around the office. Smoke rolled around him like gathering storm clouds as he leaned back and dispensed his daily bonhomie to an opposing colleague on the telephone often finishing up with the phrase: 'Well then. We will just see you in court.'

Not only did he fight like a tiger when he believed that right was on his side but he did more for young people coming into the legal profession than anyone else I know. He devoted endless time and went to endless trouble to assist those who needed his help. Many a member of the legal profession practising in Scotland today owes his presence or his continued presence in the profession to Willie. When it came to helping a friend he never ever counted the cost. He was one of the most unforgettable characters I ever knew – indeed, I can think of none more unforgettable. A man of great intellect with a superb ability to identify issues, he had a razor-sharp mind and a wit to match it. He was also a man of great emotion; and his emotional pendulum could swing probably further than that of anyone else I knew.

I remember one afternoon in 1979 he pushed the door of my room open and came in with tears streaming down his face. 'Len,' he said, 'they've killed him.' I had no idea who he was referring to and I asked him. 'Louis,' he said. 'They've killed him,' and at that he turned and walked out of my room without another word. In the event I discovered that he was referring to the killing of Lord Louis Mountbatten, murdered by a terrorist bomb in Donegal Bay. Willie had held a commission in the Royal Indian Navy during the Second World War and had served under Lord Mountbatten. They had not met for about 35 years but that did not stop Willie from breaking down in tears when he heard the news of the killing. That incident was rather typical of his psyche.

He was unique and often outrageous. His outrageousness was such that the profession in the main not only accepted it but also rather grudgingly admired it. That was Willie; that was how people viewed him. Even so, at times the letters that he wrote often made me cringe. He did not hesitate to say exactly what he thought. Not for him the diplomacy of the professional letter-writer; instead he frequently displayed a bluntness which was positively embarrassing. On occasion he was blunt to the point of rudeness. He once wrote to a professional colleague (one I may say who was a pain in the teeth and whose principal concern was trumpeting his own importance) in the following terms:

'When we first met you [to us, his partners, the pronoun was regrettably all too often the plural] we formed the view that you were a fool. Nothing has happened in the intervening 30 years to make us change our mind.' However, it must be said that his rudeness was only ever directed towards those who thoroughly deserved it.

He had a wonderful sense of humour. On one occasion an old lady (who incidentally trusted him and his judgement implicitly and used to come to see him about every little hiccup in her life) had a fire in her home. She turned, as a matter of course, to Willie for advice on what to do. The first thing was obviously to advise her to intimate a claim to her insurers. Most of us in these circumstances would have written the rather predictable dull formal letter advising the insurers of the event and asking them to forward a claim form. The predictable was seldom what one would expect from Willie McRae. Instead he wrote to Sun Alliance, the lady's insurers, in the following terms:

> Dear Sirs
> *Mrs E Neustein tae the tune o' Duncan Gray*
> Mrs Neustein's burnt her bum
> Ha ha the burnin' o' it
> She had her electric blanket on
> Ha ha the singein' o' it
> The blanket it burst into flame
> Noo she wants tae mak a claim
> Send us a form an' we'll gie it tae her hame
> Ha ha the claimin' o' it.

Not only did the insurers send a claim form but also they settled the lady's claim in double quick time and with a smile on their face!

He was an orator par excellence – a real old-fashioned rabble-rouser. When he was on his feet, whether in a court or a tribunal or on a political platform, he could charge up the atmosphere as few before or after him were capable of doing. There are still those who recall Willie McRae's many contributions to Glasgow University Union debates in the immediate post-war period and how he could whip his audience of students into a maelstrom of patriotic fervour with his fiery brand of nationalism.

In 1979 he was the Nationalist candidate for Ross and Cromarty. Brian Wilson, now the MP for North Ayrshire, was the Labour Party candidate. My old friend and former client Billy Connolly was canvassing for Brian. Billy slipped into the back of an electoral meeting in Dingwall being addressed by Willie to hear him and I well remember him telling me with unconcealed glee how he heard Willie rousing his audience to a frenzy of passion.

In 1980 the government ordered a planning inquiry to take place. It would become known as the Mulwharcar Inquiry. It was all about an application for planning permission from the Atomic Energy Authority which had caused some public controversy. All the interested parties were represented by learned and costly senior counsel – all that is except Willie's clients, the Scottish National Party, who were represented by him. The

Atomic Energy Authority was of course a party to the inquiry and was amongst those who had instructed senior counsel. That Counsel (later a Senator of the College of Justice and thus a Supreme Court judge) irritated Willie over several days. The transcript of the inquiry records Willie as saying at one point: 'Would learned and courteous Senior Counsel either bridle his arrogance or produce a display of ability sufficient to justify it, neither of which he has done so far.'

That was so typical of the kind of comment that Willie would make when the occasion required. Unfortunately all too few of his comments are a matter of record.

The unexpected was the norm for him. In the 1950s the Grand Orange Lodge of Scotland, that pillar of ecumenism and Christian charity, had as its Grand Master the Reverend Alan G. Hasson of Bonhill, a minister who was subsequently to flee to Canada and was eventually defrocked. He was a well-meaning man, no doubt, who every year around 12 July led the Orange Walk in Glasgow while riding a large white horse. This was his own tribute to King William III, who, according to history, led his troops into the Battle of the Boyne against James II in 1690 while riding a horse of similar colour. Many might be forgiven for wondering what relevance such an event has in Scotland at any time let alone in the second half of the twentieth century but that is another issue.

On the occasion to which I refer, the Orange Walk had planned to make its way along Gordon Street in the centre of Glasgow. Willie happened to be lunching in the Grosvenor Restaurant, then situated on the first floor of the Grosvenor building in that street, and at a table which gave him a grandstand view of the walk. He was with two other solicitors and a law student. Willie adhered to no particular religious denomination but he was utterly intolerant of intolerance, if you follow me. He regarded the Orange Order as the epitome of intolerance and the Orange Walk as the manifestation of that evil. He welcomed the opportunity of displaying publicly his contempt for the whole affair.

The Orange Walk turned into Gordon Street from Renfield Street and drew level with the Grosvenor. Willie's companions were astonished when he picked up a bread roll from the table, eased up the casement window beside which he was sitting and without warning hurled the roll through the open window towards the Grand Master as he rode past on his white horse. The roll missed. Willie grunted in disappointment, calmly shut the window and carried on with his conversation as though nothing had ever happened. Alan G. Hasson subsequently became a client of mine but I never did tell him of how one of my partners had once tried to hit him with a bread roll!

The Parly Road Café was an unlikely venue for a solicitor to dine. Yet Willie loved it. It was situated in Parliamentary Road in the Townhead district of Glasgow until it disappeared in the redevelopment of that area.

Townhead, for the benefit of those who do not know it, was not the most salubrious quarter of Glasgow. That was of no concern to Willie. The Parly Road Café served the best fried-egg rolls that Willie had ever encountered. Thus, even though Egon Ronay had never written of having passed that way, and even though no rosettes had been awarded by the Scottish Tourist Board or indeed anyone else for that matter, the Parly Road Café was one of Willie's favourite howffs. A cup of tea and a fried-egg roll around half past six of an evening was not only his idea of perfection but it was also sufficient to sustain him for several more hours of work.

A friend of his was then studying Higher History so that he might have enough qualifications to enter the Faculty of Law. He sought Willie's help over an essay which he had to write on Talleyrand, that great pillar of the French Revolution and close friend of Napoleon Bonaparte. Willie was an honours graduate in History and never lost his love of the subject, and so he invited his friend to join him for a cup of tea and a fried-egg roll at the Parly Road Café. Tom (his student friend) agreed with some misgivings. Perhaps he did not share Willie's penchant for fried-egg rolls.

They were seated there at their table in that rather dingy café, tea and fried-egg rolls before them. Tom was ill at ease with his surroundings and hesitant with his fare. Not so our Willie. He tackled his egg roll with enthusiasm. The yoke was soft and runny and spilled from the edges of the roll. Its fall was broken in turn by Willie's tie and then his waistcoat before resuming its descent on to the plate in front of him. Tom was fascinated by Willie's indifference to this off-stage distraction. Willie on the other hand was concentrating on the enjoyment which his egg roll was bringing him and was apparently oblivious of the dripping yolk.

'Tell me about Talleyrand,' he commanded. Just as Tom was ready to tell Willie about Talleyrand's treachery towards the Church to which he belonged and which had elevated him to the episcopacy, a female voice shrieked from the back shop: 'Senga, come oan and get yer roll.'

Willie tutted, not at the accent, nor even at the temper displayed but at the timing of the interruption. 'Never mind her, Tom. What do you think is Talleyrand's importance?' Tom had his ideas on that. He started to launch forth about the policies of Talleyrand while he was Foreign Minister in Napoleon Bonaparte's Consulate, but he reckoned without Senga's friend. For the voice repeated at an even higher level of decibels: 'Senga, this is the second time Ah've telt ye. Come oan.'

Willie did not even comment on the fact that the sentence had ended with a preposition. He simply sighed, shook his head and said: 'Right, Tom. What were you going to say about Talleyrand?'

The virago, whoever and wherever she was, clearly cared not a jot about how often she caused interruption of the history tutorial, for her scream was heard a third time: 'Senga, gonnae come and get yer roll?'

That was enough for Willie. Leaping to his feet he swung into the passageway of the café and turning round to face the back shop where he thought the voice was coming from roared out: 'Senga, for Christ's sake come and get your roll and we'll all get peace.' She did just that and Willie and Tom resumed the history tutorial without any further interruption.

Posterity will give Willie McRae his place. But before posterity makes up its mind about him let it be said loud and clear that Willie McRae was one of the most gifted, one of the most talented and one of the most generous of men.

SPEEDY

A newly qualified assistant with my firm was being sent out to the provincial court where a particular sheriff sat. There weren't many sheriffs like him. Perhaps it was just as well. His one ambition was to get through his work just as fast as possible. Laudable in itself you might think, but there were occasions when just a bit too much speed was being applied to the judicial process.

Our lad, and we shall call him Kenneth, had never experienced the speedy sheriff before and unfortunately all of us had overlooked telling him. Kenneth was going to that court to tender a plea of guilty to a charge of careless driving on behalf of a client. It was not the most heinous offence in the book but one that was important enough to the client (he relied on his licence for his job as a salesman) and so far as he was concerned it was the most important case that my firm had to deal with that day.

Imagine the scene in the court. When the case was called, young Kenneth stood up to indicate that he appeared for the accused, who was tendering a plea of guilty. He sat down. Now would be the time in any other court for the procurator fiscal to get to his feet with his notice of penalty, which would remind the sheriff (as though he required reminding) of what penalties could be imposed for this infraction of the law. He would then summarise the facts, saying no doubt what time of day it happened and what the innocent motorist was doing when this careless individual drove his car into him or whatever.

Meantime our Kenneth, having indicated that his client was pleading guilty, intended to assemble and to put in order what he had in mind to say in mitigation during the few minutes that the fiscal would take to give his summary. He was much too raw to notice the almost imperceptible shake of the head from the fiscal indicating to Sheriff Speedy that he had nothing to say about the circumstances. Kenneth did not understand why there should be this silence while apparently nothing was happening.

The voice from the bench was he thought probably directed at him when it said: 'Do you want to say anything?' The tone didn't sound encouraging. Kenneth had not met with a sheriff quite like this before. 'Yes, my Lord. I'm sorry. I had thought that the procurator fiscal might want to say something.'

'Why should he?'

Good Lord, thought Kenneth, is this some kind of a nut?

'Well, so that your Lordship would know what the facts are,' explained Kenneth, not entirely certain of the ground on which he was treading.

'I can see what the facts are. They are contained in this charge and you have just pled guilty. You are admitting these facts. Why should the Crown want to waste time and say something else?'

There was little hiding the tone of belligerence on the part of Speedy.

'Well, I just thought . . .' Kenneth wasn't entirely sure what he had just thought and whatever it might have been it was knocked out of his head by the time the next fusillade came from the Bench.

'Never mind what you thought. You are not here to express your thoughts. If you've got something useful to say get on with it.'

'Yes, my Lord,' a rattled Kenneth was doing his best. 'My client is 34.'
From the Bench: 'Ten.'
'He is married with three children.'
'Twelve.'
'Their ages are eight, six and three,' continued Kenneth, his eyes fixed firmly on his notes and oblivious to what was going on round about.
'Fourteen,' Speedy was droning out these numbers like a bell tolling mournfully in the background.
'He is a sales representative by occupation . . .'
'Sixteen.' The bell had tolled again.
'. . . and he drives about 25,000 miles per year.' Kenneth was sticking manfully to his task.
Now the noise from the Bench was like a clap of thunder: 'You have already talked me up from £10 to £16. Do you want to go on any longer?'
It was only then that our Kenneth realised the significance of the numbers that had been counted in the background like a boxing referee over an unconscious pugilist.
'Next time you are in my court, lad, you'll learn not to be so long-winded. Sixteen pounds and fourteen days to pay. Licence endorsed.'
Kenneth departed. He didn't volunteer to take any cases in front of Sheriff Speedy again.

THE JOB CENTRE

My court partners and I were sitting down one evening over a cup of coffee. It was about half past five. We had managed to get the doors locked and at last the telephones had stopped ringing. We sat down to discuss an idea of mine. I had in mind that we would employ a court clerk.

A litigation practice involves a great deal of purely administrative and clerical work. The court apprentices until now had done that work very successfully over the years but each apprentice only spent one year in the court department of the office before he went on to train in other aspects of practice. The volume of work was continually growing and it seemed to me that we had now reached the stage where we would be better with someone whose full-time job it was to act as court clerk. It would have the great advantage of continuity. In other words what we really needed was someone who would be attached to the court department of the firm on a permanent basis. Besides, there were always many other and more important jobs for the court apprentices to do without involving them in matters that were purely clerical.

By the time we had finished our coffee, agreement had been reached among us. Only one thing remained and that was to find a suitable candidate. One of us had to find the candidate and (predictably) I was given that task.

We had a choice on how to go about finding one. We could advertise. That would involve a delay between instructing the advertisement and its appearance; a further delay between the advertisement appearing and our receiving the replies and yet another delay between receiving replies and actually carrying out interviews. All of this would take time, and time is money. The second alternative was to go to one of the employment agencies that have sprung up almost like mushrooms on the professional and commercial scene in the last generation. That did not appeal to me. I regarded the whole idea of employment agencies as being a first-class rip-off. They charged something like four per cent of the annual salary of anyone engaged and frankly I could not understand why employers should use them. Obviously the higher the salary the greater is their percentage and in my experience they frequently pushed salaries up for their own ends.

The remaining alternative was that wonderful and long-hallowed institution known in Glasgow as the 'buroo'. The more modern and certainly the more acceptable title is the Job Centre. I am bound to say that my own experience of that institution was always extremely favourable. I found their staff most helpful. Their enthusiasm never seemed to wane no matter how many demands were made upon them and personally I would never go past the Job Centre when seeking staff. And so my partners resolved that I would make contact with the Job Centre and enrol their help in our quest for a court clerk.

I telephoned our local centre the following morning and soon I was put through to the member of staff who would help me. I did not catch her name. She did not offer it and at that moment I did not feel it necessary to enquire. I introduced myself and told her the purpose of my call. Her response was immediate and her reaction excellent. She made me think as I had not done the previous evening, not just on the parameters of the job, but on precisely what it would involve, what kind of individual we were seeking and what kind of salary we had in mind. It was hard work keeping up with her. I usually form a picture of the person at the other end of a telephone if I do not know them and on this occasion my picture of this woman at the other end of the telephone was coming through to me like a photographic print in a developing tank. The picture which by now had developed in my mind was of a matronly woman, in her mid-50s, bosomy, with shortish steely grey hair and reading glasses suspended round her neck by a chain.

I have a habit which is quite common in the city where I was born, bred and buttered, of using the expression 'dear' when speaking to a female – especially one whose name I did not have. To the reader it may sound condescending but it is certainly not so intended. The consequence was that soon I found myself using such expressions as: 'Yes, that is very helpful, dear'; 'Yes, if you don't mind, dear', and so on.

She told me that she would have a look amongst those registered within her own office and see if she could come across anyone whom she considered suitable. If so she would arrange for that person to phone me to arrange an interview. If she were unable to find anyone whom she considered suitable then she would circulate the vacancy to other offices in the city. She had little doubt that we would soon be able to fill the vacancy. My gratitude was immense and I expressed it fulsomely.

'Well, you've been most helpful, dear,' said I, 'and I'm very grateful to you. Incidentally I did not catch your name. Could you let me have it, please?'

From the other end of the telephone line there came two shattering words: 'John McDonald.'

I nearly dropped the telephone! When I was able to recover my composure I dropped my voice two or three octaves and stammered through the rest of the conversation before hanging up. What a brick I had dropped! I put the phone down, sat back in my chair and reflected on the enormity of my gaffe.

I could well imagine prospective applicants at that Job Centre being told that the job sounded interesting but the boss sounded a bit odd. Fortunately we decided to employ the first applicant whom we interviewed and so I never required to telephone Mr McDonald again!

THE OLD FIRM

Probably every Glasgow boy's secret ambition is to turn out for Rangers or Celtic. I achieved that ambition in 1987 in rather unusual circumstances.

My wife and I were sitting in our lounge one Saturday evening listening to Beethoven's *Pastoral Symphony*. I had spent most of the day in the garden while she had been at the fashion shop she then owned in Byres Road in Glasgow. I had a glass of my favourite brandy in my hand. We were both totally relaxed and work was the farthest thing from our minds, until the telephone rang. The caller was Bill McMurdo. Bill and I, despite our different backgrounds and differing outlooks on so many matters, had an excellent working relationship. Bill had been referred to me by the late Jock Wallace, one-time manager of Rangers, who had been a friend and a client of mine for many years. Bill had already by then built up a formidable reputation as a footballers' agent and his reputation was well merited. Among his many clients in the world of football was Frank McAvennie, who was then Celtic's centre-forward, and Bill was calling me on Frank's behalf. He told me that Frank had been asked to report to Govan Police Station at 12 noon the following day, Sunday, 1 November, and he wanted me to attend. Frank was going to be charged following an incident which had taken place on the pitch at Ibrox Park, Rangers' home ground, two weeks previously during a match between Rangers and Celtic.

Even as Bill was speaking to me the front door bell rang. Standing there was Ian Dickson, a solicitor and a partner in the well-known and well-respected Glasgow firm of MacRoberts. He explained to my son who opened the door to him that he was very anxious to confer with me as a matter of urgency. My telephone number was ex-directory and so he had been unable to telephone first. However, he knew my house and he had come to my door in the hope that I would see him.

Brian ushered Ian Dickson into our living room while I finished my conversation with Bill McMurdo on the telephone. I arranged that I would meet Bill and Frank in the Bellahouston Hotel, not far from Govan Police

Station, after 11.30 the following morning. We finished our conversation and I then went into the living room to speak to Ian Dickson.

I was positively astounded to find out that Ian had come to see me on behalf of Rangers Football Club. Ian's firm acted for Rangers at that time. His mission was to instruct me on Rangers' behalf to represent three of their players – Chris Woods, Graeme Roberts and Terry Butcher. They had all been asked to attend Govan Police Station the following morning – in their case at 11 a.m. – in order that they be charged with a breach of the peace arising out of the same incident as that in which Frank McAvennie was involved.

This was turning into one of the more memorable evenings of my life. Only ten minutes before I had been having a quiet drink and feeling totally at peace with the world and here I was now being instructed in what was the greatest headline-making case at least of that month and probably of that year.

The background was that an incident had taken place in the game. In the 17th minute the ball had been played back to Chris Woods, the Rangers goalkeeper, and Frank McAvennie went rushing in on him. It appeared to many as though Frank had slapped Woods on the face and Graeme Roberts and Terry Butcher had rushed to the defence of their goalkeeper. There had been a bit of pushing and shoving and one or two players got hot under the collar for a few moments. The incident had flashed and was over almost immediately. The referee had pulled out the red card for Butcher, Woods and McAvennie, and they were all sent off. He also showed a yellow card to Graeme Roberts.

The three red cards were the talking point all that weekend, but the footballing world had been astonished to learn on the Monday following the game that Glasgow's procurator fiscal had called for a report on the incident and that the police were accordingly investigating. Some of us thought that this was possibly a bit of window-dressing by the police and the fiscal, and I do not honestly believe that there were many people who thought that any charges in the criminal courts would result. Most expectations were that warning letters would be sent to the players involved telling them that they had better behave in the future or else! But here I was that peaceful Saturday evening in the quite unprecedented position of being instructed within minutes on behalf of both Celtic and Rangers as a result of the same incident.

I told Ian Dickson that Bill McMurdo had just instructed me on behalf of Frank McAvennie in case there was any objection on the part of the Rangers players to being represented by the solicitor who had been instructed by their co-accused. Ian did not foresee any difficulty and accordingly I arranged that I would meet the Rangers players at 10 a.m. at Ibrox the following morning.

I telephoned Bill McMurdo after Ian Dickson left to tell Bill that I was now instructed also by the Rangers players but he saw no problem about my representing all four. The view that he took, a view that I shared, was that this was an occasion when Celtic and Rangers should go forward together with a united front.

The following morning I met Campbell Ogilvie director and secretary of Rangers FC, Alistair Hood, then Rangers' operations director and now fulfilling the same role at Livingston FC, Graeme Roberts and Chris Woods at Ibrox. I had last met Alistair when he was Divisional Commander of 'A' Division of Lothian & Borders Police at Gayfield Square in Edinburgh and I had been Deputy Chief Steward for the Papal visit to Scotland in 1982. We had immediately hit it off then and I was delighted to renew our acquaintanceship. Alistair had approached every task in connection with the visit with an admirable professionalism and I knew what to expect from him. I was not disappointed. Terry Butcher was not available on the Sunday because he was in England and was not due back until the following day. The rest of us set off for Govan Police Station.

I was astonished to find the entire press corps of the west of Scotland – or so it seemed to me at the time – camped outside the office. They had clearly been tipped off but that did not trouble me because their presence could occasion no prejudice to the players. The police received us all at Govan Police Station with the utmost courtesy and the formalities of being charged with a breach of the peace were gone through as speedily and efficiently as possible. When the formal business of our visit was over, we went back to Ibrox to take stock. It was arranged that I would meet the Rangers' board the following morning to discuss the matter in greater depth.

There was still Frank McAvennie. I was to meet him just before noon. In the course of the previous evening after Ian Dickson had left and after I had spoken to Bill McMurdo I telephoned one of my then partners, Peter Watson, to tell him the good news. He and I decided that it would be politic at that stage for someone else to accompany Frank McAvennie to Govan

Police Station and Peter volunteered. Accordingly, after I left the Rangers' party I went to the Bellahouston Hotel to meet up with Bill McMurdo, Billy McNeill (then Celtic's manager for the second time) and Frank McAvennie. Peter joined us and I effected the necessary introductions. I had known Billy McNeill for many years. I had been proud to number Jock Stein amongst my friends and I had met Billy through my Celtic connections many years before. Peter took them to Govan Police Station and we all met up again at Bellahouston Hotel to hold our debriefing.

The following morning I repeated the ceremony with Terry Butcher at Govan Police Station. He was also charged with having committed a breach of the peace at Ibrox during the game. The police were going to report back to the procurator fiscal following upon charging the players and it would then be entirely up to the procurator fiscal to decide what he was going to do.

I decided that I would proceed upon the assumption that the Crown were going to prosecute the players for a breach of the peace, although I did not honestly think it was going to happen. I was invited to come along to the Rangers' board meeting the following morning. They were meeting at 10 and I was invited to come at 11. I was privileged to attend but I could not help but wonder how many Celtic supporters had been invited to attend a meeting of the Rangers' board. At the meeting David Holmes, the then Rangers chairman, made it very clear to me that he knew sufficient of my background to know which team I supported but notwithstanding that he wanted the best man for the job and he had accordingly instructed his solicitors to send for me. I was very flattered. I subsequently found out, incidentally, that between news of the charge being preferred on the Sunday and my appearance at Ibrox Park on the Monday at 11 a.m., no fewer than three Glasgow solicitors had telephoned Ibrox, not just to volunteer their services, but also to tell David Holmes that not only was I a Catholic but I was a Celtic supporter as well. Was it that they wanted to plant in his mind the thought that I would accordingly do less than my professional best for the Rangers' players? I regarded it as being an enormous tribute to the integrity of the Rangers' board of that day that they treated those offers with the contempt that they merited.

My preparations got underway. The incident had been captured on television. Scottish Television cameras had been there and the incident had been shown on the Sunday following the game. I was able to obtain a copy and I re-ran that programme focusing upon the incident many times. I discussed the matter on several occasions with David Holmes and Campbell Ogilvie of Rangers and my colleagues at MacRoberts. I was disappointed that the then board of Celtic Football Club did not display the same interest in the matter as their counterparts at Ibrox, but then the whole approach from Ibrox was so much more professional in every way than that displayed by their opposite numbers at Celtic Park.

Meanwhile the football world was astonished. Many doubted the right of the procurator fiscal to interest himself in what was going on on the park – a view with which I could not ever agree. I telephoned Sandy Jessop, Glasgow's then procurator fiscal and now Sheriff in Aberdeen, a man with whom I always enjoyed a splendid relationship. He agreed to meet me about the matter and I went down to his office, which was then in Clyde Street. After the usual badinage – Sandy was a rugby man – I got to the point. Basically I was there in an endeavour to deflect him from taking proceedings against the four players. Not only was it not necessary but it seemed to me that it was not in the public interest to proceed. I made it clear that I acknowledged his right as prosecutor in the public interest to call for a report and I heartily endorsed his doing so. It is right that the procurator fiscal should always be in a position to call for a report upon a matter which has come to his attention and it was right that the public should be reminded that footballers on the field of play enjoyed no exemption from the law. I acknowledged also that the Crown were fully entitled to take proceedings in a situation if they thought those proceedings were justified.

At the same time I made it clear that in my submission the public interest did not require him to take any proceedings. The incident itself was a very minor one. Over the years there had been incidents of far more gravity which had not resulted in proceedings and it might be said that in these circumstances it would not be proper to take proceedings for what in effect was a very trivial hiccup in a game of football. If the purpose of the Crown in having a look, calling for a report and indeed even having the players charged were to demonstrate to the world in general that they had the right to do so and if it were also to lay down a benchmark, then those objects had been served by what had taken place thus far.

I suggested to Sandy Jessop that the public interest would be adequately served if he were to write to each of the four players to say that a report had reached him, that he had caused enquiry to be made, that he was satisfied there was sufficient evidence to justify proceedings, but he had decided not to do so. The players would realise that in the event of there being any subsequent behaviour of this sort then he would not hesitate to prosecute. It seemed to me that such a warning letter, which inevitably would reach the ears of the press, would fulfil all the objectives of the Crown.

There was another matter that truly bothered me. I told Sandy Jessop that I had a genuine fear that in the event of his proceeding then something of a sectarian reaction could very well occur. We, in the west of Scotland, are but a few miles from Northern Ireland. It has always seemed to me to be a tribute to the common sense of the vast majority of Scots that the sectarian troubles of Northern Ireland did not invade these shores to a far greater extent. Rangers and Celtic constituted a sensitive area. In the view of the Rangers fans, Frank McAvennie had caused the whole thing by rushing in on their goalkeeper and slapping his face. It would not take much, it seemed to me, to persuade someone that reprisals were in order and I wondered where that might lead. To make matters worse, one of the great tragedies of Northern Ireland had occurred on the Sunday before I saw Sandy Jessop – the tragedy of Enniskillen when 11 people were killed at a Remembrance Day ceremony in that unhappy town. It seemed to me that if the Crown were to proceed then the risk of some kind of reaction was all the greater because of the tragedy of Enniskillen.

Sandy Jessop told me that he would consider all my submissions very carefully, as I knew he would, and he would let me know his decision in due course. A few days later Sandy wrote to me telling me that notwithstanding all that I had said he intended to proceed with a prosecution and the players would receive their citations in a few days' time.

I understood that there were two other incidents in the course of that game. One of them involved a Celtic player and the other involved a Rangers player. Each of them had been guilty of conduct that the procurator fiscal had regarded as being utterly provocative and amounting to a breach of the peace but he had decided not to proceed against those two players.

In due course the Crown issued proceedings against Terry Butcher, Chris Woods, Graeme Roberts and Frank McAvennie and they were all charged with a breach of the peace arising out of the incident in the 17th minute of the game. We pled not guilty and our preparations for our defence got underway.

With the assistance of Strathclyde University we were able to demonstrate from a slowing of the video that in fact Frank McAvennie had not slapped Chris Woods on the face in spite of the apparent movement of his hand. It was difficult then to see what the complaint against Frank McAvennie was. His rush in on the goalkeeper was entirely within the laws of the game. I instructed Lord Morton of Shuna (he was appointed to the Supreme Court Bench of Scotland just months after the trial), Lord Macaulay of Bragar (who was then Shadow Lord Advocate), Ranald MacLean QC (he was appointed to the Supreme Court Bench two years later) and another very distinguished Senior Counsel, Mr Robert E. Henderson QC. The Counsel whom I had chosen constituted a very formidable defence. Indeed, it was said that they were the best back four in the country.

The trial attracted maximum publicity. It lasted several days. At the end of it all Frank McAvennie was found not guilty. The charge against Graeme Roberts was found not proven whilst Terry Butcher and Chris Woods were both found guilty of a breach of the peace and each was fined. They subsequently appealed against their convictions but their appeals were unsuccessful.

I thought at the time and I still think all these years afterwards that the decision to prosecute was wrong. There was no particular public interest requiring that prosecutions get underway. There were attendant risks in prosecuting, risks which I had outlined to the Crown, although I had no doubt that they were already well aware of them. In spite of those risks they decided to proceed. I remain of the view that the public interest would have been equally well served had the procurator fiscal written letters of warning instead of proceeding.

There were, however, other and perhaps even more important results of that case. It occurred, of course, in the pre-Maurice Johnston days. Maurice Johnston was a player (another from Bill McMurdo's stable whom I had the privilege of defending) who had played for Celtic. He had gone off to play in France for Nantes then come back promising to sign for Celtic. In the event, however, on 10 July 1989 Maurice signed for Rangers. By so doing he had committed the ultimate act of treachery in the eyes of the Celtic faithful. Before him only Alfie Conn (he had played for Rangers and then for Celtic in the 1970s under Jock Stein) had played for both sides of the Old Firm since the first decade of the twentieth century. I was able to boast that I was the first person since Alfie Conn to turn out for both sides of the Old Firm. It was a matter of unending regret on my part that I did not also become the highest paid defender in the Premier League!

LEGAL AID

The practice of law is all about contact with fellow human beings and it is all about sharing problems and worries. Being in practice as a solicitor makes that contact and sharing possible. If there is one thing more than any other which has brought my profession into contact with society it is Legal Aid.

When I came into the profession in 1954 Legal Aid was something new. It had been introduced in Scotland as recently as 1950 but in its introduction it was very, very limited. It only covered the raising or defending of cases in the civil courts (and even then not all cases were eligible) and literally nothing else.

For example, you could not obtain advice or assistance with a problem from a solicitor, nor could you be represented in the criminal courts. But it did nonetheless open the doors of our profession, however slightly, to people who might not otherwise have had any contact with a lawyer at all. Until Legal Aid arrived on the scene only the very wealthy or the very poor could afford the services of a solicitor. The poor could obtain those services under the old Poor's Roll system and to the wealthy questions of expense made no difference anyway.

The old Poor's Roll made its mark upon our law and Poor's Roll cases made their contributions in our case law. I suppose none contributed more than Mrs Mary Donohue who found a snail in the bottom of a bottle of ginger beer that she had bought in a café in Paisley. She got the assistance of a Poor's Roll solicitor and when her case was determined, in the House of Lords no less, in the early 1930s the duties of people towards each other were brought much nearer an acceptable level than ever before.

Legal Aid, part of our Welfare State, really kicked open the closed doors of the legal profession to society at large. The revolution began in 1950, though it began quietly and in a way that was grudgingly accepted by the profession. When Legal Aid was initially introduced, the Legal Aid Fund, provided by central government and administered by the Legal Aid Central Committee of the Law Society of Scotland, paid the profession only 85 per cent of the fees which were due. This was in fact a kind of bulk discount, which the profession had agreed at the inauguration of Legal Aid. Consequently the profession did not quite tumble over itself to accept instructions in Legal Aid cases.

It was not until 1964 when, many years after its introduction in England, Legal Aid in criminal cases was introduced into Scotland. Even then it was only available to persons charged in the High Court and the Sheriff Court and it did not extend to cases in what were then called the Police Courts, subsequently known as the District Courts. It is, of course, now available in all our criminal courts.

In 1972 a huge step forward was taken with the passing of the Legal Aid Advice and Assistance Act. This Act enabled large sections of the community, depending upon their income, to obtain the advice and assistance of a solicitor, whether or not the matter concerned ever involved the courts. The net result of all that welfare legislation is basically that a huge percentage of the population now has access to what I regard as being the finest profession of them all. That in itself is a tremendous social revolution.

In my day, Legal Aid applications in civil cases were decided by local Legal Aid committees drawn from practising and experienced solicitors, and appointed by the Law Society of Scotland. Those committees did an enormous amount of work for minimal remuneration. I was privileged to serve on the local committee for Glasgow for about twelve years and on the Legal Aid Central Committee (the national body) for the last eight years of its life, so I was able to see for myself the huge contribution which the profession made in the administration of Legal Aid in Scotland. Parliament has laid down the financial limits for Legal Aid in civil cases. Consequently it is possible to say precisely whether or not a person will be eligible, whether that person, depending entirely upon his income and his commitments, will be given Legal Aid free or will be required to pay a contribution. There is therefore a degree of certainty which most of us would regard as desirable. Under the Legal Advice and Assistance Scheme again there are statutory limits and again there is a degree of certainty.

In Criminal Legal Aid, however, an application was determined differently. It was determined either by a justice, if the proceedings were brought in the District Court, or by a sheriff, if the proceedings were brought in the Sheriff Court. It was also the sheriff who determined whether or not Legal Aid should be made available for a case in our Supreme Criminal Court – the High Court of Justiciary. In criminal Legal Aid there were (and are) no statutory limits or allowances and an applicant was dependent entirely upon the whim of the judge before whom the application came. This of course could lead not just to anomaly but to rank injustice and it was something that our profession sought to change for many years. Some judges were notorious for their approach to Legal Aid applications and like every other human institution they could be imperfect. I once saw a sheriff in Glasgow (now no longer on the Bench) presented with a bundle of what must have been 50 or 60 Legal Aid applications. It was the last thing he had to do before leaving the Bench for the day. It took him about three seconds to flick through them and then he said to the clerk: 'All of these Legal Aid applications are granted.'

At the other end of the extreme was the sheriff who asked an applicant what his defence was. When the applicant told him the sheriff said, incredibly: 'You don't need a lawyer. All you have to do is to tell that story to the court and you will be acquitted.' It seemed to me to be analogous to saying to a man who suffered from appendicitis that he didn't need a surgeon. All he had to do was go and take out his own appendix!

Originally, when an applicant for Legal Aid in criminal cases had to lodge his application with the court he had to wait to be summoned to the court hearing. At that hearing his application would be decided in public along with scores of others. This was always quite a humiliating experience for an applicant and it could have some awful results.

On one celebrated occasion a young man's application for Legal Aid was being heard. The charge against him arose out of an encounter between Celtic and Rangers one Saturday afternoon. It was alleged that he had conducted himself in a disorderly manner on the east terracing of Celtic Park (the Rangers end), had sung obscene songs, and committed a breach of the peace. He denied the entire charge and was applying for Legal Aid. He had been cited to a particular Legal Aid Court presided over by a sheriff who seemed always reluctant to grant any application.

The youth stood at the bar of the court, perhaps somewhat fearful of the outcome. From the Bench, in the grand inquisitorial style, came the following: 'The charge is a charge of breach of the peace. Did you commit a breach of the peace?'

'Naw.'

'What, then, were you doing?'

'Ah wis just singin', your Honour.'

'What were you singing?'

'"The Sash".'

'The Sash', as is probably known, is a song that seems to have some relevance in Ulster, a song which stirs up emotions either of joy or of hatred, depending upon which side of the River Boyne one stands. Its relevance to Scotland in general and to Scottish football in particular is difficult to imagine but there are, incredibly enough in these enlightened days, some who see it differently. At the mention of this immediately recognisable song the proverbial titter ran round the court. The Bench acted as though it had never heard of such a song.

'The what?'

'"The Sash", your Honour,' and by way of explanation, 'it's a Rangers song.'

Neither the applicant nor anyone else in that Legal Aid Court was prepared for what came next from the Bench, this time not a question but a command: 'Sing it to me.'

Confusion! Never had the applicant even dreamt that he might have to do this. His reluctance to publicise his vocal efforts in that unreal atmosphere was swiftly overcome by a reminder from the Bench that he had just denied committing a breach of the peace. The Bench had to determine whether or not by his singing he had in fact committed a breach of the peace. Similar words of encouragement were to be heard from many of the attendant applicants hopefully waiting their turn. At least if they were to be refused Legal Aid they could have fun listening to that unfortunate wretch in front of them. One or two discordant and scarce audible notes were heard to come.

'Louder,' came the command from the Bench.

The notes were slightly less inaudible but equally discordant.

'I can't hear you,' said his Lordship. 'Louder still,' and the applicant got to the end of the first verse. His eyes were fixed firmly on his toecaps as though he were reading the words there. His cheeks rivalled any beetroot that mother earth has ever produced but at least, thought he, his ordeal was over.

From the Bench, 'Have you not missed out a bit?'

Silence.

'Is there not in that song, or at least in its chorus, some reference to His Holiness the Pope?'

When they sing this song the Rangers faithful make a point of chorusing something not intended to be prayerful about the Pope. His Lordship was obviously more knowledgeable of the song than he had been prepared to admit in public.

'Yes, your Honour.'

'And did you sing that chorus?'

'Yes, your Honour.'

'Your application is refused. Singing like that would be a breach of the peace anywhere.'

Those Legal Aid Courts, now mercifully gone forever, were the source of a great deal of humour. I suppose in fairness they were the source of a great deal more than humour. If a lawyer emerged having had more than his fair share of applications refused, it was always possible to dream up some new undreamt of and thoroughly obnoxious Anglo-Saxon terms for the man who had refused so many applications.

LINDA'S PROBLEM

Poor Linda was pregnant. She was only 19 and was still single but she was pregnant. Her mother, with whom she lived, was upset at first when she learnt of the pregnancy but soon gave her daughter all the support she could ask for. Linda's ex-boyfriend Harry Ward, who used to live round the corner from her in Pollok, in Glasgow, was the father.

Linda had to give up her job as a machinist as her confinement drew near and she went on to Social Security benefits, or the Social, as it was more commonly known in those parts. For the foreseeable future she was resigned to being a single parent who would be kept by the state. The Department of Social Security, however, did not quite see it that way and they told Linda to sue Harry for maintenance. She was not all that keen. She had never been to court in her life and she had no ambition to go, but the Department insisted. They gave her the address of the Legal Aid office in town so that she could get in touch with a lawyer to raise proceedings against Harry for maintenance.

With some considerable reluctance Linda and her mother duly went to the Legal Aid office and after an interview were referred to a solicitor who was prepared to undertake that kind of work and who would get Linda's claim for maintenance under way.

Tom Scott, the solicitor to whom Linda had been referred, was a man in his late 30s. He was the partner who did the civil court work in his firm and he had a very good reputation for his ability and his efficiency. He was a kindly fellow with the rare gift of being able to relate to people. Linda found that it was very much easier to tell him the whole details of her relationship with Harry Ward than she had thought it would be. Mr Scott took a statement there and then from Linda and her mother. There was plenty evidence in support of Linda's case. Harry had even admitted to her mother that he was the father. Proving his paternity would obviously not cause too much of a problem. Mr Scott also filled in the necessary application forms for Legal Aid and had Linda sign them. She had to send him a medical certificate as to when her confinement would take place and then Mr Scott would be in a position to lodge the Legal Aid application with the authorities. She duly sent in the certificate from her doctor and a few weeks later she got word that her application had been granted. The way was now clear for Linda's action of affiliation and aliment against Harry Ward.

There was a slight problem. Harry had now disappeared. Whether this was coincidence or not Linda did not know but what she did know was that he disappeared soon after he got word that she was applying for Legal Aid to sue him. Linda had thought that Harry and she would get married in due course and when she told him that she was pregnant she was sure that he would agree to marry her. However, to her disappointment, Harry did not seem to be very anxious to get married and she had the distinct impression that their relationship started to cool after she told him the news. To her considerable surprise he moved away from the district within weeks of her telling him she was pregnant and now she did not know where he was living. Even his mother claimed she did not know where he was but Linda took that with the proverbial pinch of salt.

When her lawyer told her that she would not be able to take Harry to court until she found him he was just confirming what she feared. Tom

Scott told her that he would try to trace Harry through the Department of Social Security but that could take some time. She should make her own enquiries to see if she could find him. Perhaps some of her friends would know, or even some of Harry's friends. They, however, might not be so keen on telling her! She told her lawyer that she did not know if she could get Harry's address but she would certainly try. It was when she was on her way home on the bus that very afternoon that she realised that there was one possible way of finding out where Harry was staying. Janice, the local dentist's receptionist, was a friend of hers and Linda was quite sure that Harry was a patient of that practice. Perhaps Janice could help her get his address. When she got off the bus at Brockburn Road she went straight to the dental surgery to have a quiet word with Janice.

Within a day or two Janice had come back to her. She had looked up the address of Harry Ward in the records of the practice and passed it on to Linda. Harry in fact was now living only about a mile away and still in Pollok.

Linda telephoned her solicitor immediately with the news. He was delighted. Now he could get a writ into court asking the court to make an order against Harry for maintenance for her. He would have the writ served on Harry within a day or two.

Mr Scott duly prepared the writ and he obtained the necessary warrant from the Sheriff Clerk's Office in Glasgow which would enable the writ to be served on Harry Ward. The following day the writ was sent to Harry by recorded delivery at his new address.

The morning after the writ had been sent, Tom Scott, Linda's lawyer, was in his office bright and early. He had a civil case on and he wanted to gather all his papers (and his thoughts) without the usual early morning rush. The first disturbance came at about five past nine when his receptionist rang through to him.

'I'm sorry to disturb you, Mr Scott,' she said. Tom Scott reflected that Margaret was apparently always sorry to disturb him.

'But there is a Mr Harry Ward in reception. He does not have an appointment but he wondered if you could spare him a few minutes.'

Tom had a good idea why Harry had come in. Either he would protest that he was not the father and name several other possible candidates in the way that often happens when a young man wishes to avoid his alimentary responsibilities or else he would own up and try and reach a settlement of the matter. Either way Tom did not want to entertain him. He finished the coffee that he had made for himself about 15 minutes before, tidied up his desk and then rang through to his receptionist.

'Margaret, send Mr Ward in, please.'

A moment or two later a gentle tap on the door signalled the presence of Harry Ward. The door opening followed the command, 'Come in.' Tom Scott was astonished. Harry Ward had to be well over 70 years old. In a flash he realised that he had never asked the age of Linda's boyfriend but never for a moment did he think it would be a man old enough to be her grandfather. Harry Ward was wearing a rather shabby raincoat and generally looking as though he had seen better days. On his head was the cloth cap so popular with his generation. He whipped it off as he came in. The solicitor was still thinking of something to say as he motioned Harry to sit down. The visitor opened the conversation: 'I got this through the post this morning, sir.' It was not very often that a solicitor was addressed these days as 'Sir' and Scott enjoyed the moment. From his coat pocket Harry Ward pulled out the writ which had been posted only yesterday. A grin crept across his ageing face.

'It isnae me but when I read what those two had been up to I was wishin' it had been. That's the best tonic I've had in years.'

How was Linda to know that the local dentist had two patients called Harry Ward?

THE COMMON ROOM

The present Sheriff Court in Glasgow is situated in Carlton Place, standing on the south bank of the River Clyde. Built at a cost of £28 million, it was opened in May 1986. Most of my professional life was spent in the old building in Ingram Street in the city centre. The facilities there were appalling and would not have been tolerated in any other discipline. We did eventually (in the late 1960s I think) acquire a common room, a room in the building laid aside by the administration where solicitors might wait for the calling of their cases in court. There was nothing elaborate about it. There were about 20 vinyl-covered armless chairs. They were placed side by side in the centre of the room around a cluster of low tables. There were some desk-like tables and chairs at the side, a place to hang our coats, a place to powder our noses, facilities for tea and coffee, a telephone extension from the Sheriff Court switchboard for incoming calls only and a coin box. That extension at one time could cope with outgoing calls also, although that facility was soon enough withdrawn. Perhaps it was because we all discovered too many relatives in South Africa or Hong Kong. The place was really quite grubby and would have received very few stars in anyone's rating.

Shortly before ten o'clock each morning it would become a hive of activity. The building in Ingram Street housed 14 courts and most of the solicitors involved would use the common room as a matter of course. It soon became like the old building itself, far too small and quite inadequate for its purpose.

Those of us long in the tooth remember the days when the common room was a juvenile court. Those days, however, are long gone and the profession acquired the room to themselves, uninterrupted by allegedly offending juveniles and anyone else for that matter. At least that was the theory. We thought that we were protected from interruption by the notice on the door which said 'Private'. We should have known better.

It seemed to an ever-increasing percentage of the population of Glasgow that all solicitors carried on their practices in the common room and all that anyone had to do to see any solicitor at any time was to turn up at the common room and walk right in. At least that is the conclusion most of us were driven to by the number of times a face appeared round the door and the question was asked, 'Is Mr X here?' Anyone brave enough or stupid enough to walk into the common room and ask such a question was liable to get an answer. The professional response was to say something like 'I'm sorry I haven't seen him' but that was the one least often given. Much more popular was something like 'Him? Was he not struck off last week?' or perhaps 'I think he was arrested last night.' Meantime the enquiring member of the public would withdraw and have a quiet cardiac arrest when he heard such discouraging news about his chosen defender.

Inside the common room the reaction to such a scenario was always interesting. It was usually followed by a shout directed at one of our number: 'Hey, Joe. There's a client for you. Nip out and get him before he gets away.' Solicitors waiting in the common room did not take life too seriously. Perhaps it had something to do with the tension that every pleader feels on his every appearance in court.

The telephone would ring quite often. It was always answered, eventually. The rule was that the person nearest should answer it. There was no rule about what he should say and replies like 'The uncommon room' were not infrequent. A variant that achieved popularity for a spell was 'Who's calling the Golden Shot?' On another memorable occasion a client could not understand why he kept being put through to Benbecula Airport!

In my day the common room was an institution. It was once described as the best club in Glasgow. Whether it was or not I was in no position to judge but it was certainly the cheapest. We had no annual fees. All that was required was to be a member of the profession or an employee of one.

It was in the common room that many a plot was hatched and many a wit was on display. Some years ago one of our number who, although much loved, always took himself far too seriously was due to appear to represent a client. The client at the time of the offence was an alcoholic but was now apparently reformed. Our too-serious professional brother wanted to illustrate the reformation of his client in metaphorical language. There was a simile in his mind. It came from mythology. It concerned a bird that rose from ashes but he could not remember the name of the bird. Before he went upstairs to court, very quietly, he approached one of our number who he knew had had a classical education. 'Willie,' said he, in a voice that was conspiratorial, 'what do you call that bird that rose from the ashes?'

Willie opted not to tell of the resurrection of the phoenix but chose rather to have his little joke at the expense of our self-opinionated friend.

'Oh you mean the chameleon, Joe,' said Willie, trying furiously to keep his face straight.

'Yes, thank you, yes, the chameleon,' said our Joe, intensely relieved that he could now show off his apparent knowledge when he got up to the court. He went up to Court 4. He was ready.

He was a great one for tipping off the press when he was going to be in court because he loved to see his name in print and the very thought of his use of the simile brought headlines to his mind. He was going to enjoy this latest piece of publicity. When his turn came in Court 4 our Joe stood up and intimated his client's plea of guilty. The procurator fiscal narrated the circumstances and it was now for Joe to tender his plea in mitigation. Joe went on at some length and when he came to tell of his client's reformation, the dialogue went something like this: 'And so, my Lord, my client finds himself before the court like some chameleon from mythology rising from the ashes of his former life . . .'

'Like some what?' said the sheriff whose classical education was somewhat superior to our Joe's.

'Like the chameleon, my Lord, the chameleon rising from the ashes of his former life. Like the chameleon of mythology . . .'

He was cut short by the dryness of the next question from the Bench: 'Do you not mean the phoenix?' The snigger from the public benches was the last thing our Joe wanted to hear. Then the enormity of it all dawned upon him. Willie had betrayed him. He had deliberately misled him. The perfidy of it all!

Those who told the tale were too delighted with Joe's embarrassment to pay any heed to what finally happened to the phoenix whom our Joe represented that day. Posterity, however, does record how what should have been a day of great rejoicing at the publicity his case got turned out to be a total débâcle for him. He almost skulked out of Court 4 and downstairs to the common room. There sat our Willie delighting in the mischief he had wrought.

'Willie, you're a bastard,' thundered Joe.

Willie was not bothered. He had had a great laugh at the expense of one of the more pompous members of the profession in Glasgow and he now had a tale on which he could dine out for months to come. It is said that Joe thereafter went to evening classes to improve his knowledge of classical mythology. We have no way of knowing whether that was true or not but we do know that Joe never sought Willie's advice again.

The legal profession is very nepotistic. This of course means that there was always the chance that the son or daughter of some judge or sheriff could be sitting there in the common room in pursuit of their legitimate affairs. Accordingly, the experienced solicitor would always ensure that he could account for every face that was there before expressing opinions on the quality of justice that was being dispensed. You know the kind of thing I mean. Sheriff Wilson's nephew was now a trainee and so he had cause to be in the common room in pursuit of his master's legitimate affairs. Those who knew him and possessed this valuable piece of information would never betray it, at least not until they had taken unfair advantage of it. The nephew, had he any sense at all, would make his own discreet enquiries very early in his career as to the standing of his shrieval uncle in the eyes of the profession. Should he be rated highly the boy would bathe in the reflected glory. If not rated at all then the boy would keep his mouth discreetly shut about the relationship.

'Harry, what are you doing today?' The voice that shouted the question across the common room did not need to ask. He already knew what Harry was doing today as he had overheard an earlier conversation. But he had an ulterior motive in asking.

'I'm doing a trial in Court 7 before that ignorant pig of a man Sheriff Wilson,' says our Harry in his usual gruff but honestly straightforward way.

'That's a bit over the top,' says the original questioner, 'he's surely not that bad.'

'He is ignorant in every way – ignorant of the law, ignorant of common courtesy and ignorant of common sense,' proclaimed Harry in a stentorian voice that took up the whole room and which drowned out all the conversational trivia going on.

'Harry,' said a friend quietly, who realised what the original questioner was up to. 'That boy in the grey suit next to the noticeboard is Sheriff Wilson's nephew.' Harry made a quick exit.

We once had a sheriff in Glasgow called Tommy Wood. Everyone who knew him either loved him or hated him – there was no middle ground. In all Christian charity his could never have been described as the best shrieval appointment but it was not the worst either, as some of our number were liable to forget. There was one morning when one of our number came down from Court 3 where Tommy Wood had been on the bench and nearly collapsed into one of the chairs with his gown halfway down his back. It had obviously not been a good day for him.

'What's up, John?' asked a sympathiser.

'God, I've just spent an hour before Tommy Wood. That man really is the ultimate.'

'Oh, I don't know,' said the caring voice. 'He's not the worst. Besides he's got some redeeming qualities.'

'Well, if he has, he always keeps them cunningly concealed from me,' said our John, who was obviously far from convinced about Tommy's hidden qualities. 'I was trying for about 50 minutes to get home to him just what corroboration means but I might as well have been talking to the wall for all the difference it made. And then,' said John, working himself up to his emotional peak, 'when I mentioned Morton against Her Majesty's Advocate he just laughed. He obviously had never heard of the bloody case and what's worse he didn't want to hear about it.'

John it seemed had not totally enjoyed his appearance before Sheriff Wood that morning. However the caring voice was obviously anxious that adequate charity be dispensed to the good sheriff and so he continued: 'Well, even so, the man has some redeeming qualities. He may not be the best lawyer on the bench but he's a terrific pianist, he loves a good bucket, he's a great raconteur and he won a blue at Oxford for golf.' The caring voice was almost triumphal by now. 'And I'll tell you more. His son, he's a golfer too and he got his blue at Cambridge.'

John paused for a moment's silent reflection on these pieces of intelligence and then came the classic: 'He'll be a number two Wood I suppose.'

The Sheriff Court in my day had an official known as the Trials Liaison Officer (TLO). It was the task of that hapless official to try and ensure that the courts holding summary criminal trials were proceeding nicely and that the resources of the courts were being deployed to best advantage. He or she was in constant touch with the courts and with waiting solicitors and was often engaged in transferring cases to courts that for one reason or another had become free. Most solicitors who were waiting for a trial to begin used to wait in the common room, all padded up and ready to bat. They waited there for a call from the TLO to direct them to the court that would hear their trial.

It would not be the first time that the telephone has been answered by someone of cruel wit. The scene would go like this:

The telephone rings in the Common Room. It is the TLO. 'Is Mr Laughlin there?' asks the TLO.

'Do we have a Mr Laughlin here?' asks he of the cruel wit.

'That's me,' says the young and brand-new Mr Laughlin, probably still within his first week of being qualified.

'Yes, he's here,' says Cruel Wit.

'Tell him, please, that he has been transferred from Court 5 to Court 2, which is now waiting for him,' says the very helpful TLO.

'Certainly,' says Cruel Wit and replaces the telephone. 'Mr Laughlin, the TLO says that your case has been transferred to Court 11 and they are waiting for you there.'

'Thank you very much,' says the young Mr Laughlin and he gallops off up to Court 11, which is situated in the furthest corner of the building. He gets there a few minutes later not quite understanding why the court is empty. He is much too young and inexperienced to realise that his leg has been pulled mercilessly and so he waits around the empty court thinking he is first to arrive. Meantime Cruel Wit puts on his coat, picks up his briefcase and walks out the building and back to his office.

All the while in Court 2 we have a sheriff, a sheriff clerk, a procurator fiscal depute, an accused person and a bevy of witnesses waiting upon a solicitor who has failed to appear. Some 15 minutes later the young Mr Laughlin, now realising what has happened, will rush to Court 2, breathless, clothed in embarrassment and not knowing how to cope with a situation like this. As soon as he appears in the courtroom he is met with a fusillade from the Bench: 'Mr Laughlin, I have been sitting in this court for the past 15 minutes waiting until you decided to join us. Do you have some kind of explanation for your lateness?'

'My Lord, I am terribly sorry. I understood that my case had been transferred to Court 11 and I was waiting there.'

'Well, my information is that a very clear and unequivocal message was sent to you telling you that your case was transferred to this court.'

'Yes, my Lord, a message was passed on to me by one of my colleagues but he told me it was Court 11,' explained the demoralised Mr Laughlin.

'Are you telling me that a message from the TLO was deliberately distorted by another solicitor?'

'Oh, not at all. I am sure that that is not what happened. I am sure that somewhere along the line there was confusion as to the number of the court.' Mr Laughlin was still young enough and naive enough to have boundless faith in his colleagues. He would learn the hard way.

'Well,' says a thoroughly unsympathetic sheriff, 'I do not understand how that can be. What is beyond doubt is that all these good people have been kept waiting for some reason that is not attributable to any one of them. I find it all very unsatisfactory. However, we have wasted enough time already and perhaps we might now get a start.'

Poor young Mr Laughlin. This is no way to start a day before any sheriff let alone this one. He does, however, now realise how it all came about and if he has learnt nothing else today he has learnt not to trust Cruel Wit ever again.

There used to be a noticeboard in the old common room that was of some interest. It always contained the kind of information that one would expect, namely that day's business in each of the courts. It also announced forthcoming professional events such as dinners or conferences and so on. When the common room was established what now seems to be light years ago a joint consultative committee to run the common room was also established. It was representative of the administration and the profession and it laid down some rules for the running of the common room. One of them (more in hope than expectation) was that no notice would be put up without the permission of a committee member who would initial the notice to indicate his approval. Within weeks the rule was ignored, within months it was forgotten, and soon the noticeboard became the forum for any extrovert to display his or her exhibitionism or sense of humour in any way that he or she wished. In fairness, decency was always observed and what was displayed on the board was always fit for publication, but from time to time it conveyed some little gem that was worth recording for posterity.

Pinned up on the noticeboard one day was an open letter from a young lady who was seeking a traineeship. It was accompanied by a photograph which showed her to be not just attractive but possessing those assets so valuable for inclusion on page three of one of the popular tabloids. The letter invited members of the profession who would be interested in employing her to get in touch. The young lady did not, of course, exist except in the mind of one of our number who was fishing to see what the letter might catch. He had given an address on the letter, which ensured that any reply would fall into his hands.

He was not disappointed. For many weeks thereafter he was able to cause vast amusement by producing replies from among our number which invited the young lady in question to arrange an appointment. The replies were only produced when the writer of the reply was present and when the common room was busy.

'Hello, Jimmy. I see that you wrote to that young girl the other week. Tell me, Jimmy, why did you ask her to come and see you at five o'clock some evening?'

Three dozen eyes would focus on Jimmy. We reckoned we knew without him telling us why Jimmy had asked her along as his office was closing. Jimmy would stutter out: 'Well, Bob, I knew all along that it was you who had written that letter and I just wanted to have you on.' It never sounded convincing and Jimmy scurried away determined that one day he would even the score. Perhaps he would receive the message the next time the TLO telephoned for Bob!

MALCOLM'S APPLICATION

There was once a very small and very pompous sheriff in Glasgow. As a lawyer and indeed as a sheriff he was excellent. I say without hesitation that he was one of the best lawyers before whom I ever had the privilege of appearing. At the same time he had a failing and that was his awful pomposity. He really was incredibly full of his own self-importance. One of my colleagues, in a display of wit that was quite superb, once described our small sheriff as one of those little things that are sent to try us.

But once you had made allowance for his pomposity, then appearing before him could be a positive delight. However, his pomposity manifested itself in how he viewed presiding in the old Legal Aid Court. Before the passing of the Legal Aid (Scotland) Act 1986, applications for Legal Aid in summary criminal prosecutions, as I said earlier in these pages, were made to the court in which the proceedings were taking place. The application was thereafter returned to the solicitor by the sheriff clerk with a note of when a hearing would take place. The solicitor was required to intimate the date to the accused (and the procurator fiscal) and thereafter return the application to the sheriff clerk not later than 24 hours before the hearing. Those hearings always took place in a court that was open to the public.

This particular sheriff did not approve of having to determine Legal Aid applications. He regarded it all as being beneath the dignity of his office. These matters, according to him, should be dealt with by the administration; they did not require one of Her Majesty's sheriffs to take up his important time with such trivia. As a mark of his disapproval he refused to sit on the bench when he was dealing with Legal Aid applications. Instead he would sit without wig and without gown at the clerk of court's table.

His bar officer was a great fellow. He was in many ways the complete antithesis of his sheriff and he had even more laughs than we did at the wee man's pomposity and his insistence that everything be done according to the rules. On this particular day a new apprentice, now happily in practice in Glasgow, was sent to court by his masters with a Legal Aid application which was due to be heard in that day's court. It was our little sheriff who was due to preside over the court that day and the application was late. The apprentice, whom we shall call Malcolm, had been told by his boss not to worry about the lateness of the application. He was instructed to get there immediately before the court convened, find the bar officer and give him the application. The bar officer would then slip it into the bundle (or so Malcolm was told) before the sheriff came in and no one would ever know that it was late. Malcolm toddled off to the Sheriff Court.

When he arrived at Court 3, where the Legal Aid applications were due to be dealt with, he found himself in unfamiliar surroundings. He was a few minutes late but he was relieved to see that there was no sheriff on the bench. He could see no one in a bar officer's uniform, just a dapper little man sitting at the clerk's table with a bundle of Legal Aid applications in front of him, looking at them very studiously.

Being comparatively new as an apprentice and rather unfamiliar with the Who's Who of the Sheriff Court, he realised the wisdom of the old adage 'ask and ye shall be told'. He walked up to the front of the court and straight to the clerk's table. Bending over the dapper little man sitting there he nudged him with his elbow and asked: 'Are you the bar officer?'

'Why?' demanded the dapper little man.

'Well, this application should have been lodged yesterday but my boss told me that if I gave it to the bar officer he'd slip it into the bundle before the wee bastard comes on to the bench.'

Unfortunately posterity did not record what the dapper little man said to Malcolm and he could never be coaxed into telling us. Suffice to say that that afternoon Malcolm discovered the identity of the dapper little man.

INVERNESS

I think it was a Yorkshireman who coined the phrase 'there's nowt funnier than folk'. I do not know who he was but he was right. Folk are funny. That could have been said of many a client but of no one could it have been more honestly and more accurately said than of a client of mine whom I was representing at Inverness High Court on a charge of wilful fire-raising.

His case eventually came for trial in the High Court at Inverness the week before Christmas, though it had originally been set down for trial on the last Tuesday in September. Unfortunately our Michael (for that is what we shall call him) did not bother to appear then. The Monday of that week was the September holiday in Inverness and for that reason the court was not sitting until the Tuesday. As it happens, it was also the September holiday weekend in Glasgow, and because of this our Michael was going off to Dublin for the weekend.

At 10.15 on the Tuesday morning my Counsel, Kevin Drummond, now sheriff in the Borders, and I were in our places in Inverness High Court for the opening of the circuit. Michael's was the first case due to be tried and we expected that the trial would last three or four days. We reckoned without Michael. He was nowhere to be seen. I did not know it at the time but our Michael was not even in Scotland. He had decided to have an extra day's holiday in Dublin!

The circuit opened with its customary pomp and ceremony. After the prayers and the other formalities were over, the indictment against Michael was called. There was no sign of him. His name was called three times outside the courtroom and when he failed to answer his name the Crown asked for and were given a warrant for his arrest. Accordingly my Counsel and I packed our bags and trooped back down south. It had all been a wasted trip.

When I got back to Glasgow (not best pleased I may tell you) I telephoned our Michael. He was not at home but his daughter was. She told me that he had been on the phone the previous night to say that he was staying on for another day in Dublin! The following morning Michael flew back into Glasgow airport on the Aer Lingus flight from Dublin and was promptly arrested. He was taken straight to Inverness Prison 'until liberated in due course of law'. He did not quite understand what all the fuss was about. He had only added another day to his holidays. Could they not have waited for even one day? The fact that an entire sitting of our supreme criminal court had been disrupted did not seem to amount to much in his eyes. Even the consideration that some 30 potential jurors had been brought from every part of the Highlands and Islands of Scotland (never mind the witnesses and the court officials) made no difference to Michael's view of the matter. He thought that it was a bit much; after all he had only wanted an extra day's holiday in Dublin.

Once he got to Inverness I went up there to see him. He instructed me to apply for bail. In view of the fact that he was being held on a committal warrant I could not apply to the sheriff for bail and I had to go to the High Court in Edinburgh. Predictably enough, it was refused on the ground that the court could think of no better way of ensuring his attendance at the next trial diet than to keep him in prison until then. They were quite unreasonable people these judges, said Michael. There was nothing more we could do but wait for service of the indictment again and Michael would have to remain in custody until his trial came around.

In due course his indictment was duly served and his trial was scheduled to take place again in Inverness the week before Christmas. Kevin Drummond and I travelled back up to Inverness for the trial. In view of the fact that Michael had been kept in custody we were pretty certain that the trial would get underway this time. We were right. Ours was the first case on the circuit.

By lunchtime on the first day of the trial the Crown were struggling. Only one of their witnesses identified Michael as being the person who had been observed at the scene of the fire. The requirement of corroboration being what it is, that one witness was not enough. At lunchtime we had a consultation with Michael. Our mood was bullish. The Crown had had a bad morning. It was much too early to be making any forecasts but things were much better than they might have been at that stage. Our hopes for Michael were quite high. Another few witnesses in the afternoon and the Crown were fairing no better. Our chances of acquittal were mounting almost by the minute. My Counsel and I could not believe this change in

Michael's fortunes. The previous evening at consultation when we reviewed the evidence against the client it had certainly seemed to us that the Crown might not have too much difficulty in proving their case. Yet here we were, on only the first day of the trial, and by early afternoon several of the Crown witnesses had not come up to scratch and their evidence had not been anything like as strong as we had anticipated and as their statements had indicated. No fewer than three witnesses, whom the Crown had anticipated would identify the accused, had been unable to do so when asked.

During the afternoon Kevin Drummond and I suggested across the table in the court to the Crown that it was time to throw their hand in. It was beginning to look as though they could never prove their case. The advocate depute told us he was going to call one further witness, Donald McKenzie. If Donald could not identify the accused then that was it. He would go no further. He rose to his feet: 'My Lord, I am calling witness number 22 on the Crown list – Donald McKenzie'. The macer went out to fetch Donald. In moments the door was thrown open as the macer marched in followed by an obviously self-conscious Donald McKenzie, not accustomed to being the focus of so much attention.

Lord Stewart, formerly Ewan Stewart QC, one time Solicitor General and one of the sharper forensic brains of his time, was keenly aware of what was going on and many of the exchanges between us and the Crown had drifted up to his ears. He no doubt realised that the outcome of the entire case depended upon whether or not Donald McKenzie could identify Michael as having been there just before the fire took effect. Lord Stewart administered the oath that Donald repeated in that Easter Ross accent which is always so attractive. The advocate depute took the witness through his evidence at almost indecent speed and then came to that question upon the answer to which so much depended: 'Look around this court Mr McKenzie and tell me if you see the man to whom you have been referring.' We were either going home in ten minutes or we would be in Inverness for two or three more days. We held our breath. Donald cast his eyes upward to the horseshoe gallery that goes round that beautiful Georgian court in Inverness where the High Court was sitting. He looked, I am sure, at every face in a fairly crowded public gallery. He then swung round to face the press benches behind the witness box and scrutinised every face there. He looked towards the jury and nodded in recognition at one of the members. He looked at us who were sitting at the bar of the court and then at

Michael, alone in the dock with a policeman on either side. (Talk about sticking out like a sore thumb?) His eyes met Michael's but there was not a flicker of recognition from Donald, just a momentary pause. His eyes swung away from the dock and came straight to the gaze of the advocate depute: 'No, sir, he's not there.'

Phone the wife. Home for dinner.

'I noticed,' said the advocate depute with one last valiant try, 'that you looked at everyone in the Court. I was wondering did you see anyone in any part of the court like the man you have been talking about?'

This was all very interesting but all very academic. Donald was not going to identify now. We would be down that road in no time.

Meantime, Donald, anxious to be helpful, looked fairly hard at one of the jurors and then turned towards the dock again and nodding in Michael's direction said: 'I wondered if that might be him in the dock but no. The man I saw was much heavier than him.'

That was it. Game, set and match – or at least almost. I reckoned that the advocate depute would tell his Lordship that he was not proceeding; the judge would direct the jury to return a verdict of not guilty and that would be that. Michael would be released and I would be home tonight after all.

We all reckoned without our Michael. He rose to his feet in the dock: 'He's right, my Lord. I've lost three stone since they locked me up in the prison.' He got 15 months.

THE BENCH

Melvin Belli, the American lawyer, once described judges as being lawyers with delusions of grandeur. He obviously never pled before any Scottish Bench because one of the great things about pleading in the Scottish courts is the quality of the Bench. By and large, in Scotland we are extremely fortunate with our choice of judges, whether in the Sheriff or High Courts. They are a study in themselves and there is bound to come a day when such a study of the judicial process, limited to the individuals who are there, what they do and what makes them tick, will be undertaken.

By and large the public image of judges being old, crusty and unrealistic is totally without foundation. Let me be the first to say, however, that there have been some notable exceptions during my time within the profession. They are gone, and I suppose in some ways their very passing created a vacuum. I am reminded, however, of how young policemen are, and perhaps it may be that the same judges of today who no longer appear old to me appear ancient to a pleader 25 years my junior.

Our judges are drawn from an enormous cross-section of the profession. They are no longer exclusively the sons of the well-to-do, the products of public schools and of Oxbridge. Today, by and large, they are people chosen because of their ability and because of their acceptability. By and large, they are people who enjoy the respect of those who plead before them.

They can be a motley crew and long may it continue. One of these days some bright little brainbox is going to find a microchip that can sit up there (without a bar officer) and that microchip is going to have a lot of buttons on the front and each party is going to push a number of buttons and a decision will come out. That decision invariably will be right in that it accords with the strict law; but it will lack the most important qualities of any judicial decision – a touch of common sense and a large helping of humanity. Those, to my mind, are the ingredients that have to go into the mixing bowl along with the purely legal points, and I have not yet heard of the microchip which would be equal to the task. Another missing ingredient in our judicial microchip would be that little bit of arrogance and that little touch of pomposity that from time to time is displayed by some of the incumbents of the bench.

One of the more outrageous examples of the kind of thing that I have in mind happened to me some years ago in Glasgow in a sheriff and jury trial. The charge was one of assault and robbery. The incident took place in a front garden and an old lady then giving evidence had witnessed it. Her evidence would be important. She timed the incident (which took place late in the evening) by reference to the television programme for which she was sitting back waiting. On the bench we had a sheriff (newly appointed) who was inexperienced enough to regard it as being his function to take command of the situation and to ask all sorts of questions. The prosecutor was James Tudhope, one of Scotland's most able prosecutors, a fellow for whom I had and still have the highest regard and one of the most deadly cross-examiners in the country. His fuse was short and the constant interference from the Bench with his examination-in-chief was beginning to cause an overload. The signs were becoming more and more apparent: the testiness in the voice, the gritting of the teeth, the reeling away from the bench and the ever-tightening grip on his papers.

'What programme were you waiting for, Mrs Brown?' he asked. Not that it mattered but it would help to put his witness at ease and it was thus a sound psychological move.

'*The Untouchables*, sir.'

From the Bench: 'The what?'

This was the act being played, as though he would never do anything quite as common as watch television. He probably never missed an episode.

'*The Untouchables*, sir. You know, with Elliot Ness.'

She smiled, perhaps nervously, perhaps hoping to gain understanding. The Bench was unmoved.

'Which channel is that on?' asked an icy voice.

'What?' asked a disbelieving witness.

Everybody knew *The Untouchables*, everybody that is except one overbearing Glasgow sheriff.

'Is it on channel three or channel ten?' said he, who clearly preferred terms for BBC 1 and for Scottish Television which were already by then as archaic as 2LO, the original call sign of the BBC.

It was perfectly obvious to everybody that this wee Glasgow wifie did not have a clue what he was on about. All she knew was that she pushed a button. If the programme was on she watched. If it wasn't she knew that she had to push the other button.

At that point I took a hand, largely to defuse the situation for Jimmy Tudhope, who was prosecuting. I could see he was white with anger because this character on the bench was upsetting one of his vital witnesses. The fuse had reached capacity and in a moment or two it would blow and then the sparks would fly! I stood up. I could hardly believe what I was saying.

'If it is of any assistance to your Lordship I understand that it is on the same television channel as *Batman*.'

On my way back down to my seat I realised what I had said and I thought, 'My God, he'll do his nut.' I waited for the explosion from the bench. I was even frightened to look up at this point. But the explosion did not come. Instead there came to me that lovely sound, not just music but a veritable concerto to my ears, that most welcome sound to the pleader, a wave of laughter from the jury. I was saved. I looked up. The face on the bench flushed successively pink, scarlet, crimson, and purple. He said not a word. He dared not. The jury were on my side.

That experience taught me probably a couple of lessons about a criminal jury trial. It taught me something that I had always believed yet never had demonstrated to me quite so sharply, namely that humour can be one of the most important arrows in the pleader's quiver. But it taught me also how important is the reaction of the jury. It is they who determine the case and if they don't like you or don't like the way you are presenting your case then they are not likely to dole out their favours. Equally, on the other hand, the pompous Bench is something of which one has to be careful. I do not mind these warts, these foibles, on the part of the Bench. Each and every one of them contributes to the make-up of a pleader. He adjusts himself, he adjusts his presentation, to suit the Bench. I always ascertained as early as possible which sheriff was to be on the bench for any case of mine so that I might cut my forensic cloth accordingly.

I remember being involved in a very protracted and very dull fraud trial. I was representing the second accused in a sheriff and jury trial where the accused were charged with fraud. Basically the allegation was that two people had set up a company, had placed orders galore, had falsified references, had received goods, had sold them, had not paid a single creditor, and all of this was done with the intention of defrauding the various suppliers. It was dull for a very long time because days of evidence had been taken up with what we would call purely formal evidence. We had suppliers coming from England speaking of orders they had received from the company in question. They then, according to their evidence, wrote back to the company asking for references. The references came and after that the orders would be despatched but they would not be paid. It was all so predictable and dull. Harry Flowers, one of the greats of my vintage, was representing the first accused. Neither he nor I asked any question of importance throughout the entire first day. It was totally soporific.

The second day began where the first had left off, with the same kind of evidence. The trial was taking place in June in Court 2 in the old Glasgow Sheriff Court. It was so typical of these new courts, obviously designed by people who have never had to work in one. They would have been splendid greenhouses and one wondered just what tomatoes or tropical fruits could be grown within the stifling heat that they generated. Harry and I struggled. Not with the evidence, not with the opposition but against sleep.

Eventually Harry invented a question in cross-examination which had absolutely no relevance but was put forward in what I and, I am sure, many of the jury believed to be a highly original, humorous and entertaining way. The jury enjoyed it. It was a light but brief relief. The Bench was not impressed.

A stricture came. 'Mister Flowers. Her Majesty's courts are no place for levity.' How terribly boring, how terribly wrong and how terribly unrealistic. It was in any event the wrong judicial approach because the jury instantly formed the impression that not only was the case a bore but so was the sheriff. That was totally wrong but after that comment from the Bench the jury were no longer interested in the words of wisdom that were to come from him later. They were much more interested in watching the efforts of Harry and me trying to stay awake.

We managed it but with not too much to spare!

JOE BEATTIE

Joe Beattie was one of the best and most talented detectives I ever knew. He was a policeman's policeman. If there had been 25 hours in a day, Joe would have worked them. His men would have always gone that extra mile for him. Over the years he was in charge of many high-profile cases. The inquiry into the Ibrox Stadium disaster in 1971 and, of course, the Bible John hunt were two of the better known. The latter was undoubtedly the most frustrating for him, as the man he was looking for was never found.

Bible John was the first serial killer in Scotland before the buzzword was invented. He and Jack the Ripper had two things in common: both were serial killers of women; both were never caught.

Since the late 1960s the population of Glasgow has fed on reported sightings of him and rehashes in the media have turned him into a reappearing bogeyman. Even as late as the 1990s a body was exhumed from Strathaven Cemetery for DNA testing but it turned out to be another false lead.

Joe Beattie was the detective officer charged with finding Bible John. He and his team painstakingly and to the point of obsession sifted through every piece of evidence, no matter how slight, in what turned out to be a vain attempt to find the killer.

One important witness, who had actually met Bible John, was the sister of one of the murdered women. In fact, it was as a result of that meeting, at which she claimed he constantly quoted from the Bible, that he got his name. She and her sister, subsequently to become a victim, shared a cab home with him. The witness gave a description of a man with short hair who was clean cut and who at one point showed an identification card not unlike the warrant card carried by every police officer.

She was the principal witness, indeed the only witness that the police were aware of, and, accordingly, Joe Beattie subjected her evidence to the greatest scrutiny. He even measured the inside of the cab from her eyeline to where the man sitting opposite would have been, to make sure her description was not a fantasy. It checked out in the smallest detail.

The description she gave of the identification card was very important in Joe Beattie's mind and put the man into one of the following categories:

1. A police officer.
2. A prison officer.
3. A member of HM Forces.
4. A merchant seaman.
5. A journalist.

All of these organisations had black-covered identification cards or paybooks.

Thousands were interviewed, yet Bible John seemed no nearer to being captured, no matter what steps were taken by Joe Beattie and his team. At one point every member of a Masonic lodge was questioned just because the name of the lodge was the same as one of the dead women.

One clue left by the killer was a set of teeth marks found on the breast of one of his victims. Teeth impressions were taken and a hunt through dental records began. The scope of the hunt had suddenly widened, but, serious as it was, it still managed to produce that bit of Glasgow humour. Two CID officers went to the flat of man whose dental records were similar to those on the breast. The man in question was English, very small, quiet and a professional musician with one of the city's orchestras. It had to be said that if he ever read a newspaper it would have been the *Manchester Guardian*, perhaps a couple of times a year. He had no idea who Bible John was. When the heavy knock came to the door early in the morning he looked quickly through the security spyhole and saw two men wearing trilby hats and grey-green raincoats – the favoured uniform of Glasgow CID.

He shouted through the door: 'Yes? What do you want?'

One of the police officers said: 'We want to talk to you. It's about Bible John.'

The man replied, 'No, thank you. I am Church of England.'

The CID officers then had to convince him through his letterbox that they were not the Jehovah's Witnesses that he thought they were.

As the investigation continued, however, murmurings began to be heard against Joe Beattie when he started questioning police officers and prison staff. To some parts of the establishment he was becoming a nuisance. Eventually new senior policemen were appointed and Joe was informed that, while the case would not be closed, the investigation would be downgraded. There was now, apparently, a consensus of opinion among some senior ranks that one man alone was not responsible for the murders, and thus there was no Bible John.

Certainly he was never caught and the murders concerned were never solved. That was one of the few failures in the life of Joe Beattie

Joe was a Glasgow man who had been a former RAF pilot during the Second World War. He had also been a footballer of note and indeed at one time it looked as though a promising football career was ahead of him. The Second World War put an end to that and Joe was called up to serve with considerable distinction in the Royal Air Force. Following the end of hostilities he joined the then City of Glasgow Police. In the police service he rose to the position of Deputy Commandant of the Scottish Police College at Tulliallan before he retired in the mid-1970s.

But it was as a detective officer operating out of the old Maitland Street Police Station in Glasgow that Joe Beattie will be remembered by generations of Glaswegians. He was truly a legend in his time. The stories that abound about him could fill more books than I could ever write and they are all stories which do him credit. For Joe Beattie was unique in my experience. I never heard a client say a single bad word about him.

He undoubtedly had one of the sharpest intellects of any police officer that I ever knew and certainly he had great vision. Years before it was fashionable to have computers, Joe Beattie went around advocating their introduction to the police service. Many scoffed at the idea. What use were machines in trying to catch criminals? Now we all wonder how on earth the police service could operate without them.

For many years he neighboured Tom Valentine (who was to retire some years after Joe with the rank of Superintendent) and they were a formidable duo. They complemented each other and their success as an operational team was considerable. There is no doubt that they earned the respect not just of the criminals they stalked, but also of the entire police service.

Joe Beattie was appointed to head the inquiry into the great Ibrox Disaster of 1971 when a crush barrier gave way on the infamous stairway number thirteen at the Rangers end of Ibrox Park. Sixty-six people were killed that day. Joe's investigation into the disaster was masterly and he was commended at the official inquiry which followed.

As a witness in court Joe Beattie was almost without equal. He always gave the impression of being a rather slow and cumbersome thinker but that was a role which he cultivated and developed, playing it to perfection. Joe deceived many a cross-examiner into thinking that they would have no difficulty with him. They usually learnt of their mistake quite quickly, for in fact he was usually several steps ahead of any cross-examiner. He had great experience of giving evidence and he was one of the best witnesses you could ever hope to see. He was such an original thinker that he was dangerous to the unwary cross-examiner and humour was a deadly weapon in his hands. Let me illustrate.

An identification parade was held one day in Maitland Street and Joe was the officer in charge of the parade. The suspect was being paraded in connection with an assault that had taken place a few days before. In those days identification parades did not have quite the same safeguards as they have today and allegations of unfairness were much more common. On this particular day the suspect was duly identified by the victim and by two eyewitnesses, and was then charged with the assault. In due course the case came to court and obviously the evidence of the parade was very important. The solicitor for the accused was the late Bill Dunlop. Bill was a very able lawyer but if he had one fault it was that he took his cases far too personally and he did not have that objectivity which is one of the hallmarks of the good pleader. His emotions always seemed to run too high and his style was often aggressive and confrontational. That frequently did not appeal to a jury.

In this case he cross-examined Joe with enormous vigour and the whole tenor of his questioning was directed to suggest that the composition of the parade had been quite unfair towards his client.

'Do you agree that it was your duty to ensure that those who were paraded along with my client should have some passing resemblance to him?' thundered Bill.

'I would agree with you entirely, Mr Dunlop,' said Joe, amiably enough.

'And if I were to suggest to you that there was hardly a stand-in on that parade who looked like my client, what would you say to that?' demanded Bill.

'I would not agree with you,' was Joe's measured reply.

Bill Dunlop continued with the attack: 'If my client were to say that you gave him no opportunity to view the stand-ins before the parade got under way, would you brand him a liar?' (Bill loved the dramatic.)

'No, but I would not agree with his recollection,' replied Joe, choosing his words with that caution which was typical of him.

'And if I were to suggest that that typified the unfairness of that parade, Mr Beattie, what would you say to that?' barked Bill, the sarcasm in his voice being audible to everyone.

'Mr Dunlop, that parade was conducted scrupulously. As a matter of fact,' he added, as though he had just remembered, 'it was subsequently said that that parade was the fairest identification parade that had been conducted in Maitland Street for many a year.' Joe now had a triumphant note in his voice at that recollection. Bill Dunlop was knocked back on his heels by this information.

'Really?' said he, with ill-concealed disdain, 'and who, might I ask you, Mr Beattie, said that?'

'I did,' said Joe. A wave of laughter swept the court. The sheriff could scarcely hide his glee. He obviously thought that our Bill had overdone it and had got his comeuppance. Bill Dunlop was knocked completely off his stride and there was no point in continuing his cross-examination. The accused was duly convicted.

Joe's sense of humour and his demeanour in the witness box were totally disarming and won him many friends. But, what was more to the point, these things also led to him being regarded time after time as being a very credible witness whose evidence could be relied upon. That was a very formidable position for any police officer to be in.

Let me give you another example of what I mean. Joe was giving evidence in Glasgow Sheriff Court one day in the case of a young man whom he and Tom Valentine had arrested and charged with breaking a shop window and stealing from it. The accused maintained that they had arrested the wrong man. According to him he had simply been running home when these two men chased after him and caught him. He had not broken a shop window and he had not stolen anything. The incident had taken place in Stow Street, just off the Cowcaddens in Glasgow, and one of the many poorly lit streets that still abounded in Glasgow in those days.

A solicitor who was not the most popular in the city represented the accused. He had the reputation of being thoroughly arrogant and arrogance in the courts is a particularly nasty and unhelpful tool in a pleader's armoury. In his duels with Joe over the years he had seldom come out on top. We shall call him Jim Bloggs. I hasten to say that that was not his real name and should there be any solicitor with such an improbable name then my apologies go to him in advance.

The evidence for the Crown came from Joe Beattie and from Tom Valentine, who had witnessed the whole affair from start to finish. The first witness to be called by the Crown was the shopkeeper whose window was broken. His evidence was formal: he spoke to having left his shop secure, to being called out later that night and finding the window broken and to the things which had been in the window, their value and so on. Then came Joe. He gave evidence of how he and his neighbour were in Stow Street on their way back to the station in Maitland Street when they heard the sound of breaking glass. They looked around and there was the accused at the window, helping himself to various items in it. He went on to tell how he and Tom Valentine had chased the accused and had caught him in Cambridge Street, just a couple of streets away. The man sitting in the dock was the man whom they had seen at the window and whom they had chased and apprehended in Cambridge Street. They found the articles which were shown in the court in the possession of the man they had chased and caught.

It was now for Jim Bloggs to cross-examine. His attitude in those days seemed always to be that it was an impertinence to suggest that any client of his would ever commit a crime. His line of attack on Joe was that it was not his client at the window at all. The chase had brought them around two corners. They had lost sight of their quarry on at least two occasions during the chase. How could they possibly say it was his client? Then came his moment of triumph, or so he thought. He had been to Stow Street to see the street lighting. Would Joe agree that the nearest street-lamp was about 25 yards away from the shop front and shed no light whatever on the shop window? Joe Beattie readily agreed with what was being put to him. Mr Bloggs sat down with a grunt of satisfaction. He was obviously pleased with himself for that piece of what he regarded as deadly cross-examination. He was caught off guard by the quiet and intensely polite voice that came from the witness box behind him.

'Mr Bloggs, excuse me but you forgot to ask me about the shop window, sir.' Bloggs got back to his feet, disarmed by this excess of *politesse*. 'What about the shop window?' he asked.

'It had a strip light at the top and bottom and was like the Blackpool illuminations.'

Mr Bloggs' client was convicted.

There lived within the old Northern Division of Glasgow (and thus within Joe Beattie's patch when he served in that Division) one well-known and little-loved gangster. He was widely regarded as one of the most dangerous men in the city. We shall call him Andrew. After a particularly vicious assault in Robroyston, part of Joe's Division and not gin and tonic territory, one of Joe's touts told him that Andrew was behind the assault and that it had been perpetrated by one of Andrew's lieutenants. It seemed that the victim owed Andrew money and had not paid. The price of not paying was a fractured skull.

Joe and Tommy Valentine decided that they should have a word with Andrew and with that in mind they went to see him. It was Andrew's wife who opened the door. She did not express delight at seeing the two detective officers and greeted them with the mouthful of abuse that she seemed to reserve for police officers who thought that her husband was other than perfect. But at least she let them in, if only because she knew that she had little alternative. Andrew was there in the house. Beattie and Valentine told him what it was about and that they wanted to interview him at Maitland Street. Tommy Valentine told Andrew to get his jacket. At this, Andrew's wife intervened: 'Yese are always tryin' tae f****n' crucify him,' she shouted, and at that she ran into the kitchen. Neither Joe nor his neighbour was prepared for what came next. For she came rushing out of the kitchen with a handful of nails and, grabbing Joe by the arm, she thrust them into his hand.

'There's the f****n' nails,' she shrieked. Joe's retort was immediate: 'Have you got a hammer?'

Beattie and Valentine were a wonderful double act and they could react to each other quite instinctively. On one occasion Joe had charge of an enquiry into a theft from a gas meter in a house in the Townhead district of Glasgow. That kind of crime was as common as the proverbial muck. Unless the thief was caught red-handed or had left his calling card in the shape of his fingerprints there was really very little chance of solving the crime. Unfortunately, the householder concerned did not appreciate this fact. He would come to Maitland Street Police Station practically every day asking Joe for a progress report. Sadly, but not surprisingly, there was no progress to report, but no matter what Joe told him he was not convinced and he kept coming back with a frequency that was really off-putting. Eventually after about 24 days and after the householder had made about 21 visits to Maitland Street, Tom Valentine decided to take a hand. Accordingly, on the next occasion that the hapless householder came to Maitland Street and asked to see Detective Sergeant Beattie, as he then was, it was Detective Sergeant Valentine who came to see him. He took the luckless John Kennedy into the Detective Chief Inspector's room and sat him down.

'Mr Kennedy,' said Tom, 'I'm sorry to be saying this to you but you are wasting your time coming here to ask what progress there is in solving your crime. See that Joe Beattie? He's the worst detective I've ever come across. The only thing he's ever caught is a cold. If I was you I would just forget it because you'll never get anywhere with that man in charge of your case.' The hapless Mr Kennedy walked out of Maitland Street Police Station that morning shocked by this revelation. He never did come back to enquire about the break-in to his gas meter and Glasgow acquired its only citizen who believed that Joe Beattie was the worst detective ever.

Joe Beattie died in February 2000 after many long years of illness. His bravery throughout was admirable and he never lost his sense of humour. Joannie, his widow, who had nursed him so tenderly throughout, did me the enormous honour of asking me to say a few words about Joe at the crematorium. This is part of what I said:

> Joan and the family have honoured me by asking me to say a few words about Joe. But how can any mere words pay sufficient tribute to that fine, brave man.

JOE BEATTIE

Joe and I went back a long way – to the days when I was still at school and he and Joannie were neighbours of my sister. He was the big polis up the stairs just out of the RAF who had married the lovely English girl. We met up again when I qualified and Joe took me under his wing and brought me into that huge circle of people who were his friends and for whom he would do anything he could.

We all owe a great deal to Joe Beattie, and my family and I will always be grateful to him for the help, the encouragement and, above all, the friendship that we enjoyed at his hands for 40-odd years.

An enormous number of people owe much to Joe and to what he did for them. It was not for any thanks that he did it but out of a deep sense of caring and compassion for others . . .

He had outstanding success in his chosen career both in the CID and in uniform, and he was one of that tiny elite corps, the finest police officers that I have ever been privileged to know.

He enjoyed enormous respect, from his colleagues, from the press, from my profession, from the Bench and even from the very people that he locked up. I never heard a bad word about Joe from any one of them.

And that perhaps was the measure of the man: he gained respect wherever he went. For a whole generation he was much more than just a polis from Maitland Street. Before community policing was ever invented, Joe was a community policeman; he was a counsellor before the word counselling was ever discovered; for he was an institution.

A mould has been broken. An era has ended, and life has changed for everyone of us whose lives were touched by this lovely man. But this is not an occasion for us just to shed a selfish tear at our loss. It is also an occasion for thanking God, not just for having created such a wonderful character, but also for having extended to us the privilege and the honour of his friendship. For each and every one of us who knew Joe Beattie is the better and the richer for the experience. There is an old Arab proverb which says that the best legacies a man can leave are good memories and Joe has left an abundance of good memories to us all. It is in the Gospel of St Matthew that we read: 'Well done, good and faithful servant; enter into the joy of your Master'. On Thursday of last week Joe Beattie entered into that joy, and his pain and his suffering are no more.

FREDDIE CAIRNS

The name of Freddie Cairns is not likely to mean much to many people these days. Yet for a time it was well known up and down the country. Freddie Cairns came from Parkhead in the east end of Glasgow. At the time we speak of he was a prisoner in Glasgow's Barlinnie Prison, serving a sentence of 18 months' imprisonment for housebreaking. He had a bit of a record for dishonesty but no convictions for violence.

On 26 October 1965 there was an incident in a corridor of 'A' Hall in Barlinnie. Alexander Malcolmson, who came from Shettleston, also in Glasgow's east end, and who was serving a sentence of six months' imprisonment for housebreaking, died of stab wounds sustained in the incident. Cairns was charged with his murder. It was the first murder in a Scottish prison and for that reason it attracted a lot of media attention. Cairns instructed me to defend him.

I found myself wondering if the Crown would ever be able to prove the charge. In my experience convicted prisoners who were nearby when an incident occurred in a prison always seemed to have left their powers of observation outside the gates. Most of the prisoners who were present in 'A' Hall when Alexander Malcolmson was stabbed proved to be no exception.

I instructed the celebrated Nicholas Fairbairn as Counsel for Cairns with J. Stuart Forbes (now sheriff in Dunfermline) to act as his junior. The trial began on 28 February 1966 in the North Court of Justiciary Buildings in Glasgow and it continued into the following day, 1 March. On the first day of the trial the Crown led their evidence. In spite of my earlier doubts, there was enough evidence in law against Cairns, if the jury believed it. Two prisoners claimed to have seen Cairns stab Malcolmson. That night we all conferred and we advised Cairns that he should give evidence. He had no difficulty about that. He had not stabbed Malcolmson, he said, and he would be happy to go into the witness box and tell the jury that the killing had nothing to do with him. Accordingly, the following morning Cairns gave evidence. His evidence was to the effect that he was aware of the incident, that he had seen the scuffle but he had not been involved and certainly it was not he who had stabbed Malcolmson. Those who said it was him were either lying or they were simply wrong. He had no idea who had done it. We led no other evidence.

In his address to the jury Nicholas Fairbairn was able to cast considerable doubt upon the evidence against Cairns. The evidence had been given by two prisoners, each of whom had a considerable record for dishonesty, and each of whom might have had a grudge against Cairns. The jury retired and when they came back they returned that uniquely Scottish verdict of not proven. For all practical purposes a verdict of not proven is no different from one of not guilty but many observers thought that the verdict indicated that the jury did not entirely believe Cairns' version of events. However, the matter was over – the case was closed. Cairns was sent back to Barlinnie to finish the sentence which he had been serving at the time of the murder and he was duly released later that month.

None of us connected with his defence was prepared for what came next, for immediately on his release he walked into the offices of the Scottish *Daily Express*, which were then in Albion Street in Glasgow, and said that he had something to tell them. So he had. He confessed to the murder of Alexander Malcolmson.

He was interviewed at considerable length by two of the most respected journalists in Scotland – Stuart McCartney and David Scott – and he told them his story. Not only did he confess to the murder but he also told them of how he and other prisoners had then put their heads together to ensure that the authorities would never discover the truth of what had happened that day in 'A' Hall in Barlinnie Prison. The interview took place over several days in March but it was not until July that the Scottish *Daily Express* published the story. They waited those four months because they said that they had wanted to 'clear the story with all legal authorities', whatever that might have meant. In fact they sent it to their lawyers and then to Crown Office.

When Cairns' story was eventually published it ran over a period of three days. It made excellent reading, but perhaps more importantly it had the loud and unmistakable ring of truth about it. A huge wave of indignation swept the country. Here was a criminal crowing about how he had defeated the system, politicians trumpeted. Questions were asked in Parliament. Norman Buchan, then Under-Secretary of State for Scotland, was furious and said he would take the matter up with the Lord Advocate, the government's principal law officer in Scotland. National indignation and fury grew when it was pointed out that, contrary to popular belief, Cairns could not be tried again for the murder. It had been a commonly held view that a verdict of not proven meant that the Crown could bring the accused person back to trial if ever they got more evidence. Many were surprised to learn that that is not the case and that a verdict of not proven is just as much an acquittal as a verdict of not guilty.

To use the technical term Frederick Cairns had 'tholed his assize'. He could not ever be tried again for the crime even though he now admitted having done it! But in the view of the man in the street he had literally got away with murder and it was entirely wrong that nothing could be done.

That view, however, reckoned without the ingenuity of the Crown Office in Edinburgh who have responsibility for the prosecution of crime in Scotland. Of course Cairns could not be charged with the murder again, but if he had murdered Malcolmson, as he had claimed in the *Daily Express*, then he had told lies when he gave his evidence in the High Court – in other words he had committed perjury. The Crown Office announced blandly that they were considering the matter.

The procurator fiscal of Glasgow, then Henry Herron, that most able of public prosecutors, instructed the police to investigate. Detective Chief Inspector Jack Scott of Glasgow CID was appointed as the officer in charge of the inquiry and he wasted no time in getting it under way. He went to the Scottish *Daily Express* to interview David Scott and Stuart McCartney, the reporters concerned. McCartney was on holiday when DCI Scott first called at Albion Street and he still recalls going back into the office on the day after his holiday (knowing nothing about the inquiry) to find Jack Scott sitting there waiting for him.

When DCI Scott had completed his inquiry, he took his report to Henry Herron. The Lord Advocate had instructed that the report be sent to him as soon as possible and accordingly Herron sent the report on to the Crown Office the very day he received it. By return the Lord Advocate instructed that Freddie Cairns be charged with perjury. He clearly took the view that Cairns had told the truth to Scott and McCartney and had not told the truth when he was giving evidence. No accused person had ever before been charged with having committed perjury while giving evidence on his own behalf. There was no precedent for it. The big question, then, was whether it was competent to bring such a prosecution.

Cairns was arrested and charged. He instructed me to defend him. His defence was pretty predictable – namely that he had told the truth in court and what he had told Scott and McCartney was all lies; he had done it out of bravado. When he appeared in the Sheriff Court charged with perjury he was allowed bail. In due course an indictment was served on him and he was cited to appear at a pleading diet in Glasgow Sheriff Court on 20 January 1967.

The terms of the charge were that '. . . in the course of your trial on indictment at the High Court of Justiciary in Glasgow on 1 March 1966 for the murder of Alexander Malcolmson, a prisoner in Barlinnie Prison, by assaulting and stabbing him on 26 October 1965, on which you were acquitted, and, having been sworn to tell the truth, you falsely deponed that you did not assault and stab the said Alexander Malcolmson on 26 October 1965 in the said prison, the truth being as you well knew that you did on that occasion assault and stab the said Alexander Malcolmson'.

When the indictment was called in court on 20 January I did not tender any plea on Cairns' behalf but instead I intimated a written plea to the competency of the charge. The ground of my objection to the competency was fairly basic. Cairns could never be tried again for the murder. But to prove this charge that had now been brought against him the Crown would effectively require to re-run the trial for murder. If it were not competent to try Cairns all over again for the murder of Malcolmson, how could it be competent to charge Cairns with a crime which would be proved only by proving he assaulted and stabbed Malcolmson? The point, it seemed to me, was an interesting one and it had never been decided before.

Because it was a High Court case, the sheriff who presided on 20 January (Sheriff C.H. Johnston QC) could not rule on the objection which I had taken. All he could do was simply note it and continue the case to the trial diet at the High Court sitting of 31 January. The point was a novel one and no matter the outcome legal history would be made because there was no precedent either way. Because of that fact the court authorities arranged that a Bench of three judges rather than just one would hear the debate on the competency of the prosecution case. Those judges were to be Lord Grant, the Lord Justice-Clerk; Lord Wheatley, who was destined to succeed him when Lord Grant was killed in a car crash on the A9; and Lord Strachan. It was a formidable Bench.

When we came before those judges on 14 February 1967 I had instructed R.A. Bennett QC to represent Cairns. The case was serious enough and the public interest was great enough for the Lord Advocate himself (Gordon Stott QC) to appear on behalf of the Crown. Ronnie Bennett's arguments were short and very much to the point and were effectively a reiteration of the objection which I had taken in the Sheriff Court.

Gordon Stott had always been a very persuasive pleader and that day proved no exception. His arguments in answer to our objections to the competency were unassailable. The Lord Advocate pointed out that this was an entirely different charge, which was alleged to have been committed at a different place and at a different time. There was thus no question of Cairns tholing his assize to this charge and thus no obstacle to the prosecution. The Crown were not attempting to prove him guilty of murder, said the Lord Advocate, they were interested in showing that what Cairns had said in his evidence was untrue and that he knew it to be untrue.

Unfortunately for Freddie Cairns their Lordships agreed with the Lord Advocate and repelled our objection. Lord Wheatley, never one to mince his words, said that in his opinion the Lord Advocate had 'briefly and succinctly demolished' our principal argument. If our objections were well founded, he said, then 'there would be a bonus for successful perjury'. The court unceremoniously repelled the objections to the competency of the proceedings and allowed the case to go to trial. But the trial could not go ahead straightaway because an important witness was missing. He had been a prisoner in 'A' Hall at the time of the stabbing and he had given evidence incriminating Cairns at the original trial. He had been released at the end of his sentence and now he had disappeared, perhaps not surprisingly. The Crown therefore asked the court to continue the case and allow them the opportunity of trying to find the ex-prisoner who had disappeared. The judges agreed and accordingly the case was continued for trial until some later date.

Freddie Cairns and I had one or two meetings thereafter, preparing for the trial that might or might not go ahead, depending on whether the missing witness ever turned up. But on Monday, 22 May 1967 the Scottish *Daily Express*, the same paper that had carried his confession the previous July, wrote the final chapter of Freddie Cairns' story when it carried the news that he had died the previous day. Some days before he had been taken

---

into Glasgow Royal Infirmary to undergo a stomach operation and had not recovered. He was only 26.

Perhaps his early death meant that he did not get away with murder after all.

ANTANAS GECAS – WAR CRIMINAL

The Teutonic-looking officer was tall and blond. He carried an automatic pistol with him as he carefully stepped through the mound of recently dead corpses looking for life. When he found any life in that mound he dispensed his own form of the last rites: a bullet to the head. The man was a Lithuanian named Antanas Gecevicius. He would come to be known later in his life as Antanas Gecas.

His men had massacred thousands that day with their machine guns. It was the culmination of the massacre of Jews and partisans near the city of Vilnius in Lithuania, a beautiful city that had once been called the Jerusalem of the North. According to eyewitnesses, the officer had engaged in an orgy of killing as he roamed the countryside with his troops. They were drinking vodka from bottles as they lined up their prisoners and shot them. Many other prisoners were hanged with wire and on butcher's hooks. Neither age nor sex made any difference to the treatment they meted out.

His German masters had awarded Gecas the Iron Cross and he wore that as he carried out his inhuman atrocities. He did so without mercy, without compassion. He was the very paradigm of evil. His was one of the killing squads of Lithuania, comprising Lithuanians who had volunteered to join police battalions under German command. They took orders directly from SS Reichsführer Reinhard Heydrich, and ultimately Heinrich Himmler, the key architects of the 'Final Solution' that would see millions butchered across Europe. Heydrich was in charge of the '*Reichssicherheitshauptamt*', the RSHA, which controlled the various police and secret service departments of the Third Reich. It was Heydrich that Goering instructed 'to prepare an overall solution to the Jewish question in the German controlled areas of Eastern Europe' after the Germans attacked the Soviet Union. The killing pits in the woods of Paneriai, near Vilnius, played a huge part in that solution. Jews and partisans were lined up, shot, and buried in layers on top of each other.

It was in October 1986 that Bob Tomlinson, then working as a reporter with Scottish Television, spotted a little news item in the *Daily Record*. It was at the foot of a column and it attracted little public attention at the time. A journalist with the experience and ability of Tomlinson could not ignore it. It said that at least 17 Nazi war criminals were living in Great Britain and one of them (who was not named) was believed to be living in Edinburgh. He had apparently fled from Lithuania, where he helped to murder thousands of Jews. Tomlinson read the story with incredulity. There were surely no war criminals living in Britain. Argentina, Brazil, even Australia, but surely not Britain and certainly not genteel Edinburgh.

At the end of the usual morning news conference held at Scottish Television in Cowcaddens in Glasgow, Tomlinson asked the then deputy news editor, Eric Wilkie, if he could follow up that story. Wilkie thought there was probably nothing in it but he gave Bob the go-ahead, never imagining the result. Bob Tomlinson conferred with David Scott, then head of news and current affairs at Scottish Television and began making his enquiries. These initial steps would prove to be the starting point of the most fascinating road he had ever taken in his career as a journalist.

First, he called the Holocaust Centre at the University of Yad Vashem in Jerusalem. By one of the most incredible coincidences that could be imagined, Ephraim Zuroff, who happened to be visiting the Centre, answered the telephone. Zuroff ran the Simon Wiesenthal Centre in Jerusalem and was a professional Nazi hunter following in the footsteps of Wiesenthal himself. Wiesenthal, of course, was the man who brought Adolf Eichmann back to Israel, where he was executed after trial for his war crimes. Zuroff knew as much as anyone in the world about Nazi war criminals and he was able immediately to put Tomlinson in touch with Eli Rosenbaum, a Manhattan attorney. It was Rosenbaum in New York who gave Tomlinson the name of the war criminal who was living in Edinburgh. His name was Antanas Gecas, otherwise known as Antanas Gecevicius. He was not a German as might have been expected, but a Lithuanian.

According to Rosenbaum, Gecas had been a platoon leader in a Lithuanian police battalion during the Second World War. In 1940 the Soviet Union annexed the Baltic States of Latvia, Lithuania and Estonia on the pretext that the local people had asked them to intervene and to save their countries from the fascists who were taking over. But after the outbreak of hostilities between Hitler's Germany and the USSR, the

Germans overran the Baltic States. They formed police battalions made up of locals to do their dirty work for them and Gecas was one of those who volunteered for service. While so employed Gecas had taken part in the murder of thousands of innocent people whose only crime was that they were Jewish. He had escaped capture and now he was living in Edinburgh.

Tomlinson could hardly believe what he was being told. He had to investigate. Rosenbaum faxed him a great many documents the following day and Bob threw himself into the task of studying them with great vigour and with growing amazement. He found himself reading part of a transcript of what was effectively a war crimes trial in the United States. The name of Antanas Gecas was mentioned frequently in that transcript. Among the papers that came from Rosenbaum was a copy of a statement given by Gecas to Neil Sher, a lawyer from the United States Government's Office of Special Investigations. Tomlinson realised that there was a story in what he was reading. The story would be of the war criminal who now lived in Edinburgh.

It is difficult to think of a greater libel than to call anyone a war criminal or a mass murderer or some such similar epithet. The dangers to Tomlinson and to Scottish Television in making such a programme, were they to make one, would be considerable. He would have to check out all that Rosenbaum had told him and he could use it only if it could be proved in a Scottish court.

Tomlinson conferred with David Scott. David was a journalist whom I had known and worked with for 20-odd years and for whom I had very considerable respect. Indeed, I think it is probably true to say that David Scott was one of only a handful of journalists in the country who enjoyed both the respect and the trust of the entire legal profession. David called me into the discussions.

A few years before that, Scottish Television had paid me the enormous compliment of retaining me as their principal legal adviser on news and current affairs. They reckoned that they could use the experience and expertise in media matters that I had gained over the years. In the late 1960s the Law Society of Scotland had appointed me their first ever media spokesman in litigation matters and this had brought me into very close contact with the media in general and television in particular. The experience this gave me proved invaluable. In the early 1980s there were perhaps only a handful of us in the profession who had the necessary knowledge and experience, for media law is a very specialised subject. To be involved in a story such as this was a remit that I tackled with enthusiasm.

The three of us, Tomlinson, Scott and I, sat down at Cowcaddens to talk the matter through. It would make a very good story if it were true. We had to test the truth of what Rosenbaum and Zuroff had told Tomlinson. There was only one way of doing it and that was by going to the Soviet Union. Bob would need to go there to interview those who had survived the Holocaust and who could speak of the involvement of Gecas in the atrocities of which Eli Rosenbaum and Ephraim Zuroff had spoken. In due course David got the go-ahead from his superiors and Bob could start packing his bags. It was a trip into the unknown for none of us knew what kind of response or what kind of cooperation Bob would get over there. The Soviet authorities were still very much in charge at that time and the wind of freedom had not yet reached Russia, Lithuania, Byelorussia (now known as Belarus) or the Ukraine.

The thoroughness of Bob Tomlinson's preparation is perhaps best illustrated when I tell you that he insisted that I spend an afternoon with him telling him how to ask questions of a witness! No journalist had ever sought my view on that before and I imagine that none ever will again. What Bob was anxious to do, of course, was to prevent the allegation that he had put words into the mouths of those whom he interviewed.

He and Ross Wilson, a programme director/producer of Scottish Television, set off with a camera crew to the USSR to see how much of the Zuroff allegations could be proved. Just a few months before, Ross had directed another splendid documentary made by Scottish Television entitled *Britain, A Nazi Safehouse* which had been sold to Channel 4. Margaret Thatcher had once said that there was no evidence sufficient to justify prosecution for war crimes of anyone living in Britain. Bob Tomlinson and Ross Wilson went to the Soviet Union to get that evidence.

They were not interested in trial by television and we all agreed that any evidence that they uncovered would be made available to the appropriate authorities. They left for the Soviet Union on 22 April 1987, planning to be away for ten days. Their journey took them first to Moscow to meet Madame Natalya Kalesnikova. She was the Deputy Soviet Prosecutor with responsibility for war crimes. She told them of the evidence that existed against Gecas and she told them also of the warrant that her office held to arrest him if he ever returned to the Soviet Union. They wanted him for murder.

Tomlinson and his entourage went from Moscow to Vilnius, the capital city of Lithuania, surely then one of the most backward countries of Europe. There they met and interviewed two former colleagues of Gecas (or Gecevicius as he was known there) who had served with him in the infamous Second Police Battalion. They went to Minsk in Byelorussia and on to Slutsk. They also went to Lutzk in the Ukraine and to L'vov. They got their evidence and returned to Glasgow ten days later. Within 48 hours they had organised a film crew and were on their way back to film what they had heard and seen on their earlier trip. This time they went to Moscow in Russia; to Vilnius and Paneriu and Kaunas in Lithuania; to Minsk and Khatim and Slutsk in Byelorussia; and to Lutzk and Toor and L'vov in the Ukraine. And everywhere they went there was a common theme – murder and massacre.

The result of this investigation was one of the finest television documentaries ever, a programme entitled *Crimes of War*. It included the story of Antanas Gecas, a Lithuanian who got himself a job with the Nazis after they overran his homeland. It told of how he was put in charge of a murder squad that masqueraded as a police battalion and how he was quite prepared to kill innocent people as part of his job. It is difficult to imagine anything in human activity more revolting.

Bob and Ross set about putting their programme together and I was delighted to be part of the team. We used to have early morning sessions going over what they hoped to say in the programme with reference to the information which they had brought back from the Soviet Union. I had to say whether or not in my professional judgement they could safely include it.

I remember one such early morning session. We had all met at about 8.30 a.m., Bob, Ross Wilson and myself. David Scott joined us as he usually did. He, like Tomlinson, could smell a good story when he came across one. When we finished for the morning it was about 10.40 and we all adjourned to David's office for a coffee. Going over to the drinks cabinet in his room David said: 'Well, I don't know about you chaps but I could do with a drink. How about it?' and he turned to me. I looked at my watch. It was 10.43 a.m. Too early for me. 'No thanks, David,' said I, 'the sun is not even over the yard arm yet.' David looked up at the clock on his wall for a moment and paused. He obviously found the answer up there. 'It is in Hong Kong,' he said and poured himself a gin. I felt it more prudent to stick to a tonic water.

In due course the programme was finished and Scottish Television broadcast it on 20 July 1987. It was amazingly good and reaction was swift. The critics were impressed. The programme won more awards than any other documentary that Scottish Television had ever made. It was a very moving story and in my view should be compulsory viewing for the younger generation lest they forget the inhumanity that man can display to his fellow man. We waited for a reaction from Gecas. We expected an action for libel. We were wrong. The action did not come. Instead Gecas hid from the media. Perhaps he thought that by hiding he could wash away the guilt of his monstrous crimes.

The matter rested there until two years later when, in July 1989, Scottish Television prepared to broadcast the programme again. This time Gecas moved. I had retreated by then into the calmer waters of consultancy by resigning from the partnership with effect from 1 January of that year. However, none of the remaining partners in the firm had much knowledge or experience of media law and accordingly I was still frequently consulted, especially in matters concerning Scottish Television. *Crimes of War* was scheduled to be broadcast again on Monday, 24 July 1989. It was widely known that this was going to happen and the programme had often been trailed by Scottish Television. They had already written to Gecas' solicitor advising him that the programme would be broadcast, and, indeed, that very evening I spoke to the solicitor concerned. Scottish Television were very happy to give Antanas Gecas the right of reply had he wished it either by appearing in the programme or by making a statement which they would have broadcast but neither he nor his solicitor asked for that right. In those conversations with Gecas' solicitor neither I nor Scottish Television were given any hint of what was to come later that same evening. The programme was due to go out at 10.35 p.m. and with about two hours to go to transmission the same solicitor applied to the Court of Session on Gecas' behalf for an interim interdict against Scottish Television's transmission of the programme.

ANTANAS GECAS – THE INTERDICT

Interdict is a remedy which the courts provide to prevent a wrong being committed. It is of course usually granted without the person against whom it is sought knowing of the attempt to obtain it and the first intimation is given when a copy of the interdict is served upon the opponent. Once a party becomes aware of an interdict then he must stop doing what is interdicted or he risks very severe penalties indeed. It is not the moment of granting the interdict that matters but the moment when the opponent is made aware of its existence.

To ensure that early warning is given of an attempt to obtain an interdict a caveat is often used. A caveat is a document which is lodged by a party who suspects that another may attempt to interdict him from doing something. It asks the court to advise the party lodging it of any attempt to obtain an interdict against him. The court will advise the party lodging the caveat in order to give them the opportunity of being heard where possible when the application for interdict is made. Soon after being appointed by Scottish Television as their adviser in legal affairs I had taken the precaution of instructing a permanent caveat in the Court of Session and the Sheriff Courts of Glasgow and Edinburgh. I wanted to ensure that if any party ever applied to any one of these courts for an interdict then word would be sent to the company's legal advisers.

Around nine o'clock on the evening of Monday, 24 July 1989 Gecas applied to the court for an interdict preventing Scottish Television from screening the programme. (The Court of Session contrary to popular belief *does* provide a 24-hour service.) His application triggered the caveat. The court authorities telephoned Colin McLeod, a partner of Dundas & Wilson, the corporate lawyers for Scottish Television, at his home. The message was that Antanas Gecas was applying for an interdict against Scottish Television and Colin was asked if the company wanted to be heard by the judge who was going to consider the application for interdict. Colin telephoned me at my home within moments and there then began a rather interesting chronology of events. I took the precaution of noting that chronology in my diary as and when it happened as I reckoned that one day I might be asked questions about it. I still have that diary.

When Colin McLeod telephoned to advise me of the application by Gecas, I immediately telephoned Blair Jenkins. David Scott was on holiday and Blair was then his deputy. I telephoned Blair to advise him of what was happening and for instructions. He instructed me to oppose the application for interdict. I telephoned Colin immediately. He would go up to Parliament House (the Court of Session) and oppose the application. Our ground of opposition was that what the programme said was true, that accordingly there was no wrong being threatened against Gecas and that in any event the programme had been first broadcast two years ago. We could now do nothing but wait for word from the court. Meantime transmission was drawing nearer.

At 10.45 p.m. Colin McLeod telephoned me to tell me that the interdict had been granted. We were not surprised. If the judge had refused the interdict and what Gecas maintained was true, then irreparable harm would be done to him. The balance of convenience lay with stopping the programme until the whole matter could be heard in court.

At 10.48 p.m. I telephoned Blair Jenkins. His line was engaged!

At 10.56 p.m. I dialled again. He was still engaged.

At 10.59 p.m. I got through. I told him about the interdict and that we must stop the transmission. He told me that by now all that the programme had to say about Gecas had been said. The programme was going on to deal with other matters which did not concern Gecas. Clearly if the interdict related only to that part of the programme which referred to Gecas then it was over already and we need take no other steps. I accordingly telephoned Colin McLeod in order that he could tell me the terms in which the interdict had been granted. His line was engaged. I then telephoned the Court of Session. The security people brought the clerk of the court, Ian Smith, to the phone. He was able to tell me that the interdict was 'from screening the programme'. Therefore we had to pull the plug even though there was no more to be said in the programme about Gecas.

At 11.13 p.m. I was speaking to Blair Jenkins again. We arranged that each of us would telephone Cowcaddens to take the programme off air. When I telephoned Cowcaddens the switchboard was not answering. I cursed the sloth of the operator concerned. I telephoned Colin McLeod to report to him and to ask him to join us in our efforts to get a reply.

At 11.23 p.m. Blair Jenkins telephoned me to report that he had finally managed to get through and had given the appropriate instructions. At that precise moment my television screen went blank and a continuity announcer came on after some moments to announce that Scottish Television were unable to continue the broadcast because of an interim interdict granted in the Court of Session.

It turned out that there was no fault on the part of Scottish Television's switchboard. *Prisoner Cell Block H* was due to come on at 11.05 p.m. but because of *Crimes of War* the programme schedule was behind time. The switchboard was jammed by hundreds of callers who wanted to know what had happened to their favourite programme. If only they had known what contribution they made to a rise in my blood pressure!

Gecas had instructed his interdict with a view to keeping his past out of the public domain. In fact the interdict had precisely the opposite effect. The following morning the national press carried the story of the interdict and thus the programme. Scottish Television could not have hoped for any wider publicity for their programme than the publicity that Antanas Gecas gave them by raising his action of interdict. He had succeeded in preventing Scottish Television from showing only the last few minutes of the programme. There was no reference whatever to Gecas or his activities in those last few minutes. He had accordingly achieved nothing in the way of silencing the station. What he had succeeded in doing, however, was to turn a massive searchlight on to himself and his dastardly affairs. In our camp there was rejoicing. The programme had gone out. The glare of publicity was now focused upon it. It was now the subject of a Court of Session litigation and Mr Gecas had done Scottish Television an enormous favour.

An action for interdict, however, was now before the court and it would require to be defended. Gecas had sought no other remedy and so his position would be untenable unless he also raised an action for libel. What he was saying was that the programme was untrue and it did him harm and so it should not be allowed to go out. At the same time he was not taking the remedy – an action for libel – which was open to him. We would have been able to complain to the court that it was entirely wrong for him to be able permanently to prevent Scottish Television from broadcasting the programme. If what the programme had to say was untrue then Gecas had his remedy – he could sue for defamation. Almost precisely a year after raising his interdict he sought his remedy: he served a summons on Scottish Television seeking damages of £600,000.

The basis of his action was, of course, that what Scottish Television said about him in the programme was untrue. His summons maintained that he committed no war crimes, that he was not personally responsible for the unlawful killings of innocent civilians, and that he was not a supporter of, nor sympathiser with, Nazi policies. It went on effectively to deny everything that the programme had said about him and his wartime activities. Gecas said also in his pleadings that his feelings, reputation and health had suffered severe damage. The unfounded allegations made against him, he said, had caused him to suffer greatly in these respects. He complained that his health had deteriorated and his reputation in the community had been blackened grossly. Material from the programme had been used, he said, in Soviet publications to represent him as a traitor and to blacken his name among his former countrymen. This had caused him deep mental anguish and distress. He sought damages from Scottish Television in order to compensate him for all the harm that the company had done him.

Scottish Television's defence to that action would be the best defence possible to an action of defamation, namely that what had been said about Gecas in the programme was true. Because of that we had to prove the truth about the Lithuanian villain who maintained that he was really a war hero. We would have to show that far from being a hero, he was in reality one of the most despicable of people to emerge from the Second World War.

ANTANAS GECAS – KGB GIVES WITNESS

As a consultant to my former firm I was not involved in the day-to-day activity of preparing Scottish Television's defence to the proceedings raised against them by Antanas Gecas. Peter Watson, the partner who fell heir to my practice, took charge of running the case at the Glasgow end. Whenever he required anything of me I was, of course, happy to be available but otherwise he got on with it. Those people from the Soviet Union who were going to be called as witnesses in the case would require to be interviewed and statements taken from them. That obviously would mean going to the Soviet Union to interview those whom Bob Tomlinson had seen those few years before and whose information had been the basis of the programme. The consensus of opinion among the lawyers (by now, of course, we had Edinburgh correspondents and senior and junior counsel) and Scottish Television was that I was the obvious one to undertake that task. I was asked in November 1990 if I would be willing to go and I agreed.

Accordingly, after a great deal of organisation of the trip on the part of Scottish Television, Bob Tomlinson, Alan Henderson, who is a Russian-speaking interpreter from Glasgow, and I set off for the Soviet Union on Saturday, 5 January 1991. The purpose of the visit was to gather the evidence which existed in the Soviet Union and which would be necessary in defending the action raised by Gecas. We left London Heathrow on the BA 872 at 9.40 a.m. on Sunday, 6 January. We were headed first for Moscow then to Vilnius in Lithuania and on to Minsk in Byelorussia. We expected that we would be away for about 14 days. We were going to Moscow to meet with the Deputy State Prosecutor for Nazi war crimes who was also the Deputy Prosecutor in the Office of the General Procurator for the Union of Soviet Socialist Republics. The title is a formidable one and so was the lady who occupied the post, Madame Natalya Kalesnikova. She had been most helpful to Bob and Ross when they were over and our trip would not have been possible without her help and cooperation. She was the one who had made arrangements for us to see the state prosecutors in the other countries of the Union which we planned to visit.

It turned out to be a trip that was full of surprises. The first one came when we were in mid-flight for Moscow. We were handed Soviet customs forms to complete and which would be taken from us in Moscow Airport. I found it extraordinary to be asked on that form if I had, amongst other things, any 'slaughtered fowl' with me. I did not!

At the time of our trip the entire Soviet Union was in a state of upheaval. Communism, which had held the Union together in a bear hug since 1917, was being forced to release its grip. The old order was crumbling. Freedom was beginning to assert itself. I had never been to the Soviet Union before and I found the culture shock of Moscow to be considerable. Without even leaving the airport the extremes of society could be observed. The duty-free shops were filled with goods which were brand leaders, goods like Irish Mist, Chivas Regal, Ferrero Rocher, Aramis, Kouros and Panasonic, but there was nothing at all from any of the countries of the Soviet Union. The whole place was dull and seemed to reek of poverty. Everywhere around us there were signs of a lack of money. Cheap, poor, tawdry, these were my first thoughts on arriving in the Soviet Union. Other things were noticeable at the airport: perhaps only about ten per cent of the aircraft on the ground did not belong to Aeroflot. That of course was in stark contrast to what we had seen at Heathrow – an airport that always abounds with aircraft of almost every airline in the world. Individuals both singly and in groups were hanging about, none of them appeared particularly welcoming. They would sidle up and, after a few sentences in Russian to test our linguistic abilities, they would ask, 'Change money?' Whenever we indicated that we were not interested they wandered off, usually with a final verbal salvo that betrayed a surprising acquaintance with some rather indelicate words of Anglo-Saxon origin. We had to wait around the airport for several hours after our arrival. We collected our luggage – or at least most of it – from a carousel marked as though our flight had come in from Vienna. I say most of it because one of Alan's cases did not turn up on the carousel at all. Predictably it was the case that mattered most to him for it was a case containing presents for friends in Vilnius. Alan was not alone in suffering loss: about 20 of our fellow passengers lost some part of their luggage. The thieves who abound at Moscow Airport had good pickings.

There were many surprises in Sheremetyevo Airport. While we were waiting I bought a bottle of Dry Martini in the duty free for £2.40 to keep in my hotel room. I was surprised to be given my change in US dollars. I found myself wishing (and not for the last time) that I had brought dollars with me as they were obviously very welcome. Indeed, I met an Irishman at Heathrow who told me I should bring two currencies on any trip to the Soviet Union, dollars and Marlboro cigarettes!

Going through the police control was rather different in Moscow from anything I had experienced. It seemed to take an age. The young officers concerned kept looking at me as they were examining my passport. Whenever they caught my eye they had their index and middle fingers up to their lips making it clear that they wanted cigarettes from me. I do not smoke, thus I could not oblige them.

Their customs officers did not ask to examine my cases and I was mightily relieved at that. One of my sons who had been to Russia a couple of years before had told me that ladies' tights – especially coloured ones – were a wonderful currency. I had about two dozen pairs to give out as presents or tips during my stay. It was only when I was relaxing in BA's very comfortable 767 en route to Moscow that I realised there might be a problem explaining my position if Soviet Customs looked in my luggage. They didn't and I was very grateful for that. In fact my son's tip proved to be one of the best I was ever given. Soviet hotels (at least in my limited experience) all seemed to have a maid on each floor who was on duty for 24 hours then was off for four days. I found them all to be very nice and without exception terribly helpful people, especially when they knew that the reward for the favour being asked was likely to be a pair of coloured tights. I was told that offering them money might be offensive whereas handing them over a little gift was quite acceptable. As it was I had my clothes pressed and all my laundry done for me in each of the hotels in which we stayed during our trip and all for a few pairs of coloured tights. Each maid as she came on duty would knock on my door and ask if I wanted anything. Their regular appearances at my door might have been misunderstood in other circumstances!

On the evening of our arrival Midnight Mass was being broadcast on Russian television. It came from the Russian Orthodox Cathedral in Moscow and was being celebrated by the Patriarch of the city. Boris Yeltsin, not yet an international figure, was prominent in attendance. The occasion was the Feast of the Epiphany, the day on which the Christian Church celebrates the visit to the Infant Christ by the Magi, a feast which has more prominence in other Christian countries than our own.

This was the first time that such a broadcast had ever taken place. Soviet governments could hardly be seen to be broadcasting what Marx had described as the opium of the people. In 1991, however, the government had bowed to popular pressure and so Christianity had taken an enormous and historic step forward that night. Alan, Bob and I – an Anglican, a Presbyterian and a Catholic – felt privileged to be witnessing that broadcast. While the pomp and the panoply of the Orthodox rites were somewhat strange to each of us, we felt in some way in communion with these fellow Christians who were being allowed publicly to participate in their religion after 74 years of suppression.

We stayed in an Intourist hotel in the centre of Moscow, a hotel, incidentally, which was demolished in 2002. It stood on Gorsky Prospekt and it would have been difficult to find anywhere more central. It was comfortable enough but it was not likely to qualify for a spot in any catalogue of the great hotels of Europe. My room was on the 18th floor of the hotel and I had superb views over the city. We took a brief walk outside on Sunday evening but we soon came back and from there on we left our hotel during daylight hours only. The streets of Moscow were no place for the unwary traveller after dark.

One thing that we did have time to see, however, was that one of the newly opened McDonald's had a queue that was at least 500 yards long. Pizza Hut, just along the road from McDonald's, had a queue which was about 400 yards long. Pavel, our Russian interpreter and the link between the Russian authorities and us, told us that that was something of a commonplace. That was surprising enough but when you realised that the price of a coffee and a hamburger in McDonald's or its equivalent in Pizza Hut came to about the price of the average Russian worker's wages for a month then you realised just how deprived those poor souls must have been throughout the time that communism reigned supreme.

Our appointment with Madame Kalesnikova was for 3 p.m. on Monday, 7 January. It was a strange day in Moscow. The majority of the population were celebrating the Feast of the Epiphany for the first time since the Bolshevik Revolution of October 1917. It had been transferred to 7 January because the sixth, the usual date, fell upon a Sunday. The result was that some public facilities were available but others were not. Some buses were running, some Metro trains were running, but others were not. Madame Kalesnikova, being a good Bolshevik, was not interested in the Feast of the Epiphany and she was at her office. She did, however, make a concession: she did not wear her uniform and she met us in civilian clothes. Apart from her position as Deputy State Prosecutor for War Crimes, Madame Kalesnikova was also a colonel in the Soviet Army and was the principal adviser to the Cominform on war crimes.

We went round to her office shortly before the appointed hour. It was an unbelievably shabby office for a person of such rank and status. It reminded me of the kind of office that our profession might have had one or even two generations ago. I should not have been remotely surprised, for just about everything in Moscow seemed shabby. Madame Kalesnikova was good enough to spend some time with us and she told us of the evidence which her organisation had of the participation by Gecas in war crimes in the

Soviet Union. She arranged to make available to us copies of all the documents which she had and in which we were interested. She told us that a warrant had been in existence since 1966 for the arrest of Gecas. In the event of Gecas returning to any of the republics in the USSR he would be arrested and charged with war crimes, including the mass murder of thousands of Soviet citizens during the Second World War. He would, however, be fully entitled to instruct a lawyer of any nationality to represent him at his trial and Madame Kalesnikova made it clear that the Soviet Union would cooperate to the full in assisting anyone instructed on behalf of Gecas in his defence to the charges of war crimes.

More to the point, she told us of the evidence against him which was available in the Soviet Union and I soon realised that Bob Tomlinson's thoroughness in researching the programme was such that she told us nothing that came as any real surprise. She also made it clear that in the event of Gecas being arrested and being put on trial for war crimes, the Soviet Union would welcome the attention of the world press. As a lawyer she was very proud of the fairness of the systems which operated there. At the same time she told us that if we could do anything which might assist the expulsion of Gecevicius from the United Kingdom to the Soviet Union then they would be delighted to receive him because he was one of their most wanted men. Bringing about his expulsion from the United Kingdom, unfortunately, was not something that lay within our capability.

She was quite a formidable woman and I was never entirely comfortable in her company. I found myself wondering how many people she had caused to be sent to the salt mines of Siberia! While I was given her first name I was so unsure of the woman that throughout my period of contact with her I maintained the formalities of address.

Following upon transmission of *Crimes of War* there had been such a public outcry about the scandal of war criminals living in the United Kingdom that the government had set up a commission headed by Sir William Hetherington, a former Solicitor General in England, and William Chalmers, a former Crown Agent in Scotland, to examine and report upon the position.

They had set about the task of finding out the facts with a thoroughness that was admirable. They paid Scottish Television the enormous compliment of starting their enquiry there with a viewing of the programme. Their quest had taken them to the Soviet Union in general and to Russia in particular. They had sat where we were sitting in the office of Madame Kalesnikova and she had told them the same things as she told us and showed them the same documents as she was showing us. She had some difficulty in understanding why we could not just short-cut the whole process and get copies of all the relevant material from them. But then could we really expect her to be familiar with the ways of the free world?

The Hetherington Chalmers Report, incidentally, led to the passing of the current War Crimes Act. That Act conferred upon the courts of England and Scotland the power to try persons living within their jurisdiction for crimes of war committed abroad. It was a huge step forward and extended the jurisdiction of the courts of this country far beyond anything they had experienced before. The programme *Crimes of War* was the only television programme, so far as I am aware, that led directly to a change in the law of the United Kingdom.

Having spent Monday afternoon and early evening with Madame Kalesnikova our business in Moscow was complete. We now knew what evidence was available in the Soviet Union. We had copies of various witness statements and other documents which would be useful to the defence of our case and which would help prove that this man Gecas was a war criminal. When I thanked Madame Kalesnikova at the end of our meeting for all her help she brushed my thanks aside. She pointed out to me that she was doing her duty, for it was the bounden duty of every civilised nation to help track down and punish people like Gecas. She reminded me that Britain and the Soviet Union had been allies in the fight against the fascism of Hitler and she then launched into a positive diatribe against the Nazi regime of Hitler's Germany. I found it difficult to imagine that any of our public prosecutors could be so politically inclined.

We would in due course require to go to Israel and to Germany in our pursuit of evidence to justify our assertion that this man was not just a war criminal but a mass murderer. In the meantime, we now had all that we had hoped to get from Russia. Tomorrow we would go to Vilnius in Lithuania. Napoleon had stayed in Vilnius en route to Moscow and his infamous defeat. We were making the journey in reverse. What we did not know was that the Soviets were also going to Vilnius tomorrow. We were flying there; they however were going in their tanks.

ANTANAS GECAS – TO VILNIUS

Lithuania was an experience that beats most. It all started very badly. We arrived at the Lietuva Hotel in Vilnius, a fairly modern hotel and something of an oasis in a desert of poverty, shops with empty shelves and queues whenever anything was on sale. I discovered that my camera, a Minolta XG3 SLR, had been stolen from my suitcase somewhere between Moscow Airport and arriving at the hotel. The thief had gone into my locked suitcase and torn the camera out of its ever-ready case. He had also helped himself to about £250 from the pocket of a blazer which was in my suitcase.

The air of neglect and want which we had sensed in Moscow was also present in Vilnius. There was a department store near our hotel where about one shelf in ten had something on it. I am old enough to remember wartime and rationing in this country but our shops were never like what we saw in Vilnius. I saw a huge queue in the store. I was curious and I went to investigate – it was for terracotta tableware.

The flight from Moscow to Vilnius on an Ilyushin of Aeroflot had been unbelievable. At Moscow passengers smoked on the tarmac and when they got into the plane. Cabin attendants were ancient, ugly old grandmothers whose only uniform was a hat! The cabin lights didn't work and half the safety belts didn't work either. That was bad enough but when we discovered the engines didn't work then fear and alarm began to take over! We were taken off that plane and across the tarmac to another Ilyushin that was just as bad. Meantime the smokers – and I think that was most of the passengers – carried on smoking even when we walked between two aircraft, each one fully fuelled.

The day after we reached Vilnius we met the Soviet State Prosecutor for Lithuania and he assigned three KGB agents to accompany us wherever we went. These were times of huge tension in Lithuania: borders were closed; railway stations closed and Vilnius Airport had closed the day after we flew in. Lithuania had declared a Unilateral Declaration of Independence (UDI) the previous March and now the Soviets were moving in. Where would it lead?

We were there from Tuesday till the Saturday afternoon but in that time I got what I wanted. I needed evidence, direct evidence from eyewitnesses that Gecas was a murderer, and I got it.

The evidence came from Juozas Alexsynas, a 76-year-old peasant who lived in Alytus in a small cottage. He sat there telling me how, as a member of Gecas' platoon, he had helped line up thousands of Jews, thrown them into mass graves and then buried them alive. He told me also how on other occasions they had machine-gunned thousands who had been herded into mass graves. He had been sentenced to 25 years in Siberia for his part in it all. He had been in the Lithuanian Police Battalion and Gecas had been his platoon commander. He told me of how his commander had taken a very active and a very willing part in the massacres.

I also got the evidence of Gecass participation in these mass killings from another 76-year-old called Motiejus Migonis, who lived in Kaunas. Sitting there in the homes of these old men, listening to them recount in pretty plain language the chilling details of mass murders, was something that will stay with me for the rest of my life. The barbarity and the inhumanity of it all was beyond belief.

We had to leave Lithuania in something of a hurry. On the Saturday morning we were summoned to the office of the Procurator General for the Soviet Socialist Republic of Lithuania and he told us that he had arranged for a 'safe car' to take us to Byelorussia that afternoon. I told him that we had not planned to go until the Monday but he calmly told me it would be better to go that day. Indeed if we did not go that day, he said, he could not guarantee that we would be able to leave at all, and, he said, he would no longer be responsible for our safety. It will come as no surprise to learn that we left! We were in fact taken to Minsk in a KGB Mercedes. They even had the temerity to charge us $160 for the trip!

It was on 17 July 1992 that Lord Milligan issued his judgment in the Gecas case against Scottish Television. It contained 192 pages that totally condemned Gecas as a war criminal. Many were relieved to read that judgment but I suspect that none was more relieved than I. It had been almost exactly five years before, in July 1987, that I had taken the crucial decision in that case, namely to let the programme be broadcast. I took the view that we had potentially enough evidence of Gecas' participation in war crimes in Eastern Europe to defend any claim that he might make for damages. That decision was based, I suppose, upon two things: my experience and my gut feeling. The responsibility that is placed upon a legal adviser in these situations is quite enormous and it is, I suppose, something that few are aware of. It would have been easier for me to take the soft option and advise against broadcasting on the ground that the programme might give rise to a claim for damages and thus involve the company in enormous costs and so on. The soft option did not appeal to me. I advised that we go ahead.

In the event I was right and Lord Milligan upheld the defence which Scottish Television had lodged. Had I been wrong in the decision which I made in 1987 then the consequences could have been horrendous. It is difficult to think of a worse libel than to accuse someone, falsely, of being a mass murderer. The damages could have been colossal and the costs would have been enormous. It speaks much for the courage of those at the helm of Scottish Television at the time. There must surely have been little doubt that it would have been much more economic for them to have offered Gecas some 'nuisance value' settlement of a few thousand pounds right at the start of his action. They were aware of this and they were aware that such a course of action would have saved them tens of thousands of pounds. In spite of this they decided to fight on and defend the case without regard to cost. Their journalistic integrity mattered more to them than the cost of fighting the action and they had my admiration for that view. Nonetheless, I was intensely relieved when my decision of five years before was upheld by the judgment of Lord Milligan.

Let me quote to you from parts of the 192-page judgement:

> [Gecas] committed war crimes against Soviet citizens who were old men, women and children. I am clearly satisfied that [he] participated in many operations involving the killing of innocent Soviet citizens, including Jews in particular, in Byelorussia during the last three months of 1941, and in doing so committed war crimes against Soviet citizens who included old men, women and children . . .
>
> I further hold it proved that the pursuer [Gecas] was the platoon commander of the 12th Auxiliary Police Batallion and that that platoon participated specifically in six operations . . .
>
> It inevitably follows that the pursuer committed war crimes against innocent civilians of all ages and both sexes in the course of these specific operations, it is not in dispute that he was in active

command of his platoon throughout the period mentioned . . .

[Gecas] was platoon commander in active command of a platoon which participated in war crimes generally . . .

It is clear that albeit Gecas was at the bottom of the chain of command, he was in command of a platoon involved in executing the operations . . .

The allegation that [Gecas] is a mass murderer is proved . . .

The allegation of participation by his battalion in the mass liquidation of Jews is proved . . .

The 85-year-old Lithuanian evaded justice in the end. On 12 September 2001 Antanas Gecas died in Liberton Hospital, Edinburgh. He had been undergoing medical treatment after suffering two strokes at his home in Edinburgh earlier in the year. Before his illness, the Lithuanian government had asked for his extradition to face trial for his part in the mass murder of Jews and partisans during the Second World War. The Scottish Executive considered that request, but there was general dismay in many quarters when Scotland's Justice Minister Jim Wallace announced that doctors brought in to assess his condition had expressed the view that Antanas Gecas was too ill to be moved. Accordingly the request of the Lithuanian government was not granted and Gecas thus avoided the trial that many wished to see take place.

Lord Janner, vice president of the World Jewish Congress and secretary of the all-party parliamentary group on war crimes, went on record saying: 'I regret that Gecas did not live to stand trial for his personal involvement in war crimes against humanity. He would have received the justice that neither the Nazis nor their accomplices ever afforded to their victims.'

Scottish National Party justice spokesman, Roseanna Cunningham said: 'I think there should be an investigation into the contributions of the Westminster government and the Scottish government in dealing with this case. It may be that they will have something to answer for regarding their actions over the past ten years.'

It is difficult to believe that anyone could have lived with such events. The heinous enormity of such unmitigated evil surpasses imagination. And it all began with a few lines in a newspaper and a journalist who was committed to his job.

EPILOGUE

Vita mutatur. Life changes. Not only has life changed but so has my profession. Indeed over the 40 years and more that I have been connected with it, it has changed almost beyond recognition. When I first became associated with the legal profession in Scotland, in those good old days before traffic wardens were invented and when parking meters were a thing of the future; when money was real money; when a dyke was a stone wall; when the only heroine we ever heard of was Maureen O'Hara and when I was still brash enough to be convinced that not only was I God's gift to the world in general but to the legal profession in particular, criminal Legal Aid did not exist in Scotland.

There were only about half a dozen solicitors who were likely to be involved in any criminal case of any importance. There was little reward in a criminal practice except to the specialist and consequently there was not a great deal of professional interest.

Today things are quite different. Legal Aid exists not just for civil and criminal cases but also for giving out advice. If only it had existed when Joe Friel and I ran our evening surgery in Tradeston! The advent of Legal Aid was probably the most important advance in the development of our society since the advent of the National Health Service in 1948.

In assessing any civilisation one of the touchstones has always been the quality of justice that that society dispenses. No one can doubt that the quality of our justice in the courts today is infinitely better than when I entered the profession. The improvement in that quality is due in a very large extent to the existence of Legal Aid and to the fact that men and women of ordinary means have the same access to the courts as anyone else. Equality in the eyes of the law is cardinal to any system of criminal jurisprudence. Until the advent of Legal Aid in our criminal courts that equality depended upon one thing – the ability of the accused person to pay. If he had money then he went to one of the highly paid specialists and he was given excellent service. If he did not have money then too bad, he would go to the Poor's Roll solicitor who was in effect doling out charity. The result was that a far better system of justice existed for those who could afford to pay than for those who could not. That is no longer true. Our criminal Legal Aid system is still imperfect. There are still warts, but it is a far better system that obtains today than that which obtained 40 years ago.

I am not at all convinced, incidentally, that an applicant for Legal Aid should have to go and beg for it. It is, I think, the only benefit in our Welfare State which an individual is not entitled to claim as of right. In every other case, health service, social security benefits and so on the applicant is entitled to say, 'I am a taxpayer. I have paid for this benefit of the Welfare State and I therefore claim it as my right.' It is difficult to see why Legal Aid should be any different.

The very existence of Legal Aid is the hallmark of a democracy. If you doubt that, then consider for yourselves the other systems which we know, systems where the rule of law does not obtain, systems where considerations like equality before the law are seditious or revolutionary in concept and have to be put down wherever they rear their unpalatable heads. What price do you think was equality in the eyes of the law in the Soviet Union of Stalin, the Spain of Franco or the Uganda of Amin? Let the cynics cry rubbish if they wish but our system of Legal Aid is proof that democracy and the rule of law exist in our society. Once you start making inroads on our system of Legal Aid, then the basic rights of individual members of society are being placed in jeopardy. Two of those basic rights are the right to equality in the eyes of the law and the right to equal representation in the tribunals of justice of our society. This would appear to be a principle that successive governments have chosen to ignore when tinkering with Legal Aid and making it available to successively smaller numbers of the population.

The law itself has also changed radically since I qualified in 1957, and what makes it worse for me and my generation is the fact that it has changed in just about every aspect. When I was an apprentice, our then senior partner used to display what was to me an appalling ignorance of some of the substantive law and I could never understand why. It was only in what I might euphemistically term my more mature years that I realised just how difficult it is for the practitioner to keep up to date with the law and with the changes in it. I do not exaggerate when I say that it would be possible for a solicitor to spend his entire working day simply reading new legislation, new regulations and the Law Reports. Of course were he to do that he would soon have no practice, but at least he would be up to date with the law. Legislation comes from Westminster, Europe and now Edinburgh at an alarming speed. It is frequently, due to its very speed, badly thought out and badly drafted and the result is that the courts have much more trouble in its interpretation than they should.

EPILOGUE

It is a vicious circle. The more legislation there is, the more cases are reported upon it, and all the time, at the other end of it all, is the poor lawyer who has to read it all and try and keep himself up to date.

When you look around you realise just how many areas of law have changed enormously. In the field of criminal court procedure legislation of the past 20 years has made vast changes. The law of husband and wife, of children, the law of divorce, the law of succession, the law of conveyancing are all fields of practice which have been altered radically in my time. In practically every field of human activity that the general practitioner is liable to meet, the law has been substantially changed since I entered the profession. And, of course, we now face the European dimenson in our legal system. I now understand, better than I ever did, the difficulties that our then senior partner had, and I can now view his difficulties with much more charity and understanding!

Even administration in the law office has changed. We now use fancy bits of electronic gadgetry that were never dreamt of before, such as computers, the Internet, tape recorders and fax machines. All these things are pieces of machinery that the solicitor of today takes for granted and that he could not do without in the successful running of an office. Before the days of the photocopier we actually employed typists whose entire working life consisted of sitting at a typewriter (and a manual one at that), typing out copies of letters, of documents, of court pleadings, indeed every type of written communication. What a soul-destroying existence it must have been. Today the photocopier is probably even more necessary to our society than oven chips!

Basically, however, the job of the solicitor has not changed. He is the individual dedicated to assisting humanity in its activity and in its adversity. He does so according to a code of conduct and an increasing number of regulations. He is told about the things he may not do; he is nowhere told the things he should do. He learns these by experience. There are two things which I suppose help him to discover what he should be doing: his professional conscience and his bank balance. In Scotland, rightly or wrongly, gladly or sadly, we now have a profession in which perhaps many pay more attention to the second than to the first.

The changes that I have seen are not all changes of which I approve. The introduction of advertising, which was forced upon us by an uncaring government, was one of the great acts of iconoclasm in modern times, for it helped destroy much of a noble profession. I never once advertised for a client – it was my boast that the best advert I could ever have was a satisfied client. Now advertising is the norm and the solicitor who is most likely to attract business is the one whose adverts are the slickest.

It is difficult these days to switch on a television set or open a paper without seeing them. I confess that I find them awful. We even have solicitors whose adverts claim to be quoting satisfied clients. 'You were wonderful in court last week and I just had to write to you and tell you so.' The mind boggles at where it will lead.

The other great act of vandalism committed upon the profession was the abolition of scale fees. The profession warned what would happen and the profession was right. Fees came tumbling down but so did standards. Corners are being cut now and the public suffers on account of the consequent lowering of professional standards.

But let me not sound off too much. When I look around the areas of urban population and see how the profession has taken itself out of the city centres, out to meet society where it lives, out to the likes of Castlemilk and Easterhouse and Wester Hailes, I often wonder if those who man the offices out there, in what are termed the areas of unmet need, will get the same satisfaction as I did in our five-bob surgery in Paisley Road all those years ago. If they get half the pleasure and half the satisfaction that I had then they will have no regrets.

But now I have hung up my gown. I have done my stint and moved over that others may take my place. I feel that I have trodden the boards long enough. I have walked across the stage for the last time. Now I know better than I thought I ever would how it feels to take a last curtain call.

It has been for me a rich life, rich in the pleasure I obtained from the profession which I chose. I have difficulty in imagining that any other could have given me more pleasure or more fulfilment. But life goes on, and it is not possible for any pleader to stay indefinitely there on the floor of the court in the white-hot heat of the kitchen. Pleading is for the younger man. It is an aspect of the profession that, like any other, demands its toll. I have paid that toll and now that the shadow of my life lengthens I have moved on, on across the stage and out quietly through the wings. My rewards are not measured by material things but by things that can never be bought – by memories: memories of the good times; the satisfying times; memories of the intense satisfaction at persuading a court of the validity of the arguments advanced; memories of the bad times when the result was not what was wanted and there remained the awful feeling that perhaps justice had not been done.

But the bad memories never seemed to last – perhaps it was self-protection that encouraged them to go. I suppose that, on balance, it probably *was* better than working in Asda.